The photograph shows a miniature from the St. Albans Psalter (Albani Psalter). As one can see here Christ saves all souls – "out of helle mennes souls" to quote *The Vision of Piers Plowman* (Passus XVIII, l. 373). The Psalter was created possibly between 1123 and 1135 at St. Albans Abbey near London. We are very grateful for this high quality reproduction provided personally by Dr. Helmar Härtel from the Herzog August Bibliothek Wolfenbüttel, where the St. Albans Psalter is kept.

Both compositions correspond to the apocryphal Gospel

CHRIST FREES ALL SOULS FROM THE HELL (SEE P.P. 129-130)

Christ leads the souls away from hell.

Mural painting from the Boyana Church, 13th century. The Bulgarian art critic Kiril Krustev is convinced that the anonymous Boyana artist was under the influence of Bogomil ideas. The salvation of all souls is emphasized by Avel with a shephard's stick (visible to the left), among other descendants of Adam.

Photo: Vl. Vitanov.

of Nicodemus extensively used by the Dualists.

Georgi Vasilev

Dualist ideas in the English Pre-Reformation and Reformation

(Bogomil-Cathar influence on Wycliffe, Langland, Tyndale and Milton)

On the face: scene 27 of the famous 14th century ceramic tiles series from no the longer existing church in Tring. Reproduced on foundation of M. R. James' publication *Rare medieval tiles and their story,* The Burlington Magazine for Connoisseurs. London. Vol. XLII, Jan.-Jun. 1923, p. 23. This image re-creates the episode where Christ teaches the ploughman to plough, and is transferred from the old Bulgarian apocrypha *The Legend of the Tree (De Arbore Crucis).*

© BULKORENI Publishing House, Sofia, 2005
ISBN 954-798-019-X

Georgi Vasilev

Dualist ideas in the English Pre-Reformation and Reformation

(Bogomil-Cathar influence on Wycliffe, Langland, Tyndale and Milton)

Bul
Koreni

Sofia, 2005

*This book is dedicated
to the memory of my teacher,
the great writer and humanist
Stefan Gechev.*

Introduction

The Dualist Heresy – Bridging the Island to the Continent during the Middle Ages

European genesis

When writing about the Lollards in England and their abundant literature, nearly all contemporary British medievalists perceive them as a local phenomenon, i.e. one that originated on British soil alone. It is from this point, however, that the contradictions begin. *Encyclopaedia Britannica* establishes a definition for the name Lollard, which clearly speaks of a continental origin, or at least of a continental bond: "The term comes from Middle Dutch 'lollard', a 'mumbler' or 'mutterer'; it had been applied to the Flemish Beghard and other continental groups suspected of combining pious pretensions with heretical belief."[1] One of the greatest authorities in the study of dualist movements, Ignatz von Döllinger, refers to a number of documents regarding the presence of Lollards in Europe, quoting a Bull of Pope Boniface IX, which explains that the "popularly called Beghardi or Lolhardi and Swestriones", spread in various parts of Germany, were "actually poor - *fratricelli*"[2]. This occurred in the very beginning of the 15th century as Boniface IX was Pope in the period between 1389 and 1404. This text provides several pieces of important information. The first is that the Lollards were a variety of Beghardi and fratricelli, and the second that the Lollards were in the sights of his predecessor, John XX (1316-1334)[3]. In other words, the Lollards were definitely a phenomenon in the system of medieval heresies in Europe. The third is that, since the German Lollards were Beghards, then their origin lies in the 12th century, as Malcolm Lambert has had good reason to point out in his book *Medieval Heresy*[4].

In his famous *Ecclesiastical History from the Birth of Our Savior to the Eighteenth Century*, Mosheim has collected an abundance of sources

---

[1] Encyclopaedia Britannica. Vol. 14. 1970, p. 256.
[2] Döllinger, Ign. von. Dokumente vornemlich zur Geschihte der Valdesier und Katharer. München. 1890, p.381.
[3] Ibidem.
[4] Lambert, M. Medieval Heresy (Popular Movements from the Gregorian Reform to the Reformation). Oxford.2002.3rd edition, p.200

that prove the European origin and European proliferation of the Lollards. From there we shall only quote the information of Hocsemius "a canon of Liege, in his *Gesta pontificum Leodiensium*, lib.I., cap.31 (in. Jo. Chapeavili Gesta Pontificum Tungrensium et Leodiensium, tom.II, p.350&c.) who wrote: "In the same year, (1309), certain strolling hypocrites, who were called Lollhards or praisers of God, (*qui Lollhardi sive deus laudantes vocabantur*), deceived some women of quality in Hainault and Brabant...Thus this term acquired the same import with the term Beghard..."[1] Mosheim definitely concludes that the English Lollards, the followers of Wycliffe, were called with an imported Belgian term – "be a vulgar term of reproach brought from Belgium to England, Lollards".[2]

This information is referred to and repeated in the three-volume *A History of the Inquisition of the Middle Ages* by Charles Henry Lea. Again basing himself on the sources used by Mosheim, Lea mentions that Lollard associations were established in Antwerp around the year 1300 during the plague epidemic in order to take care of the sick and, above all, to bury the dead. They called themselves Alexians – "from their patron St. Alexis, and Cellits from dwelling in cells."[3]

Reports similar to the Bull of Boniface IX and dating from the 15th century can again be found in Ignatz von Döllinger, this time in a document from the State Library in Frankfurt. This document mentions the Bull, but it also adds new and important details: some of the heretics were literate and won the sympathy of masters of theology and learned men. The heretics say they follow the life of Christ and the apostles and, what is specific, that they do not "accept any saints"[4]. Moreover, they deny the right to consecrate of any priest who commits a grave sin[5]. The last three facts characterise the Cathars who called themselves new apostles, rejected the existence of saints and the right of any priests who had committed a sin to officiate in church. The document then features other familiar Cathar characteristics, including that confession should be made directly to God and that indulgences do not count[6].

---

[1] Murdock's translation of Mosheim's Ecclesiastical History from the Birth of Our Saviour to the Eighteenth Century. Book III. Part.II. Chap.II. Boston&London. 1802, p.393
[2] Ibidem, p.381
[3] Lea, H.-Ch. A History of the Inquisition of the Middle Ages. Vol.II. London. 1888, p.368
[4] Döllinger, Ign. von, op. cit., p.408
[5] Ibidem, p. 410.
[6] Ibidem, p. 410.

In addition to the Cathar features, one can also quote echoes from the prime source – Bogomilism. The name Lollards, or "mumblers" or "mutterers" (of prayers) leads us to the observation of Anna Comnena who, on the occasion of the sentence and burning of the Bogomil leader Basil, gave a short description of him in her *Alexiad* and mentioned the Bogomil custom to mutter - ὑποψιθυείζει.[1] In turn, the definition given by Hocsemius, i.e. that the Lollards were praisers of God (*qui Lollhardi sive deus laudantes vocabantur*), echoes of the very name of "Bogomil" – "dear to God". The next detailed summary of heretical contacts between the island and the continent is found in the dissertation of the Swiss scholar (and English painter) Conrad Fueslin, *Dissertatio de fanaticis seculo XII in Anglia repertis*, defended in Bern in 1761.

At the end of the 19th and the beginning of the 20th century, various authors made discoveries mainly regarding the transfer of dualist apocrypha to the island. These were Ivan Franko in his remarkable collection *Апокріфі і легенди з украінских рукописів*[2], as well as Nikolai Ossokin with his excellent work on the history of Albigensians and their time[3], which gave important details about these relations, and Moise Gaster, who published his *Ilchester Lectures on Greeko-Slavonic Literature and its Relation to the Folklore of Europe During the Middle Ages* in London in 1887[4]. In fact, the belated isolationist notion of the categorical Englishness of the Lollards probably repeats an old Catholic thesis that the island was saved from continental heresies. This was noticed even by Conrad Fueslin, and in more recent times one can see it repeated in the *Catholic Encyclopedia*: "Till the latter part of the fourteenth century England had been remarkably free from heresy. The Manichean movements of the twelfth and thirteenth centuries which threatened the Church and society in Southern Europe and had appeared

---

[1] Annae Comnenae porphyrogenitae caesarissae Alexias. Venetiis. Ex typographia Bartholomae Javarina. M.DCC·XXIV, p.384. See:The Alexiad of the Princess Anna Comnena. London, 1918, reprinted in *Documentary History of Eastern Europe*, New York, 1970, p.8: "A Bogomil looks gloomy and is covered up to the nose and walks with a stoop and *mutters* (my italics – G.V.), but within he is an uncontrollable wolf".

[2] Франко, I. Передмова – in: Апокріфі і легенди з украінских рукописів. II. Львів, 1899

[3] Осокин, Н. История альбигойцев и их времени. Москва. 2000. First edition 1869

[4] Gaster, M. Ilchester Lectures on Greeko-Slavonic Literature and its Relation to the Folklore of Europe During the Middle Ages. London, 1887.

sporadically in Northern France and Flanders had made no impression on England."[1]

The dualist Pre-Renaissance

Now what is the meaning of clarifying this problem? Quite significant, it turns out, for since the 12th century, when the presence of dualist apocrypha in England is clearly denoted, right until the 17th (i.e. the works of John Milton) there was a significant cultural and philosophical trend in English medieval culture, which was born on the basis of dualist Bogomil-Cathar heresy. The Lollards and their iconography, the reformers John Wycliffe and WilliamTyndale, the poet William Langland, the apocryphal volumes *Cursor mundi, Aenbyte of Inwite*, as well as the Anglo-Norman variants of *The Legend of the Tree of the Cross* and *Les enfaunces de Jesus Christ*, and John Milton's great poems *Paradise Lost* and *Paradise Regained*, fall within this section of time, in this context of ideas and specific figurative thinking. Speaking of Milton, one should not forget the fact that he was also a reformer of the same temperament and dualist notion as Wycliffe and Tyndale, himself expressing his continuity of ideas from Wycliffe. Therefore, we are faced with a chain of events, works and persons who were frequently also a pinnacle in English culture. Its study will necessitate both a more careful interpretation of known facts and the addition of new ones.

One cannot but notice such a peculiar need for greater precision in the perception of the "heretical" heritage among our British colleagues. David Daniell has done a lot to distinguish more clearly the reformist work of William Tyndale so that his exceptional contribution to the development of the English language could be seen. It was clearly said that the translation of the *Authorised Version* of the Bible (1611), known as the work of King James and a circle of scholars commissioned by him, actually used 80 per cent of Tyndale's translation[2]. True, such an opinion was vouchsafed earlier by other authori-

---

[1] Here we once again fall upon a circle of contradictions – adopting the thesis of the British roots of the Lollards, the *Catholic Encyclopedia* quotes an European (this time in Flanders) origin of their name: The name was derived by contemporaries from *lollium*, a tare, but it has been used in Flanders early in the fourteenth century in the sense of "hypocrite", and the phrase "Lollardi seu Deum laudantes" (1309) points to a derivation from *lollen*, to sing softly (cf. Eng. *lull*). The Catholic Encyclopedia, Volume IX. Ed. by Robert Appleton Company. 1910, p.333

[2] Daniell, D. William Tyndale. A Biography. Ed. Yale University Press. New Haven&London, 2001, p.2

8

ties in England[1], but now it has been said so clearly and distinctly for the first time, the British and American public showing definite interest in this historical specification.

Generally speaking, it seems this is where we should recall a thought of principle significance for these studies belonging to Dimitri Obolensky, for whom the study of Bogomilism and heresies related to it meant above all to establish connections: "This connection, if successfully established, would in its turn enable Church historians to regard the Bogomil sect as the first European link in the thousand-year-long chain leading from Mani's teaching in Mesopotamia in the third century to the Albigensian Crusade in southern France in the thirteenth. Moreover, the study of the Bogomil movement has its own, and by no means negligible, part to play in the investigation of the cultural and religious links between eastern and western Europe, the importance of which is increasingly perceived at the present time."[2]

The phenomena mentioned here acquire the features of an early hidden Renaissance in British society. This phenomenon is one of particular beauty, for it was both a Renaissance at the apex (Wycliffe, Langland, Milton) and a grass-root Renaissance, in other words the literary activity and the iconography of Lollard communities.

In conclusion one is faced with the unusual question what these unbelievable interactions mean: when ideas from one culture, Bulgarian, additionally developed in the Cathar one of Provence, prove a permanent presence in a third culture, in this case English? At this point the first conclusion is that lofty cultural aspirations are indestructible. Even subjected to persecution, they migrate from one country to another, stimulate an upsurge everywhere, reincarnate and resort to mimicry until the time of full-fledged expression finally arrives. The second conclusion is probably that dualist, i.e. Bogomil-Cathar imagery and philosophy, should be viewed as a driving force of Pan-European Pre-Renaissance[3], as well as a principal ingredient of English Reformation. And third – could we presume to expect that the cultural potential of this unique philosophy has not been exhausted, that aspects of it could be resurrected, for they

---

[1] "… it is agreed on all hands that the English of the *Authorised Version* is, in essentials, that of Tyndale". The Cambridge History of English and American Literature in 18 volumes (1907-1921). Vol. IV, p.48

[2] Obolensky, D. The Bogomils: a Study in Balkan Neo-Manichaeism. Cambridge University Press 1948, p. VII.

[3] Such an opinion has already been voiced by В. Зайцев in „Богомильское движение и общественная жизнь Северной Италии эпохи Дуеченто". Минск, 1967.

feature a unique example that is also necessary for our time, managing as it once did to convince millions of people to place spiritual needs above the material ones. In other words, it developed as a culture of the masses, as grassroot amateur creative activities, an alternative of mass culture. Here the interaction between elite culture of theology and academism and the self-expression of the broad public enjoy a surprising harmony. Nor should one overlook yet another majestic aspect of this phenomenon – it is *par excellence* international while it also contributed to the germination of national literatures, i.e. it was a Pan-European bridge of creativity.

Finally, I would like to note that I am not beginning this book with polemics in mind. Although alternative to the traditional position of English historiography, it would not have been developed over a relatively short period of time, nor would the abundant facts quoted here have been collected so quickly if I had not received preliminary opinions and, most importantly, literature and published sources from the most outstanding British scholars Prof. Anne Hudson, Prof. Norman Tanner, Prof. David Daniell, Mrs. Janet Hamilton&Prof. Bernard Hamilton, Prof. René Weis, and Dr. Malcolm Lambert. My study is largely an additional interpretation of the information they have discovered and amassed. In other words, my work also relies on their research and their fellowship, which acquired a form of cooperation with an opponent. In turn, I hope that the discoveries regarding the continental connection of the Lollards with the dualist roots in Provence, Normandy and the Netherlands and, in the long run, with Bulgarian Bogomilism, which we have made with my respected colleague Krustina Gecheva[1], will also serve our British colleagues. By the way, the clarification of controversial elements will be assisted by time and the interest of the readership, as there is already a new reading public capable of undertaking its own research and academically correct comparisons. It is not by chance that the Centre d'Etudes Cathares operates by Toulouse, France, as well as a cultural circle supported by the infrastructure of the virtual society www.cathares.org.

I do not flatter myself with the thought that with my style I have succeeded in riveting the attention of this public, but the subject is so fascinating, revealing such unbelievable intellectual adventures, impreg-

---

[1] Гечева, Кр. Богомилството. Библиография (Bogomilism. A Bibliography. With titles in the original language). София, 1997

nated with bright aspirations and Calvary amidst terrible repression, that I suppose these fiery pages in our common European history will attract the interest of the reading public.

Part of the materials in this book have already been publiched in my work in Bulgarian titled *Bogomil and Apocryphal Ideas in Medieval English Culture* (The Bulgarian Image of Christ Plowman as Piers Plowman in William Langland's *The Vision of Piers Plowman*). Koreni Publishing House, Sofia, 2001. In addition, a considerable portion of my studies in English and French can be found on the site of the Institute of Balkan Studies at www.cl.bas.bg/Balkan-Studies/bogomilism/index.html or at mirror: www.geocities.com/bogomil1bg.

Expressing gratitude to British colleagues I would not like to miss the opportunity to thank Prof. Valerie Hotchkiss, whose one-month hospitality at Bridwell Library, South-Methodist University, Dallas in 2001 allowed me to work intensively with the creations of William Tyndale and the reformist treatises of John Milton. I cannot but appreciate the responsiveness of Dr. Anne Brenon, France, who placed at my disposal her publications on Waldensian-Cathar literature in England in the 17th century. I am also grateful to Prof. Thomas Butler, Harvard University, who supported my thesis even on Bulgarian soil, sending me a favourable opinion of my second doctoral thesis in 2000. I should also like to add my gratitude to Mrs. Bistra Roushkova for her translations of my texts and her pertinent editorial recommendations. My gratitude goes also to Dr. Boyka Sokolova-Leader, University of London, who translated the chapter III, also to Prof. Rumiana Zlatanova, University of Heidelberg, who send me some important sources. And my cordial gratitude goes to my mother, Stefana Vasileva, to my cousin Prof. Antonia Shivarova, and to my brother Ivan Valtchev who supported all my efforts.

Georgi Vasilev

Chapter I. Bogomils and Lollards

Spring

*...And all the flowers resurrected
with the colors of Easter eggs.*

Stefan Gechev

Facts of penetration

Two are the early references to disembarcations of heretics in England about the year 1162. The first belongs to William of Newbury (Guillemus Novoburgensis) and has been commented upon by the well-known historian Stephen Runciman. He has pointed out that the visitors came from Germany on the crest of the heretical wave mentioned by Eckbert, later Benedictine abbot of Schonau[1]. Arno Borst and Milan Loos also mention the tragic fate of this group: most of the heretics were tried at Oxford, branded, chased away, or starved to death[2]. Thus we are left with the impression that the heresy failed to get a foothold in England.

The other view, upholding the idea of the serious penetration of the Bogomil-Cathar heresy in England, was expounded by Alexander Veselovsky, Moses gaster and Ivan Franko. The facts analysed by them are from after the 14th century[3]. They study mainly how themes from the heretical apocrypha were taken over and interpreted in English culture. The central one of these themes is the "Harrowing of Hell", which reproduces chapter eighteen of the *Nicodemus Gospel*, the favourite reading of the dualists. Gaster and Franko discuss the influence of the *Nicodemus Gospel* on the miracle plays and Langland's *Piers Plowman*. The proofs are numerous. It is really surprising that these finds have been overlooked by serious authors like M. R. James, E. Chambers and E. Partridge, thus completely isolating medieval English literature from contacts with the heresy. Even Dmitri Obolensky's abundant commentary, which proves that the numerous apocrypha that spread all over Europe were, if nothing else, used by the dualists, have been neglected[4].

---

[1] Runciman, S. The Medieval Manichee. A Study of Christian dualist Heresy. CUP, 1947, p. 122.

[2] Loos, M. Dualist Heresy in the Middle Ages. Academia-Praha, 1974, p. 117.

[3] Веселовски, А. Соломонъ и Китоврасъ. Санктъ Петербургъ, 1872; Gaster, M. Ilchester Lectures on Greeko-Slavonic Literature and Its Relation to the Folklore of Europe During the Middle Ages. London, 1887.

[4] Obolensky, D. The Bogomils (A Study in Balkan Neomanichaeism). CUP, 1948, 273-274.

Some change of attitude is marked by A. Baugh and K. Malone who point out that the apocrypha were brought over to England via France in the 13th century.[1] They also note the important presence of *Nicodemus Gospel*. In our opinion the presence of the "Harrowing of Hell" theme in the *Exeter Book* (10th c.) can be seen as a heretical influence. In this scene Jesus delivers from Hell not only Adam and Eve, "but a countless multitude of folk" which is typical of the Bogomil-Cathar vision. The "Fall of Lucifer" and his angels found in the *Caedmon Ms* is another typical dualistic theme.

The odyssey of dualistic apocrypha in England has not found a satisfactory explanation and raises an important question: was the heretical presence durable enough so that it could propagate a type of non-orthodox culture, standing apart and often opposed to the official Church; could it create a milieu which could produce its own conceptions of life and patterns of behaviour in the general cultural development? Put in the terms of sociology, we shall have to find whether the heresy could create its own social and cultural infrastructure in England.

As a quoted reality the heretical communities of the Lollards of the 14th and 15th centuries have been well documented. They took part in John Ball's rebellion and were connected with the reformist efforts of JohnWycliffe[2]. However, the Lollards have been regarded as a local phenomenon, though their very name suggests a continental origin.

As I mentioned in the introduction, a number of documents about the Lollards in Germany have been collected by I.von Döllinger and Charles Lea and as far as they are mentioned in the introduction of this book they need not be quoted again in detail. Let's repeat - the *Encyclopaedia Britannica* (1970) also points to their European roots: "The term comes from Middle Dutch 'lollard', a 'mumbler' or 'mutterer'; it had been applied to the Flemish Beghard and other continental groups suspecting of combining pious pretentions with heretical belief."[3]

To enlarge upon this information we have consulted older dictionaries, which suggest a typology of the ideas connected with the Lollards. The respectable Du Cange, who used 14th c. chronicles, describes the Lollards as heretics from Germany and Belgium and adds that "in pluri-

---

[1] Baugh, A. (with K. Malone). The Middle English Period (1100-1500). A Literary History of England. Vol. 1. London, 1967.
[2] One of the sessions of the Commons received the name "The Lollard Parliament", Coulton, G. G. The Medieval Panorama. Cambridge, 1949, p. 490.
[3] Encyclopaedia Britannica. Vol. 14, 1970, p. 256.

bus partibus regni Angliae latitabant" ("they hide in many parts of the English kingdom"). John Oldcastle is referred to as "Lollardus". Du Cange provides us with the important reference to a chronicle from 1318, according to which "Lollardus quoque dicitur haereticus Valdensis"[1] ("they called the Lollard also a Waldensian"). Thus, the outlined spiritual kinship between the Lollards and Waldensians directs our attention to the roots of the Waldensian doctrine which lie in Catharism. In fact Waldo adopted from the Cathars their social vision and organisational model but abandoned their complicated dualist mythology.

In his *Dictionnaire historique* the erudite Louis Moreri (17th c.) also pointed to the German-Flemish-English triangle by referring to older sources, which he named carefully, and which reveal the beliefs of the Lollards: "These sectarians said that Lucifer and the angels that followed him were condemned wrongly, that is was rather Archangel Michael and the good angels that deserved this punishment. They (the Lollards) added inadmissible blasphemies against the Virgin, they said that God does not punish us for the faults we commit here. The authors (of the sources) say that a girl, member of this unhappy sect condemned to perish on the stake, when asked whether she was a virgin, answered that she was one on earth but would not be under it. They (the Lollards) taught also that the Mass, baptism and the extreme unction were useless; they also denied penance and refused to obey the Church and the secular authorities."[2] In his *Encyclopédie des sciences religieuses* F. Lichtenberger mentions also the Lollard prediction that "Lucifer and the demons unfairly chased away from Heaven will some day be restored there."[3]

From this we can conclude that the Lollards professed a dualistic creed marked in some cases by Luciferianism. It is hard to say, though, whether these allegations were the result of accidental contacts with continental

---

[1] Du Cange. Glossarium mediae et infimae latinitatis. T. V, p. 134.

[2] Moreri, L. Dictionnaire historique ou mélange curieux de l'histoire sacrée et profane, M. DCC. XL, t. V, p. 213.

[3] Encyclopédie des sciences religieuses, publ. sous la direction de F. Lichtenberger. Paris, 1880, t. VIII, p. 347. Both Moreri and Lichtenberger quote the popular etymology of the appellation «Lollard» as derived from the name of the heresy leader Walter Lollard, burnt in Cologne in 1323. It is possible that Lichtenberger got his note from Moreri. Another piece of interesting but unchecked information is given by Moreri: a Lollard called Basnage who had preached in Piemont had later immigrated with his followers to England.

14

Luciferians or came from the official Church, which sought to discredit the Lollards by presenting them as having a greater affinity for Lucifer than for God. The Luciferian turn is not typical of the English Lollards.

We shall go a step further in asserting that there is a great similarity of doctrines between the Lollards and Bogomil-Cathars, which can be proved by comparing their writings. I have used excerpts from the scripts of the Norwich Heresy Trials (1428-31)[1], as well as quotations from other documents which reveal a commonness with Bogomil writings on the following topics:

I. Beliefs and Rituals of Bogomils and Lollards

1. *Common Myths* – The fall of Lucifer; Satan as creator and ruler of the visible world

2. *Ritual practices* – baptism in the Holy Spirit; preference for the prayer *Pater Noster*; direct confession to God; negation of Hell and Purgatory

II. Social Ideas

1. *Preaching social justice*

2. *Negation of legal authority and oath taking; condemnation of bloodshed*

III. Anti-clericalism

1. *The official Church is seen as a community of Herod or of the Anti-Christ*

2. *Church buildings are thought of as synagogues, cross-roads or wastelands*

IV. Rejection of the official Church ritual:

1. *Negation of Transubstantiation*

2. *Negation of the Crucifix*

3. *Negation of icons (images) and relics of saints*

4. *Refusal to worship the Virgin and the saints.*

On comparing the texts one might well ask whether it is possible that phrases written in Bulgaria or Asia Minor in the 10th -11th c. can be repeated in England in the 14th -16th centuries. An explanation lies in the habit of medieval thinking concerning religious writings, which relied

---

[1] Heresy Trials in the Diocese of Norwich, 1428-31, ed. Norman Tanner. Camden Fourth Series, Vol. 20. London, 1977, mentions some episodic connections of English Lollards with the continent. Johannes Fynche de Colchester admits to have been in connection with Laurence Tyler, a Dutchman (p. 185); another defendant speaks of a book that "iam nuper venit de partibus ultramarinis ad istas partes" (p. 75).

on stereotypes. It is interesting to note, however, that the heretical writers, who also used such phrases, were allowed to adapt, change and interpret them. Unlike the official religious texts, these formulae were used as aphorisms to initiate the novice and could be developed and retold from a personal point of view. This important point was made by M. D. Lambert in his *Medieval Heresy. Popular Movements from Bogomil to Hus*[1].

In the pages that follow we shall compare parts of Bogomil (Cathar) and Lollard texts[2]. The former come from the *Treatise against the Bogomils* by Presbyter Cosmas, the *Secret Book* of the Bogomils and the *Panoplia Dogmatica* by Euthymius Zigabenus. Some of the material also comes from the collection *Sources of Bogomilism in Bulgaria, Byzantium and Western Europe*[3].

Text comparison

I. Beliefs and Rituals of Bogomils and Lollards
1. *Common Myths*
A) The Fall of Lucifer and his Angels

Bogomils

...et traxit (Sathanas) cum cauda tertiam partem angelorum Dei, et projectus est de sede Dei et de vilicatione coelorum...
(Interrogatio Johanis, *The Secret Book* of Carcassone)

Lollards

...diabolos qui ceciderent cum Lucifero di celo, qui quidem cum cadendo in terram intrarunt in ymagines stantes in ecclesiis, et eisdem continue habiturunt adhuc habitant latinantes... (Depositiones contra Margeritam, uxorem Willemi Baxter)[5]

---

[1] Lambert, M. D. Medieval Heresy. Popular Movements from Bogomil to Hus. London, 1977, p. 269.

[2] I would like to thank Dr. Lydia Denkova and Dr. Boyka Sokolova for their help with the Latin and Middle English texts.

[3] Ангелов, Д., Б. Примов, Г. Батаклиев. Богомилството в България, Византия и Западна Европа в извори. С., 1967.

[4] Heresy Trials..., p. 49. The heretic Margeria mixtes up the fall of Lucifer with another belief of the Bogomils – that the devils dwell in the churches and about the icons made in their honor (Zig.).

[5] Fasciculi Zizaniorum, ed. by W. Waddington Shiriey. London, 1858, p. 278. The commitment between Wycliffe and the Lollards seems to be mutual. In their message to the Parliament the Lollards mention his work "Trialogus".

B) Satan as Creator and Possessor of the Visible World

Bogomils	*Lollards*
Magnum regem dicunt nunc esse diabolum, ut mundi principem (Euthymii Zigabeni, Panoplia dogmatica § 40, *Patrologia Graeca*)	Quod Deus debet obedire diabolo. (John Wycliffe) (Euthymii Zigabeni, Panoplia dogmatica § 40, *Patrologia Graeca*)

2. Ritual Practice
A) Baptism in the Holy Spirit

Bogomils	*Lollards*
Baptismum nostrum Joannis baptismum esse dicunt, per aquam enim fieri, suum vero Christi, per Spiritum enim Jieri, ut ipsis videtur. (Zig. *§16*)	That the sacrament of Baptem doon in water in fourme custumed of the Churcheys litell to be pondred for as muche as whan the child cometh to yeres of discrecion and receyvyth Cristis lawe and hys commaundments he is sufficiently baptized and so he may be saved withowtyn ony other baptem (Depositions of Richard Grace of Beccles)[1]

B) Preference for the Prayer "Pater noster"

Bogomils	*Lollards*
Solam precationem appellant quam Dominus tradidit in Evangeliis, id est, Pater noster. (Zig. §19)	... item quod nulla oracio dicenda est nisi tantum Pater noster (Depositions of Johannes Baker alias Ussher de Tunstale)[2]

---

[1] Heresy Trials.... p. 121.
[2] Ibidem, p. 69.

C) Direct confession to God

Bogomils

The heretics confess and absolve themselves although they are chained by the devil. So do not only man but women and that is to be blamed (Treatise against the Bogomils, Presbyter Cosmas)[1]

Lollards

Also that every good man and good woman is a prest (Depositions of John Sky Jan de Bergh)[2]

Item quod omnis confessio soli Deo est facienda, et non alteri sacerdoti. (Depositions of Matilda uxor Ricardi Fleccher de Beccles)-"[3]

D) Negation of Hell and Purgatory

Bogomils

Item dicunt, non esse purgatorium (Prilozi za povjest bosanskih patarena)[4]

At qui sint ejusmodi, eos negant mori, sed tanquam in somno transmutari, et sine ullo labore coenosum hoc carnis in dumentum exuere, atque immortalem ac Divinam Christi stolam induere, idemque corpus et formam eamdem induere, et praeeuntibus angelis et apostolis in Patris regnune admitti, corpus au-

Lollards

Item quod Ricardus Belward docuit istum quod iste mundus est locus purgatorii, et omnis anima quamcito egressa fuerit de corpore statim sine medio transit ad celum sive ad infernum et adeo frustra fiunt oraciones vel misse dicte vel facte pro defunctis. (Depositiones de John Burell, famulus Thome Mone)[5]

---

[1] „Беседа против богомилите", с. 54.

[2] Heresy Trials..., p. 147.

[3] Ibidem, p. 131.

[4] Rački, F. Prilozi za povjest bosanskih patarena. – Starine 1869 (1), p. 139. Also in: Богомилството в България..., p. 221. On this subject see also A Neglected Byzantine Notice on Bogomils by Ив. Дуйчев in his book Проучвания върху средновековната българска история и култура. София, 1981. Dujčev discovers this notice in a polemical treatise published in London in 1624, also published in Constantinople in 1627. The dualists explained the negation of purgatory in this way: this world is the kingdom of Satanael), so this world is a place of suffering, a purgatory (even a hell in itself: "Item dicunt, in hoc mundo infernum esse, i.e. hic esse ignem et frigus et omnem malum, et non est alius infernus, nec fuit, nec erit." Salve Burce, Supra stella in Döl linger, Ign. v. Dokumente vornehmlich zur Geschichte der Valdesier und Katharer. München, 1890, p. 327. So that existential aim of the adept is to free himself, to cut relations with this world for he can return to the Father in Heaven.

[5] Heresy Trials..., p. 74.

tem, quod exuerint, in cinerem pulveremque dissolvi, numquam amplius surrecturum. (Zig. § 23)

II. Social ideas
1. Social justice

Bogomils

They scold the rich, they teach their own folk to disobey the masters, they detest the king, they blame the boyards, they suppose that people working for the king are odious to God and they instruct any servant to stop working for his lord. *(Treatise against Bogomils)*

Lollards

Also that the temporal lordis and temporal man may lefully take alle possessions and temporel godys from alle man of holy Churche, and from alle bysshops and prelates bothe hors and harneys, and gyve thar good to pore puple. (Depositions of Hawisia Moone, uxor Thome Moone de Lodne)[1]

2. Negation of the legal authority ant oath-taking. Condemnation of bloodshed

Bogomils

Neque per Hierosolymam, inquit juraveris, quonam civitas est magni regis. Magnum regum dicunt nunc esse diabolum, ut mundi principem. (Zig. §40) Item dicunt quod non sit licitum alicui defendere se ita, quod invasor possit laedi. Item dicunt quod nula potestas terrena possit uti gladio

Lollards

Also that is no leful to slee a man for any cause, ne be processe of lawe to dampne ony traytour or ony man for ony trezon or felonie to deth, ne to putte ony man to deth for ony cause, but every man shuld remitte all vengeance only to sentence of God (Depositions of Hawisia Moone)[2]

---

[1] Ibidem, p. 141. The redistribution of the property of the Church done by the lords in favor of poor people is a kind of softened Utopia, being in line with the union of Wycliffe and the king against papal authority and wealth. John Ball offered a more radical variant. In his famous sermon at Blackheath he declared servitude a thing displeasing to God, and recommended even to kill chief lords, the lawers "and finally remove from their land any one who in future proved hurtful to the commonalty." Gairdner, J. Lollardy and the Reformation in England. Vol. I. London, 1908, p. 16. As far Ball abandoned the Bogomil-Lollard requirement to condemn bloodshed he transformed himself in a revolutionary.

[2] Ibidem, p. 142.

materiali in vindictam malefac-
torum[1]".

Quod homicidium per bellum vel
praetensam legem justitiae pro temporal; causa sine spirituali revela-
tione, est expresse contraria Novo
Testamento; quod quidem est lex
gratiae et plena misercordiarum[2].

The next item shows that the anti-clerical vocabulary of the Bogomils, Cathars and Lollards was rich in repetitions – the anger of the heretics
generated a vivid language, which travelled almost unchanged across
countries and centuries and was later borrowed by the Protestants for
their discourse with Rome.

III. Anti-clericalism
1. The official Church seen as a community of Herod, or of the Anti-
Christ

Bogomils
Nostram antem Ecclesiam Hero-
dem interpretatuntur, quae Verbum
apud eos natum conetur occidere.
(Zig. §28)

Lollards
Item quod papa Romanus est Antechristus, ac episcopi et alii prelati
Ecclesie sunt discipuli Antechristi,
et quod papa non habet potestatem
ligandi et solvendi in terra. (Depositions of Johannes Skylly de Flixton)[3]

2. Church buildings perceived of as synagogues, crossroads and wastelands

Bogomils
They call the churches crossroads
and the holy mass and other divine
services done in the churches they

Lollards
Item quod omnes ecclesie materi-
ales sunt nisi synagoge, ac medicum
vel nichil deberent haberi in reve-

---

[1] God. Cassat. A. IV. 49. f. 287 (Errores haereticorum Catharorum). – Döllinger, Ign.,
op. cit., p. 323.
[2] Sequntur Conclusiones Lollardorum in quidam libello porrectae pleno parlamento regni
Angliae, regnante illustrissimo principe Rege Ricardo secundo, anno ejus circiter XVIII,
in: Fascicui Zizaniorum. Ed. by Walter W. Shirley. London, 1858, p. 366.
[3] Heresy Trials..., p. 53.

treat as garrulity (wasted words) (Treatise against Bogomils)

rencia quia Deus exaudit preces orantis in campo tam bene sicut preces orantis in tali synagoga. (Depositions of John Godesell, parchemyn-maker)[1]

IV. Rejection of official Church Ritual

1. Negation of Transubstantiation (the transformation of the eucharist into Christ's body)

Bogomils
The eucharist is not commended by God, rather is God's work, as you tell, but is like every other food. *(Treatise against Bogomils)*

Lollards
... sed quod postem verba sacramentalia a sacerdote rite ordinato prolata in sacramento altaris remanet panis purus et materialis (Depositions of Johannes Warden de Lodne)[2]
Quod substantia panis materialis et vinum maneat post consecrationem in sacramento altaris (John Wycliffe)[3]

2. Negation of the Crucifix

Bogomils
Because the Jews, crucified on it the son of God, so the cross is really offensive to God. If somebody has killed the son of the king with a cross of wood should this wood be pleasant to the king? (Treatise against the Bogomils)

Lollards
... and no more worship ne reverence oweth be do to the crosse than oweth be do to the galwes whiche man be hanged on (Depositions of Willelmus Hardy de Mundham, tayllour)[4]

---

[1] Ibidem, p. 61.
[2] Ibidem, p. 33.
[3] Fasciculi Zizaniorum, p. 277.
[4] Heresy Trials..., p. 154. The letter of Germanus Patriarch of Nicaea (1222-1240) to the residents of Constantinople contains an anathema against those who call „the resuscitating and honorable cross gallows". We cite this text from the Bulgarian version, included in: Богомилството в извори в България, Византия и Западна Европа Европа..., p. 131. One more detail – on negating the cross the Bogomils and the Lollards admit the same

3. Negation of icons (images) and relics of saints

Bogomils

Venerandas enim imagines asper-
nantur et idola gentium appellant,
argentumque et aurum et opera
manuum hominum. (Zig. §11)

...quomodo beatorum Patrum reli-
quiis inhaerent daemones. (Zig. §
12)

Lollards

... quod nullus honor est exhiben-
dus aliquibus ymaginibus sculptis
in ecclesiis per manus hominum...•
(Depositiones tions of Johannes
Burrel...)[1]

Item quod relique sanctorum scilicet carnem et ossa hominis mortui,
non debent a populo venerari, nec
de monumento fetido extrahi, nec
in cap is reponi. (Depositiones of
Johannes Skylly de Flixton)[2]

4. Refusal to worship the Virgin and the Saints

Bogomils

...they do not venerate the glorious
and pure Mary, the mother of our
God Jesus Christ and say malignant
gossips against her. *(Treatise
against Bogomils)*

Lollards

...Item quod nullus honor exhiben-
dus quibus ymaginibus crucifiixi,
Beate Mariae vel alicuius alterius
sancti (Depositions of Johannes
Reve de Becles)[3]

The great number of coincidences can be enriched even further. The appellation "good man" (boni homini), "good Christian" (boni christiani) is the title of the Perfecti, the spiritual leaders of the Bogomils and Cathars. This address is unique in the whole spectrum of medieval heresies and is typical only of the dualists.

This formula can often be found in the records of the Norwich Heresy Trials (1428-31). We read that "every good man or good woman is a prest" (p. 142) or, the variant phrase "good Christian man" (p. 153), and,

---

excess. Presbyter Cosmas informs his readers about heretics „that cut up crosses to make tools out of them". In one of the recorded proceedings of Norwich one finds: „Quam crucem iste Johannes Burell percuciebat cum dicto fagothook"–Heresy Trials..., p.76.

[1] Heresy Trials..., p. 73.

[2] Ibidem, p. 53.

[3] Ibidem, p. 108.

again, the expanded version "every man and every woman being in good lyf" (p. 142). Even the well known Latin appellation of the leaders of the dualists – *perfecti* exists in the proceedings of Norwich: the "moost holy and moost *perfit*... is very pope" (p. 141). Another Latin version is "Item quodlibet bonus Christianus est sacerdos" (p. 177) and the same sentence is also given in English translation: "Also that every good Christene man is a prest" (p. 179). To these the Latin paraphrase "fidelis homo" (p. 205) can be added.

An explanation of this appellation is provided in the proceedings which brings us back to the well-known Bogomil assertion that only the "good people" who have acquired by virtuous moral life the power to be priests should be allowed to teach, because a priest with an imperfect moral life can corrupt his disciples. The defendant Edmund Archer maintains "that every good Christian man is a good prest, and had as muche poar as ony prest ordered, be he a bysshop or a pope" (p. 166). The same assertion can be found in paragraph II of the address of the Lollards to Parliament *(Conclusiones Lollardorum)* and is confirmed by Wycliffe: "Item quod si episcopus vel sacerdos existat in peccato mortali: non ordinant, conficit, nec baptizat"[1].

In addition to the proceedings of the Norwich Trials, Norman Tanner gives detailed and convincing reconstruction of the beliefs of the Lollards. He, however, does not comment on the phrase "good man", "good Christian" which might be due to the fact that he was not aware of its specific doctrinal meaning. It is clear that even to the clerks of the Inquisition "good man" had not been very clear and sometimes they rendered it descriptively. Thus, for example, in the depositions of John Skylly de Flixton we find such a descriptive version of the phrase: "Item quod quilibet homo existens in vera caritate est sacerdos Dei et quod nullus sacerdos habet maiorem potestatem at ministranda aliqua sacramenta in Ecclesia quam habet aliquis laicus non ordinatus"[2]. Here instead of "good man" one comes across the descriptive "homo existens in vera caritate" which echoes precisely the Cathar meaning of the word "caritas" – love. Rene Nelli stresses on the lack of "caritas" as the sign of the visible world of Satan in which the absence of love causes the annihilation (Fr. neantisation) of Satan's creatures[3].

---

[1] Fasciculi Zizaniorum, p. 278.
[2] Heresy Trials..., p. 52.
[3] Nelli, R. Le phénomène cathare (perspectives philosophiques et morales). Toulouse, 1988, p. 32, p.39.

There exists yet another link between John Skylly's words and Bogomil-Cathars practices. In stressing the spiritual authority of the "aliquis laicus non ordinatus" he reproduces the radical position of the Bogomils according to which the clergy is superfluous (Euthymius of Peribleptos). Moreover, in giving the right of women to become *perfecta* (spiritual leader), the Bogomils, Cathars and Lollards were *unique in the Middle Ages for allowing women the same spiritual function as men*, an emancipation forerunning the ideas of social equality which appeared much later.

John Thomson proposes a successful interpretation of the appellation "good man":

"Some held that every good Christian or a man who was living in charity was a priest of God, and this was carried to its logical conclusion by those who held that the true vicar of Christ was the best man."[1] The author obviously takes the expression literally, without relating it to its continental history. In this way he removes it from its religious context, and intuitively reveals the basic cultural characteristics of the heresy, the fact that it enables its followers to abandon to some degree the religious myth by presenting them with an objective of self-perfection, an element anticipating the rise of Rensaissance rationalism.

The rationalist overthrow of the Orthodox ritual as undertaken by the Bogomils is parallel to the rationalist attack of the Lollards against the Catholic Church. There are records proving that among the favourite occupations of the advanced learners were literary and philosophical activities. M. D. Lambert notes the spontaneous formation of reading circles[2]. He mentions as an example the cultivated tastes of Sir Richard Sturry who "had a copy of *Roman de la Rose* and was acquainted with Chaucer and Froassard"[3]. Lambert's list can be continued with the impressive documentation collected by Margaret Deansly in *The Lollard Bible*[4].

Another comparison is also pertinent in speaking about the rationalism of the heretics. The approach used by the Bogomils for explaining Christ's miracles is similar to the objections raised by the Lollards against the magic scenery of Catholic mass.

---

[1] Thomson, J. The Later Lollards 1414-1520. Oxford University Press, 1965, p. 248.
[2] Medieval Heresy..., p. 240.
[3] Ibidem, p. 242.
[4] Deanesly, M. The Lollard Bible (And Other Medieval Versions). Cambridge, 1920/1966.

Bogomils	Lollards
They do not believe that the people were nourished in the desert with five loafs super only. They say these were not loafs but the gospels of the four Evangelists and the fifth – the Acts of the Apostles.*(Treatise against the Bogomils)*	Quod exorcismi et benedictiones facte super vinum, panem, aquam, et oleum, sal, ceram, et insensum, lapidem altaris eecclesiae muros, super vestimentum, calicem, mitram, crucem et baculos peregrinorum, sunt vera practica necromantiae potius quam sacra theologiae. *(Conslusiones Lollardorum)*[1]

John Thomson has underlined the rationalist way of thinking of the Lollards[2] and Norman Tanner has paid attention to the fact that the heretics tried at Norwish "were accusing the Church of using magic, thus reversing the roles played in the trials of witches"[3].

These almost perfect coincidences and astonishing similarities point to the common roots of Bogomilism and Lollardy. Yet, it is surprising that given the well-studied problem concerning the views and beliefs of Lollards, there has been no attempt to trace down their Bogomil-Cathar roots. Here we would like to present the results of our survey and analysis.

First, we should mark the achievement of the brilliant trio A. Vesselovsky, M. Gaster and I. Franko, dating back to the previous century. In this field it is really they who first formulated the problem of cross-cultural influence[4]. Their achievement deserves to be brought to light again. It was only in 1960 that M. A. Aston took a step in their direction by trying to discover resemblances between Lollards and Cathars in her study of their social conditions and dissemination: "Lollards, like Catharists and earlier continental heretics, and like friars themselves, flourished along

---

[1] Fasciculi Zizaniorum, p. 362.
[2] We adduce the view of John Thomson in details: "The rationalistic element in Lollard thinking is not confined to calling images stock and stones and to denying transubstantiation. It can be seen also in the denial that the priesthood had any special power and in the claim that water which had been blessed by a priest was no better than the water which had not." – The Later Lollards, p. 248.
[3] Heresy Trials..., p. 20.
[4] The German authors quoted by I. Franko are of special interest: Reischshen, R. Die Pseudo-Evangelien von Jesu und Marias Kindheit in der romanischen und germanischen Literatur. Halle, 1879; Wülker, R. P. Das Evàngelium Nicodemi in der Abendländischen Literatur. Padeborn, 1872; Horstman, C. Altenglische Legenden. Padeborn und Heilbron, 1878.

the main roads, and found supporters among the trades people of large towns."[1] The proximity of certain basic Lollard ideas with those of the Bogomils was stressed by M. D. Lambert: "In East England the crucifix was attacked in terms oddly reminiscent of the Bogomils; 'no more credence should be done to the crucifix'[2] it was said, 'than to the gallows which thieves be hanged on'." This author succeed in establishing a long line of indirect but real links between the Bulgarian and the English heresies. According to him the heretics described by Eckbert of Schonau are "blended with Bogomil influenced group"[3]. Let us recall here the fact that the German-speaking sectarians who landed on the English coast in 1162 have been supposed to be an affiliation of the community mentioned by Eckbert.

Certainly, the movement across countries and ages produced visible distinctions between the views of Lollards and Bogomils. *La couleur locale* is a deviation as regards the origin. Here we shall outline some of those differences.

First, the Bogomil assertion that the world of the Old Testament was the world of Satanael did not appear in Lollard thought. There was a predominant appeal for mercy and denial of bloodshed as motivated in the *Conclusiones Lollardorum* as "expresse contraria Novo Testamento".

While the Bogomil and Cathar perfecti denied marriage as a carnal continuation of the human race in the material world created by Satanael, the Lollards were not inclined to dogmatic abstinence.

They only removed matrimony from among the regulative functions of the church by saying that "only consent of love in Ihu' Christ betuxe man and woman of Christene beleve ys sufficiant for the sacrament of matrimony withoute contract of wordes or solemnisation yn churche."[4] Nor do we find the Bogomil-Cathar restriction to the consumption of meat, rather the Lollards showed their independence to the official church by saying "that no Cristen peple is bounde to taste in Lenten time, Ymbrin Days, Fridays, vigiles of seyntes ne other tymes which ben commanded of the Churche to be fasted" and even "it is leful... to ete flesche"

---

[1] Aston, M. A. Lollardy and Sedition 1381-1431. – Past and Present, apr. 1960, p. 15.
[2] Medieval Heresy, p. 268.
[3] Ibidem, p. 63.
[4] Heresy Trials..., p. 111.
[5] Ibidem, 115-116.

as often as appetite comes[5].

Another local feature can be detected in the replies of some of the defendants in Norwich who asserted that while the sacrifice of Christ is "precious and profitable" the death of St Thomas is unprofitable[1]. Can this disagreement over the holiness of St Thomas be read as a sign of the temporal coalition between the Lollards and the royal institution against the papacy?

Cultural activity of the Bulgarian and English dualists

Textual comparison has hitherto been the center of interest. At this point we would like to direct our attention to the most attractive aspect of the heresies – their ability to develop imaginative thinking. Both Bogomilism and Lollardy involved their followers in cultural activity which was surprising for the Middle Ages. Catharism on its part was a major creative stream in the Provençal culture of the 12th century. As different authors have pointed out the Bogomils "contributed particularly to the advancement and propagation of literacy" (D. Mishev); there were schools in practically all of their communities and they loved lecturing (S. Georgiev). According to D. Angelov, these medieval dissenters were one of the principal intellectual forces which brought about major democratisation "of letters and education in Bulgarian society during the 9th-10th centuries"[2].

During the past century V. Jagič concluded that by its intensive effort of copying texts, literary and educational activities and by imbibing the broader views of the apocrypha, and views wider than the dualistic tenets Bogomilism transformed the cultural effort of Simeon's and Climent's age[3] into a popular enlightenment.

Books had a prominent position with Lollards as well. In the records of the Norwich Trials there is ample information that the heretics prac-

---

[1] Ibidem, p. 57.
[2] Ангелов, Д. Българинът в Средновековието. Светоглед, идеология, душевност. Варна, 1985, с.28.
[3] Ягичь, В. Исторія сербохорватской литературы. Казань, 1871, с.96. The position of A. Lombard is similar as he views the Bogomil literature as a continuation of the work of Cyril and Methodius, of their translations in the vernacular of some parts of the Scriptures. See Lombard, A. Pauliciens, Bulgares et Bonhommes en Orient et en Occident. Genève et Bâle, 1879.

ticed reading in secret societies or at home, and that many of the texts were translated in English. The *Pater Noster, Ave Maria* and the *Credo* were translated in English (in lingua anglicana script, libros in anglicano idiomate scriptos)[1]. Robert Cavel (capellanus notatus de heresi) reports that he had seen the heretics in their private schools (in scolis privates eorundem)[2].

Margery Baxter (notata de lollardia et heresi) mentions a Carmelite friar expounding the gospel in English[3]. According to Norman Tanner "clearly schools existed in which heresies were taught systematically" (Colchester, London and other places)[4]. Malcolm Lambert also treats the Lollards first of all as a reading community, stimulating self-teaching"[5], and mentions a small group of "academically trained" Lollards such as Nickolas Hereford, Philip Repton, John Aston and John Purvey, who was Wycliffe's secretary over the last years. More detailed research is necessary to illuminate the relations between this highly educated group and the Lollards of the lower strata. Its presence, however, suggests the existence of a well-developed Lollard culture which had real summits. *Given these facts, it is possible to assert that the Bogomil Cathar and Lollard heresies generated important literacy. We can also say that in Bulgaria, France, England, as well as other countries, the heretics brought about cultural innovation and, to our opinion, they can be recognized as one of the driving forces of the Renaissance of the 12th century.*

Anne Hudson mentions a Lollard library, containing three types of books: 'schedule', 'quaterni' and 'libri', though she does not specify their nature because it "can only roughly be asserted from episcopal and chancery records"[6].

John Thomson has been less hesitant and has produced according to Margaret Deansly – another excellent scholar of Lollardy – "an excellent and up-to-date bibliography of all printed and unprinted sources"[7]. This is how Thomson describes the collection of James Willis from Chilterns

---

[1] Heresy Trials..., p. 69, 73, 100.
[2] Ibidem, p. 93.
[3] Ibidem, p. 48.
[4] Ibidem, p. 69, 73, 100.
[5] Medieval Heresy, p. 257, 240.
[6] Hudson, A. Some Aspects of Lollard Book Production. – In: Schism, Heresy and Religious Protest (Studies in Church History, 9), 1972.
[7] Deanesly, M., op. cit., p. VII.

in the mid-fifteenth century: "St Paul's Epistles, the Apocalypse, and St Luke's Gospel". Another Lollard possessed "a book of St John the Evangelist"; there is a reference to a copy of the Epistle of St James (Reg. Chedworth. Line.)[1].

Margaret Deansley provides information about a Lincoln Lollard who used the *Nicodemus Gospel* in English (Reg. Chedworth. Line.)[2]. This gnostic book also suggests a Bogomil-Cathar circulation.

Concerning *The Book of St John the Evangelist* we would like to note that this might be the other title of *The Secret Book* of the Bogomils since *The Secret Book* contains the revelation received by John personally from Jesus Christ. In favour of such supposition is the notice of M. Gaster from a century ago: "The Apostle John, the author of the *Apocalypse*, which answered so well to their system, was the beloved apostle of the Bogomils, and many a book and revelation is ascribed to him."[3]

The culture of the heretics was an open one, the Lollards knew not only the strictly dualist selection of writings. There are numerous references to other texts such as the *Old Testament*, to a book of Solomon (perhaps *Proverbs*, or the *Song of Songs* as John Thomson suggests), a copy of Tobit, etc. John Thomson mentions also perfectly orthodox books and that one suspect person owned a copy of the *Canterbury Tales*.

The heretics' *affinity for books* emerges as one of the inherent characteristics of their culture, accounting for their poetic feeling and rich imagination. According to A. Galahov "the apocrypha were overflowing

---

[1] The Later Lollards, p. 242. We have to recall the doctrinal affinity of the heretics for some of the quoted books. The Epistl. Corinth. 1 was used as a crucial argument in some Cathar writings (esp. Anonymous Cathar Treatise–beg. of 13th century–included in: Liber contra Manicheos of Durand de Huesca). The beloved phrase of the Cathars from the Epistl. Corinth. 1 was:"Though I speak with the tongues of men and angels, and have not charity I become as sounding brass, or a tinkling cymbal... and though I have all faith so I could remove mountains, and have not charity, I am nothing..." See also Nelli, R. op. cit., p. 12. Another valid criterion for proving the Bogomil nature of the cited titles is proposed by Thoma Thomov. He indicates that even in Historia... manichaeorum qui et pauliciani dicuntur Petri Siculi (IX century) the literary choice of the old dualists that was inherited by the Bogomils is described this way: "Quintum est quod nullum recipiunt Veteris Testament! librum, deceptores ac fures prophetas appellantes... nec nisi sancta quator Evangelia et apostoli Pauli quatordecim Epistolas Joannis tres sancti, Judae catholicam, et apostolorum Actus...", Patr. Graeca, t. CIV, col. 1255.
[2] The Lollard Bible, p. 363.
[3] Ilchester Lectures.... p. 49.
[4] The Later Lollards, p. 243.

with poetic details and answers to most curious questions"[1]. M. Gaster has observed that for their imaginative mind "the Biblical story becomes a biblical romance: truth and fiction are inextricably mixed"[2]. This is a sure mark of individual interpretation. Bogomils, Cathars and Lollards were not simply literate but were aware of the creative dimension of literature.

Let us at this point sum up the cultural similarities which have been discussed. First, the literature of the Lollards, no matter how scanty the information about it, coincides in its principal titles with the literary heritage of the Bogomils and Cathars. Second, the aspiration of the Lollards to read and preach in English (lingua Anglicana) made translation one of their major occupations, which was an important contribution to their national culture. The culmination of this process was reached with Wycliffe's translation of the New Testament, a turning point marking the official recognition of the English language as an ecclesiastical tongue. The heretical inspiration behind Wycliffe's efforts can be detected also in his translation of the well-known gnostic *Evangelium Nicodemi*. J. Gairdner quotes the exclamation of a chronicler of that time: "This Master Wycliffe translated into the English, not angelic tongue the gospel (in anglica linguam, non angelicam)"[3]. In this way the Scriptures could be administered "to the laymen and infirm persons according to the requirements of the time and their individual wants and mental hunger"[4].

This, in our opinion, is a major achievement of the heretics on a European scale: almost everywhere they translated the *New Testament* into the vernacular, adding to it the apocrypha, and thus helping the processes of formation of a national literary language, the new letters for the laymen. Thus for instance, Provençal became so subtle and rich that Dante was deeply impressed by its beauty and wrote sonnets in it.

One of the successful attempts to place the English biblical translations in their European context was undertaken by Margaret Deanesly in 1920 in her impressive work *The Lollard Bible*. She compares the early English versions of the scriptures with the translations of the French,

---

[1] Галаховъ, А. Исторія русской словесности - древной и новой. I. СПБ. 1880, с.198.
[2] Ilchester Lectures..., p.p.25-26.
[3] Gairdner, J., op. cit., p. 101.
[4] Ibidem.

Italian, German and Flemish heretics (see the Appendix). Her approach is authoritative particularly given that at the beginning of the 14th century the famous Inquisitor Bernard Gui had registered in his manual *Practica Inquisitionis* that the translations into the vernacular were the most certain way of unveiling the heretical activities of Cathars, Waldenses and Beguins[1]. About the Cathars he writes that "... they read the Evangelia and the Epistles in the vernacular" (legunt the evangeliis et de epistolis in vulgari)[2]. The remark about the Waldenses reads: "... they possess commonly the Evangelia and the Epistles in the vernacular" (Habent autem evangelia et epistolas in vulgari communiter)[3]. Similarly, the Beguins are referred to as users of the vernacular though their books are not differentiated: "the mentioned Beguins have the books of Brother Petrus Johannis put into popular language" (habent libri... ex latino transpositos in vulgari)[4].

The practice of the Lollards to "teach God's precepts in English" (precepte Dei in lingua anglicana)[5] resemble closely ones described by Inquisitor Gui, who could hardly imagine that his notes would ever become the object of a comparativist study.

The spiritual awakening brought about the heretics had another important behavioral consequence – in the atmosphere of cultural revival there began a process of an *initial awakening of the interest in human personality*.

The leading personalities among the heresiarchs have been remembered in history along with sovereigns, conquerors and the fathers of the Church – Bogomil, Jeremiah, Nikita (the leading person at the Council of Saint-Felix de Carman), Jean de Luglio, John Wycliffe, Jan Huss. They define the prototype of the human being who has found realisation by his free thought and creativity. Malcolm Lambert's observations concerning England speak of the impulse of the Lollard "to search out the truths of Scirpture for himself" by way of which the individual acquires the ability of self-teaching[6]. The first step is to inculcate the primary aphorisms and gradually, when becoming more learned, to make one's way to interpre-

---

[1] As Beguins he understands the Franciscan Fratres Minores, followers of Pierre-Jean Olieu (Petrus Johannis Olivi).
[2] Gui, B. Manuel de l'inquisiteur (édité et traduit par G. Mollet). I. Paris, 1926, p. 26.
[3] Ibidem, p. 62. See also the Appendix.
[4] Ibidem, p. 142.
[5] Heresy Trials..., p. 73.
[6] Medieval Heresy..., p. 240.

tation, ask questions and find answers. The way in which Lollards attracted new sympathizers and guided them to the depths of knowledge is similar to the one practised by the Bogomils and described by Euthimius Peribleptos (early llth c.). They first gave a small piece of their knowledge to the neophyte and they increased the portion until they revealed the full scope of their knowledge[1].

The heretic Margery Baxter presents a case in point, her statements, eloquence, the richness of her language, all testify to the high quality of Lollard culture.

* * *

Given the vast scope of the problem, at the end of our study it might be helpful to suggest the directions in which more research needs to be done.

First, in spite of the work dedicated to Wycliffe and his ideas, as yet no detailed and convincing explanation of the origins of his dualistic views has been given. It will also be interesting to look into the durable interest of Sir Thomas More in the heretics sustained under the cover of a controversy with them[2].

Second, the profound knowledge of the accused Margery Baxter of Martham of dualistic myths, should direct attention to the higher level of Lollard culture, the translation of numerous apocrypha in English, a layer of literature left almost without scholarly attention for many years. It is enough just to mention the influence of the *Nicodemus' Gospel* on *The Vision of Piers Plowman* and the miracle plays.

Finally, an endeavour which deserves to be undertaken is the elucidation of the problem of the Lollard contribution to the Reformation, where "by the time that the Roman establishment was succeeded by the Anglican, the Lollardy was developing into Puritanism"[3]. (Max Weber has

---

[1] The art of communicating with people deserves to be quoted as seen by Euthymius Peribleptos: "Cum eos viderunt illud facile suscepisse, etiam alia eis dicunt et ita paullatim, et non nisi longo temporis cursu discipulos impietatem vix decent", Patr. Graeca, t. CIV, col. 55.

[2] A serious initial effort in this direction is M. Deanesly's. Her study of biblical translations of the Lollards begins with the information from the Dialogue by Sir Thomas More. The Lollard Bible, p. p. 2-6. The same title is included as an appendix in t. V of Gairdner, J. Lollardy and Reformation in England.

[3] The Later Lollards.... p. 253.

stressed the importance of Protestant ethics for the development of capitalism and its social role.)

The material discussed in this paper seems to suggest as a final conclusion that Bogomilism, the Bulgarian spiritual ferment, in its indirect and modified ways has left a mark on the spiritual climate of England.

Appendix: Cathars and Waldenses

According to M. Deanesly the Waldenses were the first to start translating the Scriptures and the Cathars "borrowed from them a devotion to the study of vernacular versions of the Bible"[1]. In return, the Waldenses should have adopted from the Cathars the "consolamentum". This view contains two inaccuracies. The first is that the Waldenses did not practice the "consolamentum". The second, and more important, is the assigning of the priority of the translation into the vernacular to the Waldenses, since the Cathars historically and culturally precede them. Waldo started preaching at the very end of the 12th century, while at the Council of Saint-Felix de Caraman in 1167 the relations between the numerous and well established Cathar sects were settled. The Cathars did not translate the whole Bible but especially the *New Testament* which they considered their spiritual guide.

Attention should be paid to one very significant detail, which is mentioned by many authors. The prayer *Pater Noster* (Matth, 6) in its Cathar version ends with the words: "For thine is tlie kingdom, and the power, and the glory, for ever. Amen." This phrase is missing in the Vulgate.

C. Schmidt explains this as follows: "The biblical versions that were in Cathar service in Italy and in France were translated not after the Vulgate, but from an original Greek text – the same which was used for the Slavonic version accomplished by Cyril and Methodius. The apocrypha that came in the Cathar sect were again of a Greek provenance"[2]. The same conclusion is reached by J. Ivanov Bogomilski knigi i legendi. Sofia, 1925, p.111 - in Bulgarian[3]. C. Schmidt and N. Ossokin, backed up by other historians, remind us that some of the perfecti, the Cathar leaders, were highly educated people who knew Greek and Hebrew. Waldo did not know Greek, nor is there any information that any of his disciples did.

---

[1] The Lollard Bible, p. 42.
[2] Histoire et doctrine de la secte des Cathares, Aibigeois. II. Paris-Genève, 1849, p. 271.
[3] Иванов, Й. Богомилски книги и легенди, С., 1925, с.111.

Chapter II. Traces of Bogomil Movement in English.
The Case 'Bugger'

The linguistic trace

A traditional way of checking how far a certain phenomenon has become involved with the history of a given country is to see whether that phenomenon has left any traces in its language. In our case the answer is simply "yes" - there is such a word as "bugger" in the English language, a transformation of the French "bougre" as the Cathar heretics in Southern France were called. The *Oxford English Dictionary* also quotes other variants of "bugger", as well as "buggerie" which is connected with the first entry. The whole lexical nest includes "bowgard, bouguer, buggerage, buggerer, buggar, buggeress and buggerly". "Buggery" also has several forms: "bugery", "buggerey", -*arie*, -one, "boggery", "bowgery", "bockery" and so on. This paper will deal with the topical meaning of "bugger" – a sodomite (a buggery - sodomy), particularly as it is also a legal term or, to quote the OED "In decent use only as a legal term".

Naturally, this most prestigious dictionary of the English language also provides the etymology of the word "bugger": "Bugger. Also bowgard, bouguer (ancient French - bougre): Latin - Bulgarus, Bulgarian, a name given to a sect of heretics who came from Bulgaria in the llth c., afterwards to the other "heretics" (to whom abominable practices were ascribed), also to usurers."[1] The correct statement is also added that, in the said medieval period "the name was particularly applied to the Albigenses".

This valuable reference, however, is mainly left for limited academic usage, while the popular usage of "bugger" continues as a legal term for sodomite (as a technical term in criminal law - to quote the OED). In addition, this reliable information is not always given in the academic circles themselves. For example, *The Oxford Dictionary of English Etymology* quotes a similar form - "bowgard" (and "bouguer"), but claims that the Bulgarians were heretics "as belonging to the Greek Church, sp. Albigensian"[2]. This is a serious mistake, because the Greek and the Al-

---

[1] The Oxford English Dictionary. I. Oxford, At the Clarendon Press, 1933, p. 1160. The dictionary provides another, less studied historical meaning of the word "bugger" -usurer. It suggests that the heretics dealt in money-lending because the money provided their independence from the feudal power and hierarchy.

[2] The Oxford Dictionary of English Etymology, ed. by C. T. Onions, 1966, p. 124.

bigensian churches have never been connected. What is more, if one follows the logic of events, the Albigensian Church is a sort of opponent of the Greek one insofar as the Albigensians are genetically linked with the Bogomils who, in turn, are against the Orthodox (Greek) church on principle. A similar confusion of the Bulgarian Bogomil church and the Greek (Orthodox) church can also be found in *Webster's Third New International Dictionary*, where the word "bugger" is given only with the meaning of sodomite, "from the adherence of the Bulgarians to the Eastern Church considered heretical."[1] It is true that the Catholics accuse the Orthodox Church of heresy and vice versa - Catholics are considered a kind of heretics by Orthodoxy, but this controversy between the two official churches has nothing to do with the Bogomils and the Cathars, i.e. with "the bougres", "the buggers".

Therefore, we are faced with the task:

- to confirm the historically correct meaning of the word "bugger" ("bougre") as a variant of the national name Bulgarian;

- to see what religious and political circumstances have loaded it with negative twisted meanings.

And if the results of this study prove convincing they could be offered to English linguists and lawyers. It is within the scope of their ability to restitute the initial meaning of "bugger" and, in the name of the new communication between the people, to free the Bulgarian national name of the hostile imagery of past antagonistic ages. There is natural evidence in this respect. In French, for example, the negative connotations of "bougre" imposed by the Inquisition have been swallowed by the positive evolution of the same word with the meaning of "brave homme". One finds a similar line of evolution in the English language, preserving almost the same meanings of "bugger". To quote *The Oxford English Dictionary*, there exist "often, however, in English dialect and in U.S., simply = 'chap', 'customer', 'fellow'." It is interesting to reconstruct this cultural and historical development and the region and the social strata which outlined it. One can assume that French linguistic practice has shed the negative connotations imposed on "bougres" because the French have reconsidered their attitude to the Cathars with the passage of time, perceiving them as the carriers of a highly developed for

---

[1] Webster's Third International Dictionary. Massachusets, 1961, p. 291

the Middle Ages civilisation[1]. On the other hand, arriving in England under the negative stamp of the Inquisition, this word was locked in the artificially acquired negative meaning and the mass conscience lost its real history, nor did it have occasion to restore it.

To the best of my knowledge, the first more comprehensive attempt to restore the historical truth in England was made by Moses Gaster in 1887. Quoting C. S. Faber, he wrote: "Boggard" a Northern provincial appellation of a foul fiend evidently resolves itself into *Bulgard, or* Bulgarian, the very common designation *of the Albigenses*, whose dealing with Satan was notoriously a general belief. "[2] *As* was already mentioned, in the next century *The Oxford English Dictionary* marked the connection "bougres/buggers" or "heretics who came from Bulgaria in the 11th century" with "Albigenses" (Cathars). It is also pointed out that, according to R. Brunne Cron. of 1330, "bugger" entered the English language with the double meaning of sodomite and heretic: "þe Kyng said & did crie, þe pape was heretike... and lyued in bugerie". The combination "þe bougre and þe heretike" is found in Ayenb. of 1340[3]. It is important that the OED admits that sodomy was ascribed to the heretics. The dictionary of Funk & Wagnalls uses a slightly stronger word to show the imposition of foreign meaning on "bugger": "Bulgarian heretics to whom abominable practices were imputed."[4] But it was Eric Partridge who finally pointed out the truth, i.e. that the "bougres" or Bulgarian heretics were

---

[1] Indeed this process of self-emerging attributing of new words meaning begins by the end of sixteen century. For example during the verb rabougrir appeared in French in 1600 and the verb abougrir was introduced, even earlier in 1564, is introduced the verb abougrir, describing an ill growing plant, waning down due to drought and inclement conditions. These verbs could be applied to the condition of people. The context is clear - the French have witnessed that the Cathar heresy persecuted by the internal crusades and the Papal inquisition, has declined and became an example of wilting. Next the word bougre gains a new meaning indicating a chetif (week), faible (feeble) person. The reflective derivative verb se rabourgrir appears in 1690 according to Le Robert, Dictionnaire de la langue francaise. (Paris, volume VII, 1985, page 985). Similar is the interpretation of the Grand Larousse encyclopédique, Paris, 1963.volume VII, p.974: "arrêter le développment normal" - translating: to stop, halt a normal development. The meaning of the same word in Provençal dialect is close: to suppress or smear a person. (Lou trésor doú felibrige – Dictionnaire Provençal-Français. T.I. Paris, 1932, p.40).

[2] Gaster, M., op. cit., p. 78. To appreciate the contribution of Faber and Gaster in clarifying this problem we should mention the fact that in the Etymological Dictionary of the English language, published by W. S. Keat in 1879-1882, Oxford, the word "bugger" is missing.

[3] The OED, v. I, p. 1019, 1160.

[4] Funk & Wagnalls New Standart Dictionary of the English Language. N.-Y., L., 1933, p. 341.

vilified. He showed how "bugger" originated "from ML Bulgarus, a Bulgar, hence a heretic and, *by lay slander* (italics - G.V.), a sodomite."[1]

Who was the author of this slander? After the first two marches against the Cathars, undertaken by Pope Innocent III and the Northern French kingdom in the beginning of the 13th century, the populace of Provence and Northern Italy sympathised with the victims because of their education and moral purity. It was then, too, that the Catholic clergy launched a vilifying campaign against them[2].

Why were the poor bougres, persecuted and burnt at the stake, also presented as sodomites? Since the heretics and particularly their leaders were paragons of virtue and the fact that they did not spare themselves or their strict moral conduct were noticed by most of their contemporary chroniclers, an arbitrary allegation had to be found which could fire the imagination of the uneducated ordinary people by ignominious means so that they would substitute their admiration for complete denial. It is obvious that the psychological mechanism of this scheme was well-planned.

Yes, the Cathars, whose name means "pure" in Greek, were people who seemingly had no human weakness because they had given up the ways of the sinful world like eating meat or shedding blood. Ordinary people thought of them as living saints capable of working miracles. But, the propaganda of the Catholic Church "specified", the Cathars denied the carnal relations between people because they had such with... animals[3]. But no one has seen such a thing, nor is there evidence of such

---

[1] Partridge,E.A Short Etymological Dictionary of Modem English. L., 1959/1966, p. 63.

[2] R. Nelli has explained the relatively late negative connotation of the word „bougre":"In the beginning the troubadours (i. e. the 13th century - author's note, G. V.) did not lend a negative meaning when they mentioned the name „bougre" as, for example, in the *Song of the Crusade against the Albigensians*. It was only later that the word acquired a disparaging connotation and became a term of abuse in the mouths of those who persecuted „the Bulgarian heresy" - Catharism" (Participation in a discussion published in the book of Топенчаров, Вл. „Две жарави - един пламък", София., 1982, с. 174).

[3] This slander spread over a considerable territory. Borislav Primov has noted the existence of the word „buzzerone" in Italian with the meaning of „homosexual", „sodomite" and the participle „buzerans" in Hungarian which means „a man sexually involved with another man". According to B. Primov, both the latter and the verb „buzeral", meaning „to trouble", „to pester", have come to the Hungarian from the Italian through German of Serbo-Croatian mediation. Примов, Б.,Бугрите (Книга за поп Богомил и неговите последователи), София, 1970, с.с.305-306. To corroborate this link we shall mention that A. Prati indicates that the Italian term for sodomite „buggerone" originates from the word Bulgari (Bulgarians)- „that had turned to Manicheans and therefore suspected in sodomy sins."(Vocabulario etimologico italiano.

actions. No one has seen it, the ecclesiastic "interpreters" explained again, because the Cathars fornicated secretly, in the night. And it was that fornication which wore them out, not the fast and prayer to which they claimed they had dedicated themselves.

Many authors have pointed out that the church frequently resorted to calumny in dealing with the heresies, including one of the most famous scholars of Catharism, Charles Schmidt. It is strange that in the past it was even taken up by creative personalities who were familiar with the depths of heretic philosophy like, for example, Joachim of Fiore. Nevertheless, objective scholars like Lev Karsavin, who had no personal sympathies for the Cathars and considered them a force destructive to medieval Christian civilisation, wrote quite frankly: "It is not by chance that, beginning with Bernard of Clairvaux, many writers, saints, prelates and monks tried to discredit the morality of the heretics and spread rumours of how they sinned during their nightly gatherings. And if these allegations are few, this only proves one thing - their complete groundlessness."[1]

Therefore, the conclusion that comes to mind is that the word "bugger" entered the English language in the first third of the 14th century as an echo of the negative campaign the Catholic Church had launched in Southern France against "les bougres" - the Cathar heretics. That is why neither the Englishmen of the Middle Ages nor those that live today perceive it as the national name "Bulgarian" but as a negative epithet, frozen in signifying a perversion. It has undergone the greatest deformation in comparison to other words whose initial meaning was shifted when they

---

Torino, 1951, p.180). D.Oliveri in his dictionary Dizionario etimologico italiano, concordato coi dealetti, le lingue straniere e la topoonomastica (Milano. 1953, p.106) indicates that the „Bulgarians were accused in sodomy practices as adherents to the patarene heresy." D. Oliveri draws similarity to the contamination of the French word bougre with the meaning of a sodomite pervert. B. Primov's observation is confirmed by Du Cange who points out that the Spanish word „bujaran" is loaded with the same negative meaning - „masculorum concubitor", i.e. „one who lives with a man" (Du Cange. Glossarium mediae et infimae latinitatis, t.I, p. 772). Although it has acquired a pejorative content this term it to all means and purposes a trace which outlines the large geographical territory of „Bulgarian", i.e. Bogomil influence.

[1] The noted Russian historian and philosopher quotes the opinion of more sincere Catholic chroniclers. One of them characterised the Patarene Diotesalva as „respected, with honest conduct and dignified bearing" (aspectu venerabilem, honestum incessu et exteriori habitu). Karsavin also quotes another chronicles: „They say that the heretics are virtuous and accomplish miracles" (Dicebant quod heretici faciebant virtutes et miracula). Карсавинъ, Л.П. Очерки религиозной жизни в Италиі XII-XIII вѣков. С-т Петербургъ, 1912, с. 54. See also the Appendix to this chapter.

entered the context of heretical culture. In 1931 J. L. Seifert gave two examples which confirm the pattern of such a shift. He pointed out that the national name "Fleming" (flamendr) entered the Czech language during the international heretical communications and remained there with the distorted meaning of "singer", while in the 16th c. the word "Waldenses" (Vaudois) began to acquire the meaning of "sorcerer" under the influence of the mixing of late trends in the Waldensian heresy with sub-cultural phenomena like alchemy and astrology[1]. An additional, secondary designation of "bugger" as a result, as an echo of those events, can also be seen in the fact that in those times the usurers in Provence and Lombardy were called "bougres".

Hidden identity

The logic of linguistic quest presupposes another question: isn't there any other indirect trace connected with this or another encounter of the island with the dualistic heresy? Should one open *The Oxford English Dictionary* at the entry of "publican" one will find information about such an earlier arrival of a heresy on British soil in 1160. The evidence is provided by William of Newburg (Guillelmus Novoburgensis) and is interpreted by Stephen Runciman and Milan Loos. It is the result of the wave which spread from Germany and was recorded there by Eckbert, Abbot of Schonau. A group of some 30 uneducated people who denied baptism, marriage, the Eucharist and Catholic unity and were led by one Gerhard came to England - these people William of Newburg calls "publicani"[2]. Stephen Runciman further adds that, in 1167, heretics with the name of Poplicani or Deonarii were caught in Burgundy and tried in Vezelay on the charges that they denied the cross, holy water, churches,

---

[1] Seifert, J. L. Die Weltrevolutionäre (Von Bogomil über Hus zu Lenin). Amalthea-Verlag. Zürich-Leipzig-Wien, 1931, p. 52, 111. The Czech dictionaries give a rather different meaning of 'flamendr", i. e. "vagrant", but etymologists point out that it primarily entered the Czech through the German as signifying a "merchant from Flanders" - Machek, V. Etymologický slovník jazyka českého. Praha, 1971, p. 146. As many historians have pointed out it was the merchants who were among the main propagators of the Cathar heresy in Europe. One should also mention that, quoting C. S. Faber, M. Gaster also mentioned how the name Vaudois (Waldensian) was loaded with the meaning of "sorcerer" - Gaster, M., op. cit, p. 78.

[2] Runciman, St. The Medieval Manichee (A Study of Christian dualist Heresy). CUP, 1947, p. 122.

donations, marriage and the holy orders[1].

Finding that the heretical group of "publicani" which arrived in England was related to *Flemish and Burgundian* heretical communities, St. Runciman has in fact pointed out the two main channels by which heretics and, what is more important heretical apocrypha, would again come to the island over the next two centuries. Those were actually *the Flemish-German and French (Norman-Burgundian) ways of influence* (author's italics - G.V.). But Runciman also cared to reveal the root of the name "publicani" or "poplicani", suggesting that this is a Latinized phonetic transcription of the Greek word Paulicians. The western followers of the heresy came into direct contact with one of the sources in Constantinople where the resident Paulicians presented the strictly dualistic, or Dragovitsa branch of the Bogomil church[2]. And, according to Stephen Runciman and the majority of the scholars, it was the dualists from Constantinople who were among the propagators of the heresy in that period.

The view that the Cathars were called "poblicans" in Northern France and England was voiced as early as 1849 by the outstanding scholar Charles Schmidt, who also quoted a list of old chroniclers who mentioned that name[3]. Some of them are given in Du Cange's *Glossarium*. The latter truly mentions the "popelicani" as early as 1017, while the *Chronicle* of Rodulphus Coggeshalensis from the time of Louis VII (1137-1180) says that it was thus that the "popular tongue" called the heretics who had spread to many parts of France[4]. At the Third Lateran Council of 1179 quoted by Du Cange, the names of the heretics Cathars, Patrenes (Patarenes) and Publicani were placed next to one another, with the explanation that they had spread in Albi, Toulouse and elsewhere[5]. From

[1] Runciman, St. The Medieval Manichee... Milan Loos (Dualist Heresy in the Middle Ages. Akademia-Praha, 1974, p. 117,125) mentions a barely studied case of probably Cathar heresy in England, mentioned in Guilberti Foliot Epistola CCL (Ad Rogerium Wigorniesem episcopum) PL 190, col. 935-936: "Quod super his textoribus sentiamus, qui vestra nuper ingressi diocesim..." It was a typical Bogomil-Cathar detail that they preached in the popular tongue: "Qui corde conceptas haereses in vulgus spargendo praedicant."

[2] The Medieval Manichee, p. 123.

[3] Schmidt, C. Histoire de la doctrine de la secte des Cathares ou Albigeois. T. II. Paris-Genève, 1849, p. 280. Schmidt quotes Muratori as the first historian to deduct the direct Cathar-Paulician link (Antquit. ital. med. oevi, V, 83). He also quoted the authoritative opinion of Mosheim that the Cathars were Paulicians who, coming from Bulgaria and Thrace, spread their doctrine in Italy and the rest of the West (Institut. hist. eccl., 379) - p.261.

[4] Du Cange, op. cit., t. VI, p. 412 says about the "Publicani": "that is how our Manichaeans are called".

[5] Concilium Lateranse III, cap. XXVII, De hereticis, Mansi, t. 22, col. 232.

Magna Chronica Belgica of 1208, again after Du Cange, we learn that the Popelicani professed both principles, i.e. they were dualists.

Among modern scholars, Stephen Runciman's opinion is shared by Femand Niel[1] and particularly by Borislav Primov why pays special attention to this matter. Although he uses Du Cange's *Glossarium* most frequently, he has sufficient reason to conclude that all the forms of "Publicani", "Populicani", "Poblicani" and "Popelicani" originate from the Latin name of the Paulicians - "Pauliciani"[2]. The Dragovitsa Paulician church around Plovdiv[3], known for its extreme dualism, was a sort of rival in the infiltration of the Bulgarian Bogomil Church to the West. With time, regardless of the theoretical discussions between the adherents to the moderate (Bulgarian Bogomil Church) and the extreme (Dragovitsa Church) dualism, in Western Europe the two religious communities began to be perceived as variants of one phenomenon - Catharism, *both indicating that Bulgaria was the original source of that heresy* (author's italics - G. V.).

Back on British territory, one sees that while the word "bugger" was pushed back because of its derogatory deformation of meaning, the heretics who found firmer foothold in England under the name of "publicans" and later on, maybe bearing in mind the tragic continental fate of the "bougres" (the annihilation of the Cathar civilisation in Southern France), succeeded in adopting an aspect more acceptable to the Church in England. Although one could object that, at the end of the 12th century, it was "publicans" who were tried, branded and chased out of Oxford, it seems that after several decades of persecution they contrived various means of adaptation and mimicry which to a certain extent led the heretic communities out of the sphere of direct conflict with the ecclesiastic power. A case in point is the fact that the heretics managed to "change" to a definitely positive aspect the etymology of their name by a skilfully translated parable from the New Testament.

---

[1] Niel, F. Albigeois et Cathares. PUF, Paris, 1959, p. 59.

[2] Примов, Б. „Българското народностно име в Западно Европа във връзка с богомилите". - Изв. Инст. Бълг. Ист. 6, 1956. Always correct to the smallest detail, Ch. Schmidt does not forget to recall the exact phonetic way of producing „Poblicans": παυλικιανοί or παυλικανοί was pronounced by the Greeks as „Pawlikani" from which the French can spontaneously produce the form of „Poblicans". This last, by the way, is the Old French pronunciation of „Pauliciens".

[3] D. Obolensky, relying on P. Safarik and N. Filipov, also located the Dragovitsa church (Ecclesia Dugunthiae) in or around Plovdiv, near the Dragovitsa River. Thus he had reason to question the claim of Fr. Rački (later adopted by Dr. Dragojlovič and others) that the Dragovitsa church was located in Macedonia. -Obolensky, D. The Bogomils (A Study in Balkan Neo-manichaeism). Cambridge, 1948, 158-169.

To this end the Cathars and the "Publicans" used Christ's parable of the Pharisee and the publican (tax collector) (Luke 18:10-14), while the publican with his unpopular profession honestly admitted to his sins in the temple, the Pharisee placed himself closer to God and above the others. Christ condemned such hypocrisy and pointed out that the humble publican had greater chances for God's mercy. Identifying themselves with the publican (*publicanus* in the Latin translation of the New Testament) the "Popelicani" or "Publicans" succeeded in symbolically placing their much-suffering heads under the protective force of Christ's preference. At the same time, by the logic of this interpretation, their persecutors (inquisitors, Dominicans and bishops) proved in the place of the Pharisees. This comparison was used even in Southern France, but there it was rather a means of polemising than of mimicry. There is just such a quotation by the famous 14th century inquisitor, Bernard Gui, who has recorded how the Cathars from Southern France called their persecutors from the Catholic Church Pharisees and saw themselves in the position of the persecuted Christ and the apostles: "sicut docuit Christus et apostoli ejus... cum tamen ipsi sint boni homines et boni christiani, sicut pharisei persequebantur Christum et apostolos ejus."[1]

There are also facts indicating one of the ways in which this approach was transferred to England. It was frequently used by Guillaume de Saint-Amour (1202-1272), rector of Paris University, in his epic struggle against the tidewater of Catholic orders in the emancipated University of Paris. One finds that a sermon of his, reprinted four centuries later by an English Reformation publication, had the objective of using "old authors" to expose the "mistakes and malpractices of the Roman Church"[2].

The dauntless Guillaume de Saint-Amour, to whose courageous struggle nearly a whole chapter of the *Roman de la Rose* is dedicated, called his opponents from the religious orders "falsely pious" who love the loftiness, fame, vanity, showiness and bows addressed to them. At the same time the "publicans" are presented as "men of the world who, even if they are sinners" do not pretend they are saints and admit to their sins. That Guillaume de Saint-Amour was familiar with Cathar mythology is also indicated by the following passage in the same sermon. He points

---

[1] Gui, B. Manuel de l'inquisiteur. I. P., 1926, p. 24.

[2] Scriptorum veterum (quorum pars magna nunc primum e MSS. Codibus in lucem arodit) qui Ecclesiae Rom. Errores & Abusus detegunt & damnant necessitatem qui Reformationis urgent. Londini, MDCXC.

out that the clerical Pharisees have become pseudo-apostles, just as the angel Satan was transfigured into an angel of light", i.e. Lucifer: "ipse per enim angelus Satanael transfigurat se in angelum lucis"[1]. This could be the shortest version of the Bogomil legend about the fall of Satan and at the same time a purely Bogomil-Cathar hint that the earthly order (including that of the church) was established by Satan.

This hereticised, or at least deviating from the canon parable became a popular image in English literature: Wycliffe used it in his sermons; it is mentioned in the *Chronicle* of 1340 (Ayenb. 175) quoted above which speaks of "Þe bougre and Þe heretike", and the same sermon is mentioned by Chaucer. In its traditional and untraditional interpretation, the underscored image of the publican was used by Shakespeare, Robertson, Milton and Bunyan. In other words, when one looks at the respective page of the OED one sees that the publicistic-imagery meaning of this word has prevailed, its more frequent usage being connected with that anti-Catholic and Reformist spirit with which it had once been loaded by the "publicani" heretics in Southern France. This is a linguistic reflection of the ostensible change of identity with which the old "publicani" or "popelicani" covered their Catharo-Paulician origin and presented themselves as followers of the publican from the Gospel of St. Luke.

Thus the names "bugger" (Bulgarian) and "publican" (Paulician), which respectively started from the Bulgarian Bogomil Church and the Paulician (Dragovitsa) dualist Church near Plovdiv - in both cases from Bulgarian territory, travelled the long route through Bosnia, Dalmatia, Northern Italy, France, Germany and Flanders to be taken to the island and adopted by the English language with those changes, even distortions, which the long and difficult journey had imposed on them. The reconstruction of the cultural epic is a humanist task: in this way one leaves the layer of meaning imposed by the rule of the stronger (which is always deforming) and reveals the cultural and civilisational synthesis of ideas and conduct which took place during the Middle Ages perceived as the age of introversion. In our case, the depth of philosophical ideas, the rich imagery and inventive discussion indicate that dialogue between cultures is a historical law. That that law today becomes a calling of mankind and that the real connection between the "ego" and the "other" is in the mutual revealing of their spiritual essence. Sooner or later this will

---

[1] Scriptorum veterum..., p. 46, 49.

happen - a stand which Tsvetan Todorov aptly defends in his well-known book *La conquête de l'Amérique. La question de l'autre* (1982). A similar kind of retrospection is applicable not only to the space that is external to Europe, but also within that of its own history. Thus the chronicle of some tragic centuries is substituted for, or at least complemented with its alternative - the resurrection of even today important quests of the spirit which, one must say, were even then expressed in a surprisingly rational form.

Appendix: The good name of Bogomils and Cathars

The opinion of serious scholars coincides with the conclusions of L. P. Karsavin about the moral purity of those heretics. Such is the stand of Ch. Schmidt and this is how N. Osokin sums it up: "Even in the eyes of the strictest moral judgement the Cathars would be worthy of the name they have chosen for themselves" ($\kappa\alpha\theta\alpha\rho\acute{o}\varsigma$ = pure)[1].

A whole list of recorded observations can be provided in this respect. First Euthymius of Akmonia (after 1034) wrote that the ungodly Churila preached "He who does not leave his wife cannot be saved" and that, in addition, the heretics "teach the men to leave their wives and the women to leave their own men". It seems that in order to invalidate such ascetism Euthymius accused Churila of "raping a maiden in some abandoned mill"[2]. In his famous *Panoplia dogmatica* (the beginning of the 12th century) Euthymius Zigabenus described how strictly the Bogomils kept the fast. In addition to the Fast of Lent, they "on the second and the fourth day and the Friday of every week fast right up to the ninth hour". In order to throw a shadow on the strict conduct of the Bogomils and without quoting any facts, Zigabenus in turn makes the publicistic remark: "If, however, someone invites them to dine they immediately forget their instructions and eat like elephants. Hence it is clear that they also behave outrageously, although they denounce fornication as if they were without flesh and body." (P. Gr., t. 130). We find the same approach in Presbyter Cosmas (10th century). On the one hand he admits the ascetic self-denial of the Bogomils from this world and its pleasures: "...they declare themselves inhabitants of the heavens and the men who marry and live in the world they call servants of Mammon." On the other, howev-

---

[1] Осокинъ, Н. „Исторія Альбигойцевъ до кончины папы Иннокентія III". Казань, 1869, c.204.

[2] Ficker, G. Die Phundagiagiten. Leipzig, 1908.

44

er, he did not miss the opportunity for an insinuating remark - without, of course, quoting facts Cosmas calls their fast "hypocritical": "Actually the heretics are like sheep: meek, submissive and quiet. Their faces are seemingly pale with the hypocritical fast"[1].

I will quote two of the more popular Western sources: Salve Burce's description and that of the inquisitor Bernard Gui. In 1235 Salve Burce wrote: "Dicunt enim omnes, scilicet Catheri, quod in matrimonio temporali est fornicatio, dicenda malum Deum istum, Diabolum istud ordinasse." (The Cathars say that marriage on Earth is fornication, that the bad god, the Devil, has ordered so.)[2].

Bernard Gui (the beginning of the 14th century) describes how the Cathars keep strict fast and, in addition to the regular fasts "et per totum anum residium diebusjejunant in pane et aqua in quolibet septimana... Item, non tangunt aliquam mulierem" (the whole year they fast on bread and water three days a week...Also they do not touch any woman)[3]. There is no attempt at calumny in these documents and the facts are given as they are. In Salve Burce one finds an important detail which, either because of misunderstanding or because of the intentions of Catholic propaganda, served as the basis for a rumour against the Cathars.

The Cathars believed that they were children of the Good God and it follows from this that they considered themselves brothers and sisters, members of one spiritual family. That was why they thought that cohabitation with one's own wife was equal to incest with one's mother or daughter (Item dicunt; jungere se cum uxore sua aut con matre aut con filia aut on alia uxore unum et idem peccatum esse, quantum est Deo, sed qantum est mundum, scandalum est)[4]. It is with exactly this interpretation that Raynier Sacconi, for example, speculated. With the zeal of a renegade (a former heresiarch) he did not hesitate to use for anti-Cathar propaganda the twisted claim that "multi credentes eorum tam uiri quam mulieres non tient magis accedere ad sororem suam et fratrem.-.etc." (both men and women have no fear of having intercourse with a sister or a brother of theirs... etc.)[5]. Still, considering the good name the Cathars

[1] „Беседа против богомилите". - In: „Стара българска литература 2. Ораторска проза". София, 1982, с. 31.
[2] Döllinger, Ign., op. cit., p. 54.
[3] Gui, B. Manuel de l'inquisiteur, édité et traduit par G. Mollat. I. Paris, 1926, p. 18.
[4] Döllinger, Ign., op. cit., p. 54.
[5] Sacconi, R. Summa de Catharis. - Archivum Fratrum Praedicatorum (Roma), XLIV, 1974, p. 45

enjoyed among the population, Sacconi stipulates that some of the Cathars did not do that because they were ashamed.

Right to the end of the 14th century the populace in Southern France retained the strong memory of the high morals of the Cathars, particularly of their leaders - the "perfect" (perfecti).[1] Jean Duvernoy quotes a number of opinions of ordinary people, recorded in the Régistre de Jean Fournier published by him. A farmer who was led out of the secret Cathar meeting (around 1303) because he seemed slightly suspicious exclaimed: "But, sir, I too want to receive my part of the Good!"[2]. Another 14th century exclamation has been recorded: "Since the heretics were chased from Sabartes there is no longer good weather in the area"[3]. This is followed by the emotional statement that after the heretics were driven away "the land does not produce anything good"[4]. Jean Duvernoy also quotes another document, dating from around the year 1300 - the Régistre de Geoffroy d'Ablis (Paris, Bibl. Nat., ms. Lat. 4269, f 16v) in which a similar belief has been recorded that the Cathars brought happiness and plenty and that one could not do evil in the day one had seen one of the perfects. Sometimes the goodness of the Cathars was given natural dimensions. A notary from Soual (Tarnes) says: "When the heretics lived in these lands we did not have so many storms or lightning. Now that we are with Franciscans and Dominicans the lightning strikes more frequently."

A similar collection of examples of the good deeds of the Cathars is provided by Richard Abels and Ellen Harrison in their study *The Participation of Women in Languedocian Catharism*.[5] One of them, however, is particularly interesting in our case. The following has been recorded in the famous MS 609 (f 157v) about one of the witnesses with Catholic orientation: "he never believed that the heretics were "good men"; he believed, however, that their works were good, even their faith was bad" (credebat quod heretici numquam fuerunt boni homines; opera tamen

---

[1] Duvernoy, J. L'acception: "haereticus" (iretge). -In: The Concept of Heresy in the Middle Ages. Paris-La Haye. I. 1976-77.

[2] Duvernoy, J. Le Régistre d'inquisition de Jacques Fournier 1318-1325. t. I, Touluose, 1965, p. 437.

[3] Op. cit., t. III, p. 335.

[4] Ibidem, p. 307.

[5] Abels, R. and E. Harrison, The Participation of Women in Languedocian Catharism, Medieval Studies, Toronto, 41, p. 245

eorum credebat esse bona et fidem malam).

There are truely cases when the intellectual subtlety of denying marriage by comparing it to incest was sometimes wrongly interpreted by later deformed imitators. They were not familiar with the rich philosophy of Catharism and gave a more primitive expression of their anti-conformism. Johannes Hartmann (1367) claimed that incest with mothers and sisters was allowed "because just as the calves were given for food to the people, women are given for the use of free spirits."[1] These, however, were no longer Cathars but the sect of free spirits. Finally, to conclude the documentary supplement on this subject, it is only fair to quote the case of Belibaste (14th century) who really was known for his penchant for the flesh, although those were times when the Cathar church had already been destroyed by persecution and the self-control which the perfect strictly kept between themselves was no longer possible.

The spiritual purity of the Bogomils and the Cathars remains a high moral example for that age against the background of which the dissipated clergy was extremely embarrasing to medieval society. Presbyter Cosmas used strong words against the "laziness and ignorance of the shepherds" and upbraided the Orthodox priests that they sheared their flock without caring about it.[2] Pope Innocent III sent special scorching letters and punished the steeped in corruption Catholic clergy in Southern France. The rigorism of the "perfect" (Bogomil and Cathar leaders) was so consistent that they themselves were aware it could not be achieved by their ordinary audience. That was why the Cathar community allowed those ordinary people to have a family and live in the world within the limits of the rules in the Scripture. It was in fact the Bogomil-Cathar purity which attracted enthusiastic followers of the heresy, for they saw in it the opportunity to begin a spiritually dedicated, undivided and morally ennobled life.

---

[1] Seifert, J. L. Die Weltrevolutionäre..., p. 45.
[2] „Беседа против богомилите", с. 74.

Chapter III. The Heresy and Women

Women's emancipation and the Bogomils

During the 12th century, if not slightly earlier, Western Europe lived through a period of economic and social upheaval, termed by many historians the 12th century Renaissance. One of its aspects is the considerable emancipation of women, mostly in Southern France, a development which spread over to Italy, Flanders, and later, England. One can detect social zones where real emancipation was achieved. These were created in the socio-economic climate of the Cathar communities who followed heretical dualist ideas. Similar developments can be observed among the Waldenses, who were generically close to Cathar ideas. It is important to remember that the dualist streak came from Bulgaria, cutting across to the west through Bosnia, Dalmatia and Northern Italy. One of the most important characteristics of the Bulgarian dualists, Bogomils and Paulicinians alike, was the complete social liberation of women.

Bogomilism has attracted much of scholarly attention, but new research has come up with new questions – especially those concerned with the status of women. As we know, women achieved a high degree of emacipation in this movement.

For our purposes, we will try to explain this fact a) by considering an element of Bogomil theology and social practice and b) by tracing some of the paths of transmitting these developments to Western Europe.

Bulgarian heretics had a different conception of woman compared to official religion – they did not regard her as Adam's rib, nor as a creature inferior to man, nor as an object for material and sexual domination. This difference underlies the central myth of Bogomil heresy, according to which, the human soul was an angel of God placed within its mortal clay wrapping of a body by scheming Satan. That is why, the idea of spiritual growth among the Bogomils required a complete ascetic denial of this world, which was imagined as a secondary creation of Satan, not God; such was the way of returning to the heavenly realms of the Good Father /the Good God. By entering an evolution of purification in the form of strict asceticism, the adepts were offered the chance to 'divest' themselves of their bodies as if the latter were merely clothes (stola), and thus set their souls free at the moment of the body's death.

The body would remain on earth as ashes and would never be resurrected.

The Bogomil myth contains some remote echoes of the imagined greater responsibility of woman for the fall. According to it, women are incarnations of the souls of angels of the second heaven (angelo secundi coeli)[1], while men have incorporated the souls of the angels of the first heaven (angelo primi coeli). But, all in all, the basic aspiration of the Bogomils to abandon everything pertaining to the material world (omnia corporalia and visibilia)[2], created by Satan (Lucifer), and get back to the real, yet invisible one, of things spiritual (omnia spiritualia et invisibilia), places both men and women in the same position of being able to deny earthly materialism.

This theologically motivated equality was supported by an equality in ritual - women had the right to be ordained and give absolution. In a word, women had the right to be spiritual leaders which has always been a bone of contention for the Orthodox and Catholic clergy. Here is an early testimony of such a reaction coming from Presbyter Cosmas, an anti-Bogomil polemicist: "The heretics absolve themselves, though they are tied up with devilish fetters. This is done not only by the men but by the women also, which is most damnable"[3].

The equality of men and women also finds expression in the fact that women were allowed to become leaders, a role traditionally occupied by men ; men, on their part, were granted the spiritual ability to give birth to God's Word, the Logos, which enabled them to adopt the position of Mothers. According to the Bogomils, both women and men could be Mothers of God's Word (θεοτοκοι).

Dimitar Angelov, the well-known scholar of Bogomilism, often comments upon the high status of women[4]. A good example is the story of the heretic leader Irina of Thessaloniki, who lived in the 15th century[5].

We are not trying to suggest that the genesis of the idea of women's

---

[1] Interrogatio Joannis (The Secret Book of the Bogomils/ - in Иванов Й., „Богомилски книги и легенди", С., 1925, с.78

[2] Rački Fr., Prilozi za povest bosankih patarena - in Starine 1869 (1), p.318

[3] Презвитер Козма, „Беседа против богомилите" - в „Стара българска литература(2). Ораторска проза", София, 1982, с.257

[4] Ангелов Д. „Богомилството", София, 1993, с.257

[5] „Пространно житие на Теодосий Търновски от патриарх Калист" - в „Стара Българска литература (4). Животописни творби", София, 1986, с.с.452-453

equality is Bulgarian. The Bogomils inherited it from the Manicheans through the mediation of the Paulicinians. Yet, unlike the Manicheans, who kept their teaching secret, locked in a small, closed elite groups, this belief became a wide social practice among the Bogomils who brought it later to the West. The civilizational aspect of this attitude can hardly be overestimated, for women were not just introduced to the sacrament of the religious ritual, but were given access to working with 'the Word', whereby achieving the full scope of their culture's potential. Their participation in an activity, traditionally reserved exclusively for males, is strikingly modern and marks the emergence of a humanistic streak in cultural and social behaviour, a striking feature, prominent in the practices of the Cathars of Provence and the Lollard circles in England.

In a dissertation defended in Lausanne in 1920, Archimandrite Stephane Gueorguiev describes the collective discussion of sermons and apocrypha, typical of the Bogomils. The Bogomil longing for the depths of literacy (as Presbyter Cosmas ironizes the heretics) includes women without any restriction. The bishop-monks Leonce and Clement, who had Bogomil convictions, were accused in Cappadocia (1143) during an official trial of allowing women-heretics to "read the holy gospels and to officiate together with Clement". As if this was not enough, these women were ordained as deaconesses by the same Leonce and Clement (see the Appendix).

This new reality, in the long run, brought about important changes, both in the Orthodox and, particularly, in the Catholic tradition. The impact of Bogomil practices was for the first time brought into focus by Stefan Lazarov, who noted that the Bogomils "encouraged even their enemies to think in a broader, more humane way in the sphere of art"[1].

A significant change concerned the representation of the Holy Virgin, in both the Orthodox and Catholic traditions, a change caused by the impact of the popularity of the Bogomil conceptions of the place of women.

A basic Bogomil tenet is that all souls can be saved, so there is no need of the Day of Judgement. Such an idea seriousliy invalidates the power of the Orthodox and Catholic churches, which curb disobedience by threatening the sinners with the eternal fires of Hell. Under the pressure of Bogomil ideas, the Church felt the need to introduce some degree of mitigation of such eternal punishment in order to prevent the growing

---

[1] Лазаров Ст. „Проучвания върху културата на богомили и катари: театър, музика" (Автореферат на дисертация), С., 1989, с.4

sympathy towards the more merciful heretics. A degree of mildness was introduced into the system by borrowing an idea whose origins were in heretical literary imagery. The Orthodox Church started to propagate the apocryphal (better described as non-canonical) tale of *The Descent of the Holy Virgin*. This story, as Moses Gaster and others point out, is an imitation of the apocalyptic books written in defence of the Bulgarian dualists, especially, *Visio Paoli* and *The Descent of Christ into Hell*[1]. In the same manner in which Apostle Paul descends into Hell to describe the torments of the sinners (such as corrupt clergymen who persecuted heretics), is the Holy Virgin made to visit the underworld. Stirred by the suffering of the sinners, she asks her son Jesus Christ to give them some respite, from Maundy Thursday to Pentecost. The reinforcement of the female principle in the official Christian myth was the answer, or rather, the adaptation of the Orthodox Church to the conditions of the contest for women's emancipation so powerfully apparent in Bogomil spiritual and social life.

In this first, Bulgarian, part of this chapter we define three major elements, rooted in the practices of Bogomils, which suggest a new place for women in society:

- full participation in religious ritual,
- the right to engage in literary activities,
- a changed attitude of the official church regarding women, brought about by their emancipation in Bogomil communities.

The heresies, which followed in the wake of the Bulgarian heretical tradition, preserved these three elements until, in the South of France, new opportunities for cultural realisation appeared and brought about new modifications in the position of the official church.

---

[1] „Ходене на Богородица по мъките" - in „Стара българска литература (1). Апокрифи", С., 1982, с.247 or the „Descent of the Holy Virgin". It is interesing to quote Moses Gaster: „The „Descent of Christ to Hell" itself gave rise to a remarkable imitation, „The Descent of the Holy Virgin", and it is easy to imagine the influence it would have on the popular fancy, especially as it was from the beginning regarded as the clue to the mysterious life after death, and therefore gave an opportunity to entering into all possible torments, while the original Gospel only spoke of a place of waling and ghashing of teeth". Gaster, M. Ilchester Lectures on Greeko-Slavonic Litterature and its Relation to the Folk-lore of Europe During the Middle Ages, London, 1887, p.52 One has to pay attention to a theological subtility. The anonymous Orthodox author of the „Descent of the Holy Virgin" has his way to discuss with the dualist: he puts them in the inferno because they refused to preach the name of Our lady, as they negated the material nature of the Christ's body. This detail reveals „The Descent of the Holy Virgine" as a remake-reply against the Bogomils.

Women in Catharo-Provençal Civilization

The place of women in Cathar communities in the South of France has been well studied. A few monographs deserve special mentioning, among them are the two volumes by Jean Guiraud,[1] which pay considerable attention to Cathar women. G.Koch's monograph[2] (1962) has also been of great use to the present study. R. Nelli's book *La vie quotidienne des Cathars au Languedoc au XIIIe siècle* (1969)[3], devotes an entire chapter to women. Le Roy Ladurie (1975) has also collected interesting empirical data about the social life of women under Cathar influence[4]. In 1979 R. Abels and Ellen Harrison published an excellent article, *The Participation of Women in Languedocian Heresy*[5], which is undoubtedly the best work in the field. One of the latest studies is Anne Brenon's *Les Femmes cathares*[6] (1992). Clearly, the problem has been studied in some depth, yet the empirical material also lends itself to interpretations, somewhat different from those offered so far.

Starting with Ms 609 and having considered other sources as well, R. Abels and E. Harrison give the following figures concerning the number of women perfectae: "the ratio between sightings perfecti and perfectae would still have been three to one"[7], and further, that "of 719 heretical ministers named in Ms 609, 318, or slightly less than 45% were women"[8]. The authors apply the term perfectae-class, which suggests the existence of an identifiable stable body of people . There is proof that the perfectae functioned among the women of the community and that, when there were no perfecti at hand, the women had the right to give the consolamentum, the last unction, to male Cathars (See Döllinger, t.II, s.165). Cathar women were the first to create charitable institutions which we find in medieval towns much later. Jean Guiraud describes their schools,

---

[1] Guiraud J. Cartulaire de Notre Dame de Proulles, precede d'etude sur l'Abigeisme languedocien au XIIe et XIIIe siecles, t.1-2, Paris, 1907

[2] Koch G., Frauenfrage und Ketzertum in Mittelalter /Forschungen zur mittealterlichen Geshihte 9; Berlin, 1962. Quoting according Abels R.and E. Harrison - The participation of Women in the Languedocien Catharism - in Medieval Studies, t.41, Toronto

[3] Nelli, R. La vie quotidienne des Cathars au Languedoc au XIIIe siècle, Paris, 1969.

[4] Le Roy Ladurie E. - Montaillou, village occitan de 1294 à 1324, Paris, 1975/1982, p.-p.383-385

[5] Abels R. and E. Harrison - The participation of Women in the Languedocien Catharism - in Medieval Studies, t.41, Toronto

[6] Brenon A., Les Femmes Cathares, Paris, 1992

[7] Abels R. and E. Harrison, op. cit, p.226

[8] Ibidem, p.225

boarding-houses, hospitals, workshops for poor women. Anne Brenon has pointed out correctly that these charitable and caring activities, typical of the Cathar communities in Languedoc at the beginning of the 13th century, began to grow in French towns only during the late Middle Ages[1].

Female Catharism had an institutional impact on the aristocracy. Guiraud speaks of the tradition among the lower and impoverished aristocracy to send their daughters, who were excluded from the inheritance of land, to Cathar pensions and boarding-houses so that they would be provided with a decent living. Abels and Harrison mention the same practice[2]. There is the curious example of Raimon IV (1194-1222), who in order to get rid of his second wife Beatrice, made her convert to Cathar asceticism. Similarly, Raimon-Roger de Foix "agrees" to let his wife part with him, in order to follow the secluded life of Cathar nuns[3]. This is an example of the permeation of Cathar precedent into law , which helped solve problems raised by female inheritance, which suggests that Catharism was found acceptable when it came to solving social problems. Cathar hostels, of the type of nunneries, were established in various places - in 1209 there were six of them in Montesquieu, in Saint-Martin-de-la Lande there were ten. Such institutions were familiar in Le-Mas-Saintes-Puelles, Laurac, Vitrac, Villeneuve-la-Comptal and Cabaret[4].

The strongest historical memory of the participation of women in social life is borne out by Provençal culture. Le Roy Ladurie remarks on its integration and rationalisation of the place of women on the level of everyday life. Provençal culture was open to "an exchange of ideas", where a woman's words had the same scope and freedom of play as that of men. There is "an insatiable aspiration in Occitan women to acquire and preserve their language"[5]. As in contemporary feminism, there is an attempt to overcome "the disempowerment through silence" and "to

---

[1] Brenon A., op. cit., p.215. A.Brenon as Guiraud did before her enumerates the Cathar institutions: house for the neophytes, hospital/asylum, craftsman's workshop, shelter - p.215.

[2] Abels R. and E. Harrisson, op. cit., p.217: "Because of poverty, the minor nobility turned to the heretical convents to place their unmarried daughters and widow female relations." The authors mention also the education role of such establishments: "Cathar convents occasionally functionned as seminaries for daughters of the rural nobility" (p.232).

[3] Nelli R., La vie quotidienne des Cathares du Languedoc au XIIIe siècle. Paris. 1969, p.p. 106-107

[4] Abels R. and E. Harrisson, op. cit., p.p. 22-229

[5] Le Roy Ladurie, Montaillou, village occitan de 1294 a 1324, Paris, 1975/1982, p.p.383-385

democratize access to the spoken and written word."[1] The complete encounter between the woman and the word was achieved in the literature of Provence, and more precisely, in the amour courtois genre. There woman is not subject to man but is an object of veneration. This does not mean that feudal attitudes had completely changed, but that in spite of all, an unheard of enhancement of the status of women was achieved, though mostly as a verbal gesture. The realities of life were as if compensated for in a symbolic literary gesture. After the trouvères had sung Roland's glory in the chanson de geste, the Provençal troubadours raised the lady of the heart to celestial heights.[2]

This aesthetic emancipation might also be interpreted as a projection of the equalising of the status of men and women among the Cathars. Scholars like Raul Manselli object against "any attempt to draw a parallel between Catharism and the amour courtois poetry"[3]. Yet, writers like Denis de Rougemont and René Nelli believe that such a link is legitimate, though they have not unravelled its complex convolutions and psychological motivations. A point which is important to remember is that most of the troubadours shared Cathar ideas. Piere Cardenal's poems often read as dualist treatises and Piere de Corbian, though he wrote a Prayer to the Virgin in which he glorifies the mother of God, also believed that she had conceived through her ear, and that Christ had come out of her like a ray of light, without damaging her body[4]. These are traditional docethical views, typical of the dualists, by way of which they deny Christ's material nature, identify him with the Word (the Logos), which every purified human being is capable of conceiving within him/herself.

Bernard Sicart de Marvejols, like many other troubadours, levelled severe criticism against the Catholic Church, the major enemy of the Cathars. That the amour courtois poetry was rather an act of the emancipation of women is suggested by the appearance of women poets

[1] Long E., Feminism and cultural studies - in Critical perspectives on media and society, ed. By R. Avery and D. Eason, New York, London, 1991, p.117

[2] The troubadours knew well the name of Roland. See Peire Vidal of Toulouse, who says: "My audacity is equal in this of Roland and Olivier, while in art of love I am equal to Berart de Mondesdidier's art of love..." - in J. Robaud, Les Troubadours (anthologie bilingue), Paris, 1971, p.220. But in the troubadour's poetry the image of Roland was displaced by the admiration towards the beloved lady.

[3] Manselli R. Dolore e morte ella esperienza religiosa catara - in Todi, Presso di l'Academia Tudertina, 1967, p.258

[4] Corbian Pierre de, Prière à la Vierge - in Anthologie des troubadours XIIme - XIIIme siècles (édition refondue). Paris, 1974, p. 367. Pierre de Corbian shares practically the same heretical vue that is criticized in the "Descent of the Holy Virgin".

(trobaritz), like La Comptesse de Die and Marie de Ventadour, who, in her poetic manifesto, declares *The Equality of Sexes in Love* (*L'egalité des sexes devant l'amour*)[1]. The development of women's poetry was interrupted in the 13th century when Pope Innocent III and the French kings began a crusade against the Cathars in Southern France. As Alfred Jeanroy, a scholar of troubadour poetry has noted, these were not times favourable to the flourishing of new literature because "the Inquisition had a firm grasp on all spiritual life"[2].

Next, we shall consider the alternatives offered by the Catholic Church to the emancipation achieved by Catharism. Unfortunately, the first of the measures was physical extermination - over one million people were destroyed. Mercy was not shown to women as an act of examplary punishment. The well-known Song of the Crusade against the Albigenses (*La Chanson de la Croisade Albigeoise*) tells of the woman ruler of the town of Lavaur - dame Guiraude, thrown into a well on May 3rd, 1211 and stoned to death. The author of La Chanson, Guillaume de Tudèle, though in favour of the crusader's cause, could not refrain from praising her goodness and generosity[3].

Later came a time of more peaceful methods. Dominique d'Osma, the father of the Dominican Order, established Notre Dame de Prouilles, with the explicit intention to re-educate Cathar women from good families. This monastery was rather rich, as its documents testify, and had the support of the Vatican. But even then, according to R. Nelli, "women went on choosing the Order of Cathars, wherever it still existed, because it ensured their equality and made the oppressive nature of patriarchal power more bearable"[4]

Catholic literature about women was neither original nor attractive. The diversity came again by imitating its heretical counterpart. An example of such borrowing is the famous *Legenda Aurea* by Jacques de Voragine, a collection of lives compiled at the end of the 13th century. The book contains catholicised versions of some heretical apocrypha, including *The Tribulations of the Virgin*, which was the official reply of the Eastern

---

[1] Anthologie des troubadours XIIme-XIIme siècles, p.198. J. Roubaud in his anthology "Les Troubadours" qoutes the names of some other women poets like Avalais de Porcaraiques, Na Castelloza, Clara d'Anduse, Bieris de Romans plus one anonymous poetess.
[2] Jeanroy A., Introduction in "Anthologie des troubadours...", p.29
[3] Tudèle, Guillaume de, La Chanson de la Croisade Albigeoise (Cansos de la Crozada), editee et traduite par Eugene Martin-Chabot, Paris, 1976, vol.5, p.165
[4] Nelli R., op. cit., p.108

Orthodox Church in its cultural struggle with the dualists. In this text, the Virgin begs the ireful Jesus Christ to have mercy on sinful mankind; as a result of her intercession he sends Dominique to begin working for mankind's salvation from heresy[1]. Jean Guitton also thinks that the rise of the cult of the Virgin is a reaction against "the mistakes" of the heretics, and was meant as protection against the "dangerous degeneracy of the amour courtois poetry" (sic)[2]. In so far as the Virgin was represented as benign to sinners, the possibility for mercy and forgiveness in the Catholic world became much wider and allowed for milder relationships among human beings. The appearance of a system of nunneries in this period became a way of making up for the shattered system of Cathar homes . These became the new centres of social care for women and their cultural needs, in spite of the limitations set upon them by the dogma. Having destroyed the Cathar centres of women's social and cultural realization, the Catholic Church had to create analogous formations.

Lollard women - outstanding personalities

The generic links between the dualist Bogomil and Cathar heresy point further in the direction of the Lollards and serve as a testimony to its pan-European nature, a question we have discussed elsewhere[3]. Here, we shall continue following the thread of the place of women in social groups, exposed to dualist ideas. Although there was a considerable distance in time between the Cathar civilization of the 12th-13th century and the fact about the life of the Lollards in England in the 15th century quoted here, the cultural and historical role of women Lollards was the same on principle. The achievement of equality between men and women is best demonstrated by the permission granted Lollard women to conduct services, as the Norwich trials testify. This has been declared in the testimonies of women at the trial. As Hawisia Mone put it: "every man and every woman being in good lyf oute of synne is a good prest and hath [as] much poar of God in all thynges as ony prest ordered, be he pope or bisshop". A similar statement was made by Sibilla, John Godsell's wife.

These, however, are not statements made only by women. John Sky-

---

[1] Voragine J. de, La légende dorée - traduite de latin par T. de Wyzewa, Paris, 1920, p.p.402-403

[2] Guitton J., Le Christ équartelé (crises et conciles dans l'église), Paris, 1963, p.196

[3] See Chapter I.

lan, accused at the same trial, repeats the same words verbatim:"Also that every good man and good woman is a prest"[1]. Fifty-one men and nine women were accused of heresy.Yet, in some respects, the women were the more active part in it. Norman Tanner writes that "Margery Baxter and Hawisia Mone appear to have been active Lollards and not mere followers of their husbands!"[2].He correctly places John Burrell and Margery Baxter as major characters in the trial. The Inquisitor's notes from the interrogation of the latter clearly state that she was independently involved in heretical activities (ipsa tenuit, credidit et affirmavit articulos sive opiniones subscriptas - p. 42).

Hawisia Mone also revealed her talent to dispute well. Matilde, wife of Richard Fletcher, was described as a prominent heretic (notata et multipliciter diffamata de heresi - p.131). Katerina Wryght, wife of Roger Wryght, was also described as a "well-known suspect as a fervent follower of heresy "notatata et vehementer suspecta de crimine heretice pravitatis" (p.194). Isabelle Chapleyn was also proclaimed a "well-known" heretic (multiplicater notata - p. 198).

The Lichfield and Coventry trials of 1511-12 provide similar data about the activity of women. Among the 45 persons put on trial, one third were women. Again, they were not just their husbands' followers, but were rather among the leaders. John Gest confessed that he had been persuaded for eleven years by his wife Johanna to enter the heresy "circiter xi annos elapsos solicitationibus Johanne, uxoris sue incidet in heresim."[3] Another woman, Alice Rowley, "appears to have been one of the busiest and most important working members of the sect."[4]

The most outstanding personality in the whole of the three-year process in Norwich, was also a woman. Margery Baxter transcends all the clichés typical of the discourse of both inquisitors and heretics. She was the only one who freely spoke of her religion in an outburst of spontaneity, freely told the Bogomilo-Cathar myth of the fall of Lucifer in her own rendition (p.49) and the legend of the bee, which stings the tongue of traitors, which suggests a possible acquaintance with the *Physiologus*, an important literary and philosophic book of the Middle Ages. By

---

[1] Heresy Trials in the diocese of Norwich 1428-31, edited by Norman P. Tanner, London, 1977, p.147

[1] Ibidem, p.26

[3] Fines J., Heresy Trials in the diocese of Coventry and Lichifield, 1511-12 - in Journal of Ecclesiastical History, vol.14, 1963, p.p.161-162

[4] Ibidem, p.162

abandoning the formulaic language of the dogma, Margaret Baxter infused the trial with most surprising metaphoric expression, or as a modern feminist might say, hers was "a self-articulation within the subculture"[1]. She provides a strong example of the link between liberal religion and literacy, typical of Lollard sub-culture, which, because of its greater openness, can be regarded as the avant garde cultural space of the times. According to Malcolm Lambert, the latter included the variants of the Wyclifite Bible, which was then translated into English, as well as other vernacular collections of the Lollard sermons, functioning of professional writing - offices etc.[2] The cultural significance of the translation can hardly be overestimated, given "how strongly the ecclesiastical authorities held the view that it was the translations of the Scripture that were the cause and root of all trouble"[3]. This literary production had a high academic quality and is among the most important literary legacies of the period.

Documents testify to the active role of women in this field. Alice Rowley confessed that she had used "good bookis"[4], while her husband was in the habit of reading to her "from St.Paul's Epistles"[5]. There are other records of such family readings in the Proceedings of the Norwich trials. Authors as different as A. Lombard, M. Gaster, Yordan Ivanov, R. Abels and E. Harrison have pointed to the profusion of heretic literature, which was part and parcel of a wide and free literary context, shared by heretics and orthodox alike. In England, this also brought about a new understanding of women by the official church – the appearance of nunneries and a vast body of literature addressed to women testifies to this processes. Such popular pieces are *Hali Maidhad, Seinte Margarete, Sawales Warde, Ancrene Wisse*, two of them containing key-motifs from the founding dualistic myths, disseminated by Bogomils, Cathars, and Lollards.

In their introduction to the collection *Medieval English Prose for Women* the editors Bella Millet and Jocelyn Wogan-Browne re-construct

---

[1] Long E., Feminism and Cultural Studies - in Cultural perspectives on media and society, p.120

[2] Lambert M., Medieval Heresy, 1977/1992, Oxford, p.249

[3] Fines J., op.cit., p.165. These words seem to be an euphemism when John Foxe gives the information that in 1542 Thomas Bernard and James Morden were burned because "the one teaching the Lord' Prayer in English, and the other for keeping the Epistle of St. James translsted into English." - see W. H. Summers, The Lollards of Chiltern Hills, London, 1906, p.97

[4] Fines J., op. cit., p.162

[5] Ibidem, p.166

this topic from Hali Meidhad, without discussing its heretical roots: "Had man been content to replace the angels in God's creation and not to imitate Lucifer's disobedience, our nature could and should have been like that of the angels."[1] This is a close repetition of the myth about Lucifer's rebellion and fall, as told by Margery Baxter, but already coming from the pages of the official religious literature. Another visible dualist quotation can be found in *Sawles Warde*. It concerns is the descent into Hell and the ascent to Heaven[2]. This is a typical variant of *Visio Paoli* and *Nicodemus Gospel*, apocalyptic writings distributed by the heretics. Such characteristic free compilation and reproduction is also visible in *Seinte Margarete*, which contains borrowings from the popular eastern apocrypha about the virgin Juliana.

The forth text, *Guide for Anchoresse* also reveals traces of heterodoxy. There are some essential and stylistic reminiscences of *The Letter from Heaven* (same *Legend of Sunday*, or *Lord's Letter*), which was widespread in the Middle Ages and was an essential book for the Flagellantes, with an Eastern provenance, as Moses Gaster explains. Jesus is called Paraclete (the Consoler) - a way of naming him, used mostly by the Eastern dualists[3].

Two important features emerge from Medieval English Prose for Women. First, the two editors themselves point out that the context of these lives was the debate of the official Church with the heresies and the new realities created by life in their social groups and the Islamic conquest. The Catholic Church had used such compilations to create its own popular literature in its struggle against the Cathars – as is the case of Jacques le Voragine's *Legenda Aurea* which includes apocrypha subjected to a pro-Catholic re-wording.

---

[1] Medieval English Prose for Women, ed. by B. Millet and J. Wogan-Browne, Oxford, 1990, p.XV

[2] Ibidem, p.109. A precise quotation is more expressive here:"…we should look from the vision of hell to the joy of heaven, feel fear from the one, love towards the other…" The text also includes three allegories of the type used in the "Le Roman de la Rose" and that is an indication of an influence of the French medieval luterature. **Fear** relates about inferno whereas **Reason**, helped by the **Prudence** and **Fortitude in God,** describes the Paradise.   ·

[3] M. Gaster gives an information how the apocryha reached England: "Roger of Hovedene gives this "Letter from Heaven" in his Chronicle under the year 1201 and says that it had been brought in this to England by Abbot Eustachius of Flays. The Letter was directly copied thence by Roger of Wendower into his own Chronicle. An Anglo-Saxon translation is said to be in existence at Corpus Christi College in Oxford.", p. 67.

The enhanced interest in women in medieval England was a reflexion of the dynamics of the Renaissance of the 12th century. The editors of Medieval English Prose for Women have avoided the temptation of specifying the developments included in it as typically English and see them as an "influence not only of the literary tradition, but of the French courtly literature and the Latin prose of the twelfth century Renaissance"[1]. The authors prefer the formula "transmitter or transformer" (we shall say, both), and pay attention to the element of Jewish and Eastearn apocrypha[2]. It remains for us to narrow the focus to a clearer picture, as M. Gaster, I. Franko and D. Obolensky have already done, by specifying the heretical character of these apocrypha. Millet and Wogan-Brown have hinted upon this by seeing in *Hali Meidhad* an apparent closeness to heterodoxy[3], although they play down the importance of this fact.

A few rather clear conclusions can be drawn at the end:

First, that Bogomils and Cathars, as well as the heresies close to them, were a powerful force of change in the cultural and social processes in the way they placed women in religion in an equal position with men. As a result, women's cultural activities brought about an important element of mildness, mercy, elegance, psychological depth and an interest in finer literature to the life and literature of the period. Mores and behaviour become milder, to be elegant in manners became a matter of prestige.

There is some truth in the observation made by Alfred Jeanroy who noted that while in Southern France the troubadours explored an unprecedented spectrum of literary genres, in the North, which was less affected by the heresy, the amour courtois was unknown, while the poetry of the trouvères was rather schematic, bearing testimony of the pride of the aristocracy in recounting the glories of battles, rather than the beauties of the world of emotion.

Ladies' attention towards the troubadours and the jongleurs created a more "open society" - the poets and the singers were accepted in the feudal milieu as equals. The emancipation of poets was parallel to that of women and is an example of a high degree of early democratisation.

In the North, the epic poem was the only flowering genre about 1160. In the South of France, according to Alfred Jeanroy, there was a rich variety of literary forms, a sign of a cultivated taste[4]. The leading role of

---

[1] Medieval English Prose for Women, p.XIV
[2] Ibidem, p.XXIII
[3] Ibidem, p.XVI
[4] Jeanroy A., op.cit., p.16

Provençal literature was admitted by Dante and Petrarch who saw themselves as its followers[1]. In England, after the suppression of John Bull's rebellion, the dualist heresy lost the ground for free development but created social groups which brought about a peak in the literature of the period. As the proceedings of the Norwich trials clearly show, women were natural leaders in this literary revival.

Bogomil-Cathar and Lollard emancipation of woman is an undeniably important spiritual component of the 12th century Renaissance helping the rise of a provisional cultural model – an early forerunner of modern civilization.

Appendix: The right of women to ordain and to shrive according to the practice of Bogomils, Cathars and Lollards

A. BOGOMILS
Tenth century:
"The heretics absolve themselves, though they are tied up with devilish fetters. This is done not only by the men but also by the women which is worthy of castigation."[2]

Twelfth century (1143): Heresy trial of the monks-bishops Leonce of Balbissa and Clement of Sasimes: "...he ordained women for deaconesses letting them read prayers and the holy Gospels, and serve mass along with Clement." καὶ χειροτονῆσαι γυναῖκας διακονίσσας, καὶ ἐπιτρέπειν αὐταῖς τὰς συνήθεις ἐκκλησιαστικὰς αἰτήσεις ποιεῖσθαι καὶ τὴν τῶν ἁγίων εὐαγγελίων ἀνάγνωσιν καὶ συλλειτουργῆσαι ταύτας μετὰ τοῦ Κλήμεντος.[3]

B. CATHARS
Beginning of the fourteenth century:
Depositions of Raymunda Valsiera for the Inquisition in Languedoc, describing how Cathar women can practice the "Consolamentum", the

---

[1] See for example J. A. Cuddon, Dictionnary of Literary Terms and Literary Theory, London, 1977/1991, p.p.1007-1008: "The troubadours (who composed in langue d'oc) had a very considerable influence on Dante and Petrarch, and indeed on the whole development of the lyric (q.v.), especially love lyric in Europe."
[2] „Беседа против богомилите", с. 54.
[3] Gouillard J., in Quatre procès de mystiques à Byzance. IV. Les évêques "bogomiles" de Cappadoce, Paris: Institut des études Byzantines. 1978, p. 74.

sacrament of the Cathars: "...that this power from the hands of the good men upon the good men, and from the hands of the good women upon the good women...that the good women possess the mentioned power and they can receive it for exercising on men and women, and if so it is that good men are absent [the adepts] can by saved by good women, the same way as good men do". ("...quod dicta potestas transiret de manibus ad manibus bonorum hominum ad bonos homines; et bonarum mulierum ad bonas mulieres quia, ut dixit, ita sunt bonae mulieres, sicut et boni homines; quae bonae mulieres, sicut et boni homines; quae bonae mulieres dictam potestatem habent et possunt recipere in fine homines et mulieres, si tantum sit, quod non sint praesentes boni homines, et ita salvantur per bonas mulieres, sicut per bonos homines.")[1]

C. LOLLARDS

Fifteenth century:

Lollards' depositions at the heresy trials in Norwich :

"Also that every man and every woman in good lyf oute of synne is a good prest and hath [as] much poar of God in al thynges as ony prest ordered, be he pope or bisshop." (Hawisia Moone, uxor Thome Moone de Lodne).[2]

«Item quod quilibet fidelis homo et quilibet fidelis mulier est bonus sacerdos.» (Sibilla, uxor Johannes Godsell de Dychingham).[3]

"Also that every good man and good woman is a prest." (Johannes Skylan de Bergh).[4]

Margaret Aston mentions that the Lollards produced some women preachers. The question, however, of whether there were Lollard women priests does not have a definite answer yet, according to her. Aston gives the case (after Henry Knighton, 1391) of a Lollard woman that had taught her daughter to celebrate mass but not to consecrate the sacrament.[5]

---

[1] "Errores Manichaeorum: Confessio Raymundi Valsiera de Ax". - in Döllinger, Ign.v., Beitrage zur Sectengeschichte des Mitte latter, t. H-Dokumente vornehmlich zur Geschichte der Valdesier und Kathurer, München, 1890, p. 165.

[2] Heresy Trials..., p. 142.

[3] Ibidem, p. 67.

[4] Ibidem, p. 147.

[5] Aston, M., Lollards and Reformers (Images and Literacy in Late Medieval religion). The Humbledon Press, 1984, p. 62, p. 69.

Note: 563 years after the trial of Norwich (where it was established that the heretics gave women the right to shrive), the Anglican Church, unique among the Christian churches, ordained 32 women as priests in March 1994; in this we can discern the distant influence of the tradition of the English heretics. In its centuries-old disputation with the Vatican, the Church of England used almost the same critical qualifications and epithets as the heretics who preceded it.

The rigid position of the Catholic Church against the ordaining women was corroborated by John Paul II on July 27, 1994. He explained that since Jesus had chosen only men for apostles, there is no justification for changing the situation today. According to Reuters (the source of the information), this position will almost certainly be maintained by subsequent popes.

Chapter IV. John Wycliffe
and the Dualists

Our bread over another substance
[ouer bread over othir substaunce]

While so far we have followed the daily life and ritual practices of the heretics, the time was come to observe how prominent individuals charged the teaching with a reformation potential. At the beginning of this study, this author would like to specify the usage of two basic terms. "Cyrillo-Methodian version" of the Bible, and particularly the New Testament, signifies the text that was finally translated and compiled by the disciples of St. Cyril and St. Methodius. As we know now, the Slav apostles translated only a selection of New Testament texts dedicated to feast days and used in service (Aprakos)[1], while the complete version was the work of their disciples. One way or another, the approach of Ss. Cyril and Methodius and their school of translation remained a characteristic feature of the translation work done later in Ochrida and Preslav. It is this and copies there of that are indicated when speaking of Cyrillo-Methodian versions.

Similarly, this author has taken into account the now generally accepted opinion of British and American medievalists that, most probably, John Wycliffe himself was not directly responsible for the translation of the New Testament. Today, the idea that John Wycliffe was not the author of the translation of the New Testament into English prevails among English and American medievalists. In the introduction to her book, M. Deanesly mentions a "median" version and texts created in the circles of Wycliffe's followers[2]. The *Cambridge History of English and American Literature*, in turn, mentions a translation by Nicholas Hereford, as well as a revision of the translation made by John Purvey[3]. The situation is most probably summed up best by V. Hotchkiss: "Although often given credit of the translation of the Vulgate into English, it is now generally thought that Wycliffe was not directly responsible. Nonethe-

---

[1] Кирило-методиевска енциклопедия. I, 1985, p.p. 631-632.
[2] The Lollard Bible and Other Medieval Versions by Margaret Deanesly. M.A. Cambridge University Press, 1920/1966, p. VII..
[3] Cambridge History of English and American Literature in 18 volumes (1907-1921). Vol.II. The End of the Middle Ages, p.p.29-30.

less, he certainly inspired his followers to undertake this project."[1] And, since it seems one should agree with the *Cambridge History of English and American Literature* that the history of those early translations should be deciphered and written additionally[2], this author has chosen a rather more different approach. Besides adopting the more general concept of "Wycliffite translations" we shall concern ourselves with a later version, dating from the 1400-1450 period[3]. Presumably, as a result of the repeated copying and passage of time, in this case there will already be a distance from the original. And, should one find characteristic features inherent to Wycliffe's philosophy in this text, they would be even more valid for the manuscripts considered to have come out under the direct supervision of or been edited by Wycliffe himself. We could add one important observation in this respect: repeated comparison between the later 1400-1450 version and the copy ascribed to Wycliffe's own hand[4] revealed a coincidence of the fundamental interpretations and peculiar terms used by Wycliffe himself. A proximity and coincidence that, by the way, resounds in the theology Wycliffe expressed in other works. Generally speaking, this study is in the sphere of ideas and is the first of its kind. And there is still abundant material for studying Wycliffe's ideas and thought, regardless of the currently ongoing revelations about his literary heritage. In our case, the main approaches are frequency analysis and hermeneutics. Since the version we have used is on CD, it allows a precise quantitative description of Wycliffe's specific vocabulary. For a number of objective reasons, this author could not use previous editions of Wycliffe or other direct sources connected with the Wycliffite translation circle[5].

---

[1] Hotchkiss, V. Outlawed English. – In: Formatting the Word of God. Ed. by V. Hotchkiss and Ch. Ryrie. Dallas. 1998, p. 65.

[2] The Cambridge History of English and American Literature, Vol. II., p. 30. Hargreaves, H. also shares the opinion on the difficulties involved in reconstructing "the history of Wycliffe's Bible" (The Marginal Glosses to the Wycliffite New Testament. – Studia Neophilologica. Upsalla. 33, 1961, p. 300).

[3] Wycliffite Manuscript. The New Testament. England, 1400-1450. Ed. by Bridwell library and Octavo edition. CD.1999

[4] The Holy Bible, containing the Old and New Testament with the apocryphal books, in the earliest English versions made from the Latin Vulgate by John Wycliffe and his followers. Edited by J. Forshall and Fr. Madden. Vol..IV. Oxford, MDCCCL. Although this edition was not used in our case, this author does not underestimate its value. It is a great publishing achievement, with an excellent introduction and analysis that is topical even today.

[5] Literature on the subject quotes as such: New Testament, translated out of the Latin Vulgate by John Wyclif, about 1378. Ed. by John Lewis. London, 1731; New Testament

Open any modern official edition of the Bible in English (for example *The Holy Bible. New Revised Standard Version.* Oxford, 1989) and read the Lord's Prayer and you shall see that there God is asked to give [us] "this day our daily bread". In Wycliffe's English versions of the Scriptures however, begun about the year 1380, one finds a rather different text, i.e. **"oure bread ouer othir substaunce"** Math. 6:9-13 [give us this day our daily bread over another substance][1]. Why the difference? Why such an unusual sounding in which, besides the translation, there is obviously a small comment of the translator himself? The answer on principle was indirectly provided by Yordan Ivanov, a noted Bulgarian philologist and historian. In his well-known book, *Bogomil Books and Legends*, he wrote that the Bosnian Bogomils read the Lord's Prayer in just such a way, pronouncing "give us our daily bread of another substance"[2]. A similar version can be found in the Lyonnaise rendition of the Albigensian Scriptures: "E dona a noi lo nostre pa qui es sabre tota cause" ["the bread that is above all else"]. Similarly there is one Old Italian version: "Il pane nostre sopra tucte le substantie da a nnoi oggi" ["our bread over any substance"].

Since the Bogomils gave the Cathars the quoted version of the Cyrillo-Methodian translation of the New Testament (subsequently translated into the Latin by the Cathars), we shall turn to the idea that John Wycliffe did not translate the Scriptures from the Vulgate, as the printed editions of his version later stated, but from a Cyrillo-Methodian version. By the way, even today the Bulgarian version of the Lord's Prayer reads "our daily substantial bread" which is much closer to the Greek original "τὸν ἄρτον ἡμον τὸν ἐπιούσιον", where the word "ἐπιούσιον" means literally "suprasubstantial". In other words, the Cyrillo-Methodian version is closer to the Greek original than the Vulgate "our daily [quotitianum]

---

translated from the Latin, in the year 1380 by John Wiclif, D.D. To which are prefixed Memoirs of the Life, Opinions, and Writings of Dr. Wiclif, and an Historical Account of the Saxon and English Versions of Scriptures, previous to opening of the fifteenth century. 4to. London, 1810; New Testament. The earlier version. By Lea Wilson. 4to. London, 1848; MS Bodley 959 Genesis-Baruch 3.20 in Earlier Version of the Wycliffite Bible. Ed. C. Linderg (Stockholm Studies in English, 6, 1959; 8, 1961; 10, 1963; 13, 1965; 20, 1969.

[1] The Holy Bible, made from the Latin Vulgate by John Wyccliffe and his followers, vol. IV, p. 18.

[2] Иванов, Й. Богомилски книги и легенди. София. 1925, с.113. The same fact is quoted in "Slovník jazyka staroslověnskeho. Lexicon linguae palaeslovenicae. t.II, p.322: "**ИНОСОУШТЬНЫ**" (Tetra-evangelium Nikojanum, Serbia XV, Cyr. Num.indicis A.-23).

66

bread". In fact, the term "supersubstantialem" is used in the various Vulgate versions, in Matthew and in Luke (11:2-4), but it is practically excluded from the liturgical and sacramental practice of the Catholic Church. What is more, to pronounce "suprasubstantial" [supersubstantialem] instead of "our daily bread" [panem nostrum quotidianum] in the Lord's Prayer was considered a sure sign of heresy in the Middle Ages. According to Collectio Occitanica, Inquisition records from Carcassonne, in Lombardy Bernard Oliva, the heretical bishop from Toulouse, pronounced 'panem nostrum supersubstantialem' (dicendo in oratione Pater noster: panem nostrum supersubstantialem) when he said the Lord's Prayer[1].

Even in the 19th and the beginning of the 20th century, many authors paid attention to the fact that the Bogomils lay the stress on "our bread of another substance".

In this case we shall list just a few of them because, both in Bulgaria and abroad, one encounters a conservative underestimation of this detail and an inability to decipher its theological significance[2]. H. Puech and A. Vaillant underscored the concept described by Euthymius Zygabenus that "Bogomils created their haven, the true eucharistic bread that is ἄρτος ἐπιούσιος, by which they acquire the blood and flesh of Christ everyday"[3]. Zygabenus mentions the special word ἐπιούσιος by which they characterised the bread: τὸν ἄρτον γὰρ, φησὶ, τὸν ἐπιούσιον[4]. N. Osokyn also noted the "Greek practice" of the Bogomils and the Cathars: they sang the Lord's Prayer after the Greek fashion, substituting "our daily bread" (quotidianum) for the words "our supernatural bread" and adding at the end "яко твое ест царство" (Thy Kingdom come) etc.

---

[1] Döllinger, Ign. V. Dokumente vornehmlich zur Geschichte der Valdesier und Katharer herausgegeben. Munchen. T. II. München, 1890, p. 38: "...dicendo in oratione Pater Noster: panem nostrum supersubstantialem". This case was also quoted by Y. Ivanov.
[2] One should mention here that there are only a few good interpretations of Bogomil and Cathar theology, including Raicho Karolev's 19th century work, those of H. Puech and A. Vaillant, as well as Edina Bozoki, among others. In the case of Bulgaria, the cause was the fact that, after 1944, research of the Bogomil movement fell under Marxist interpretation, with their teaching seen above all as a social movement. In the West, powerful Catholic influence was a barrier before studies of the finer peculiarities of dualistic philosophy. There is not s single study in this sense in Great Britain.
[3] Puech, H. A. Vaillant. Le traite contre les Bogomiles de Cosmas le Prêtre. Paris. 1945, p. 245.
[4] Patrologia Graeca, 130, col. 1313.

adopted by the Eastern Church with good reason"[1]. Jean Guiraud, a scholar who studied the Cathars and was their opponent centuries after they existed, claimed that "they dared to adjust even the word of Christ", taking the liberty to read the said part of the Lord's Prayer in their own way[2].

At this point I would like to undertake a rather more comprehensive explanation of the Cathar concept of the Lord's Prayer that C. Schmidt made in 1849: "... they interpreted 'daily bread' in the sense of food for the soul and, instead of the simple formula from the Scripture, 'Give us today our superstubstantial bread', ending with the words 'for Thine is the kingdom and the power and the glory in all eternity'. Since these words cannot be found in the Vulgate, the opponents of the Cathars who were not familiar with the original text, accused them of misrepresenting the Bible in this particular place. This accusation the latter did not deserve because on this point their version, made on the basis of a Greek source, was more correct than the version of the Western Church."[3]

It was exactly Schmidt who gave the explanation, repeated a century later by Yordan Ivanov. He pointed out that, in the Greek original, the expression from Matthew "τὸν ἄρτον ἡμον τὸν ἐπιούσιον", repeated also in Luke, was translated as "panem supersubstantialem" (Matthew) and "panem quotidianum" (Luke) in the Vulgate. He added that the latter expression "was more accepted in the (Catholic – author's note) Church than the former one"[4].

Dualistic arguments in Wycliffe

One could actually say that Wycliffe's "oure breed ouer othir substaunce" is rather more than just a translation. It is a strongly accentuated comment, for it substitutes the word "supersubstantialem" for three whole words **"ouer othir substaunce"**, intended to endorse the supramaterial notion of the Word as spiritual bread. On other occasions, and in open polemics with the Catholic Church in England at that, John Wycliffe re-

---

[1] Осокинъ Н. Исторія Альбигойцев до кончины папы Иннокентія III. Т. I. Казань, 1869, с. 214.
[2] Giuraud, J. Cartulaire de Notre Dame de Prouilles, précédé d'une étude sur l'Albigéisme languédocien au XIIe et XIIIe siècles. T. 1-2. Paris. 1907, p. CXXII.
[3] Schmidt, C. Histoire et doctrine de la secte des cathares ou albigeois. T. II. Paris-Genève. 1849, p. 117.
[4] Ibidem.

peatedly supported the view that the Word was spiritual bread and true communion: "Teneamos ergo quod, virtute verborum Christi, panis fit" ("We consider bread the virtue of Christ's·word")[1]. There is an undoubted coincidence with the dualistic thesis, to mention even Euthymius Zygabenus (early 12th century), according to whom the Bogomils called "the Lord's Prayer bread of the communion" (ἄρτον μὲν γὰρ κοινωνίας ὀνομάζουσι τὴν προσέυχην τοῦ, Πατερ ἡμῶν)[2]. We have the same coincidence with the Albigensian thesis that "God's word is this bread", recorded by the Inquisition at the beginning of the 14th century.

Albigensians	*John Wycliffe*
Verbum Dei esse ille panis.	...Restat igitur ut panem cotidianum acceptamus spiritualem, praecepta divina cotidies opportet meditari et operari.
(Acta inquisitionis Carcassonensis contra Albigensis a. 1308 et 1409. – Döllinger, I. II, p. 28)	
	(Wyclif, J. Operis evangelici. Lib. III et IV. London, 1896, p. 285)

This definitely dualistic interpretation prompts one to look for other dualistic themes in Wycliffe. And there are so many of them and so well expressed that one wonders how they have not been noticed until now. To the best of this author's knowledge, none of the contemporary scholars studying Wycliffe has made even a single such observation or assumption. In the first third of the 20th century, Leo Seifert alone expressed the opinion that Wycliffe was very close to dualism[3]. To fill in this unsubstantiated void, we shall hereafter quote some of Wycliffe's fundamental dualistic theses, compared to those of the Bogomils and Cathars and grouped in the following manner:
- dualistic theogony;
- dualistic criticism of the Church and the rites;
- social views.

---

[1] Confessio Magistri John Wycliff. – In: Fasciculi Zizaniorum Magistri Wycliff Cum Tritico. Ed. by Walter Shirley. London, 1858, p. 120.
[2] PG, 130, col. 1313.
[3] Seifert, L. Die Welte revolutionäre. Von Bogomil über Huss zu Lenin. Wien. 1931.

DUALISTIC THEOGONY
The Devil as master of this world

It was a fundamental Bogomil tenet that the Devil was creator and master of this world. This explains Wycliffe's well-known Seventh of all the 24 Conclusions refuted by the Synod in London in 1382, one that continues to amaze British medievalists.

Bogomils and Cathars	*John Wycliffe*
In 1211, the anti-Bogomil council in Tarnovo convened by Tsar Boril anathematised, among other things, "those who claim that the Devil is the autocrat of this world".	Item quod Deus debet obedire diabolo.
(Попруженко, М. Синодикъ царя Борила. София, 1928, с. 92)	(XXIV Conclusiones Wycclyf damnatae Londoniis in synodo – Fasciculi Zizaniorum, p. 278)

The fall of Lucifer and his angels

The other part of the dualistic myth about the pride and fall of Lucifer and his angels also features repeatedly in the works of Wycliffe. True, he called upon Isaiah, obviously to defend himself from his numerous opponents from the Catholic Church. Both Bogomils and Cathars themselves also frequently quoted this theme according to Isaiah.

Bogomils and Cathars	*John Wycliffe*
Et (Sathanas) obserabat gloriam, quae erat moventis coelos, et cogitavit sedem sua ponere super nubes coelorum et volebat Altissimo similis esse.	…de Lucifer Ysa XIV. 13 dicitur: In celum ascendam super astra celi exaltatio solum meum.
(Interrogatio Johannis, or the Secret Book of the Bogomils).	(Wycliffe, J. Summa in theologia. Tractatus tertieus. De civili domino. London, MDCCCXXV, p. I)
	Argumentum patet de Lucifer cum suis complicibus apostatis (Ysa XIV.12-15) de primus parentibus in state innocencie. (Ibidem, p. 373).

It is essential to know that the English reformer leant on this myth to attack the Pope, comparing him and his court to the fall of Lucifer and his angels. In the commentary column in English on the same page, the publisher has summed up the result of the comparison thus: 'Angels, our first parents and the apostles have sinned, much more may the pope with his whole college sin.'[1]

Incarnation of the souls of angels in the human body

This important part of what is called "secondary" or Satanic creation in the West, to use the Bogomil terminology, also found place in Wycliffe's views. He developed the thesis of the dual human nature, i.e. flesh and soul, explaining that souls were probably angels implanted in human bodies. Wycliffe did not reveal his source, mainly out of caution, he just said he had taken the idea ex fide scripture. By this expression he underscored both the orthodoxy of the source and the reliability of the knowledge.

Bogomils and Cathars

Et praeterea excogitavit et fecit hominem ad similitudinem ejus vel sui, et praecepit angelo tertii coeli intrare in corpus liteum. Et tulit de eo et fecit aliud corpus in formam mulieris, et praecepit angelo secundi coeli introire in corpus mulieris.

(Interrogatio Johannis, or the Secret Book of the Bogomils)

John Wycliffe

... quomodo homo est duaram naturam utraque (p. 2)...scilicet corporis et anime (p. 35)... Loquendo itaque de anima opportet ex fide scripture supponere esse spiritum creatum mole invisibilem et incorruptibilem possibilem per se esse ut angelus.

(Wiclif, J. De compositione hominis. London, 1884)

DUALISTIC CRITICISM OF CHURCH AND RITES

Wycliffe's Catholic adversaries persecuted him even after his death. In addition to the fact that his bones were exhumed and burnt, there were claims that he was guilty of 700 transgressions against the Roman Church and its practices. Wycliffe's probably most attacked thesis was his rejection of transubstantiation, the conversion of the bread and the wine in the altar into the blood and body of Christ. As we well know, this rejection was a fundamental tenet with both the Bogomils and the Cathars.

---

[1] Wycliffe, J. Summa in theologia. Tractatus tertius. De civili domino. London, MDCCCXXV, p. 373.

Rejection of transubstantiation (conversion)

Cathars

... quod nullus debebat credere quod illa hostia, quam Capellanus ostendit populo in missa, esset corpus Christi, et quot erat nisi panis.

(Acta inquisitionis Carcassonensis contra Albigensis a. 1308 et 1309. – Döllinger, I. II, p. 18)

John Wycliffe

Quod substantia panis materialis et vinum maneat post consecrationem in sacramento altaris.

(XXIV Conclusiones Wycclyf damnatae Londoniis in synodo. – Fasculi Zizianorum, p. 278)

At that, the heretical Wycliffe made an important addition, one that should be acceptable to any reasonable theologian: that the bread and the wine of the host acquired the meaning of moral participation unto Christ, that they were **efficax ejus signum**. It is regrettable that the synod refused to accept this nuance, offered by Wycliffe on the basis of St. Augustine's famous interpretation of the three aspects of the communion.

Only God giveth absolution, to Him we confess without a mediator

This fundamental dualistic attitude to an internal communion with God, inherited by the Protestants today, was also a familiar position of Wycliffe's.

Cathars

Item credunt quod nullus possit pacere nisi Deus, et dicunt quod homo sive sacerdos dat tantum consilium.

(Tractatus de hereticis. – In: Dondaine, A. La hiérarchie cathare in Italie. Archivum Fratrum Praedicatorum. Rome, 1950, p. 319)

John Wycliffe

Contrition belongs to the mind alone, and it is not an object of sense, inasmuch the contrite confesse to the Lord.

(Great Voices of the Reformation, 1952, p. 26)

Item quod si homo fuerit debite contritus, omnis confessio exterior est sibi superflua, vel inutilis.

(XXIV Conclusiones, Fasciculi Zizaniorum, p. 278)

Wycliffe developed this view in severe criticism of the decree of Pope Innocent III, Omnis utrusque sexus, according to which people who had not been granted absolution by Catholic priests could not be saved. The uncouthness and pointlessness of such an assertion were refuted categorically: "No one can believe that a man may not be saved without a confession of this kind, for other wise all the dead from Christ's ascension to the time of Innocent III are lost – a horrible thing to believe."[1]

Sinner priests have no right to officiate

Another dualistic rule, i.e. that priests who sinned could not serve believers, was also adopted. To that Wycliffe added his famous assertion that earthly rulers who sinned lost their right of property and power. In other words, to use the modern political terminology, he created a situation of impeachment by the attitude to God.

Cathars	*John Wycliffe*
Sacerdotes Romanae Ecclesiae non possunt solvere et ligare cum sint peccatores; et cum sint immundi, nullum allium possunt mundare.	Item asserere quod nullus est dominus civilis, nullus est episcopus, nullus est prelatus, dum est in peccato mortali.
(Collectio Occitanica, t. VII. – Döllinger, II, p. 6)	(XXIV Conclusiones..., Fasciculi Zizaniorum, p. 280)

The Catholic Church is fornicatress

We know that John Wycliffe reached the point of complete rejection of the Catholic Church and the Pope and recommended that the civil power deprive the church of its endowments. He defended a similar opinion directly in a letter to Richard II, but with much sharper expressions in the spirit of the Cathar allegation that the Pope was "involved with the Devil", i.e. Antichrist, that can be found in his other texts.

Cathars	*John Wycliffe*
Item quod ecclesia romana non est Ecclesia Dei sed meretrix...	Item quod si papa sit praescitus et malus homo, ac per consequens membrum diaboli, non habet potestatem supra fidelis Christi sibi datam.
(Tractatus de hereticis, p. 318)	
	(XXIV Conclusiones..., Fasciculi Zizaniorum, p. 278)

---

[1] Great Voices of the Reformation (Anthology). New York, 1952, p. 27.

... quod ex hujus abondantia, curia Romana contra legem Christi multis peccatorum generebus insolscit.

(Ibidem, p. 263)

Rejection of excommunication (excommunicatio)

Like the Cathars, Wycliffe rejected excommunication, one of the most severe sanctions of the Catholic Church, as invalid and immoral, thus rendering its authority ineffective to a certain degree. Wycliffe must have enjoyed quite considerable authority and social support for, although the London Synod of 1382 condemned his views, the reformer was not excommunicated.

Cathars	*John Wycliffe*
Si ecclesia Romana eum excommunicaret propter hoc, qui non vult jurare, vel alium, non crederat se esse excommunicatum.	Item quod sic excommunicans, ex hoc sit heareticus, vel excommunicatus.
(Confessio Petri Maurini de Monte Alionis, XIV cenutry. – Döllinger, Ign., p. 231)	(XXIX Conclusiones, Fasciculi Zizaniorum, p. 279)

SOCIAL VIEWS

Wycliffe's social views are a matter of such richness and complexity that they will probably be the source of plenty of studies to come. In this paper we shall mention only two essential cases of ideas and practice shared by the dualists and the British reformer.

Rejection of oath

Considering how underdeveloped medieval legislation was, the oath was an important legal tool to subject ordinary people to the worldly and ecclesiastic authorities. By rejecting the oath, the dualists actually refused involvement with the structures of authority in society that they considered unjust and subject to the Devil. Thus ordinary man was provided with social involvement as a democratic choice in a hint of the first modern right of civil society. One cannot but notice that John Wycliffe considered the oath as "superfluous among the perfect", mentioning one of the fundamental terms of Bogomils and Cathars, i.e. perfecti. In other words, he used the language of the dualists.

Cathars	*John Wycliffe*
Item dicunt, quod nullum juramentum possit fieri sine peccato aliqua de causa.	Under videtur ad sensum suum prohibere simpliciter iuramentum, quia videtur iuramentum superfluere inter perfectos.
(Cd. Cassanat. A. IV. – Döllinger, Ign., p. 323)	(Wyclif, J. Operis Evangelici. London, 1896, p. 188)

Rejection of liturgy

Even the Bulgarian Bogomils called the liturgy something superfluous, a view that was later transferred among the Cathars. Wycliffe was also one of its radical supporters, being in harmony with the familiar Bogomil protestation that the apostles did not conduct liturgies.

Bogomils	*John Wycliffe*
You say that not the apostles established the liturgy and communion but St. John Chrysostom; that more than three hundred years passed from the Birth of Christ to the time of St. John.	Item pertinater asserer non esse fundatum in evangelio quod Christi ordinavit.
	(XXIV Conclusiones..., Fasciculi Zizaniorum, p. 278, 281)
(Презвитер Козма. „Беседа против богомилите". – „Стара българска литература. 2. Ораторска проза". София, 1982, с. 36)	

Rejection of indulgences

Just like the Cathars, John Wycliffe rejected the sale of indulgences.

Cathars	*John Wycliffe*
Item de indulgenciis quas facit ecclesia romana nuhil credunt.	Non sunt indulgencie nisi a Domino Jesu Christo.
(Tractatus de hereticis, p. 318)	(Wyclif's Latin Works. Opus Evangelicum. I, II. London, 1895, p. 480)

Icons and the cross

Quite naturally, there are some specific differences in this parallel. Although he was an adherent of dualism, John Wycliffe retained a certain desire to arrive at a compromise with the official church on some problems. For example, he did not reject the presence of images in church. Partially adopting the dualist criticism of icons and the cross, he only warned against extreme veneration of the latter and the former.

Cathars	*John Wycliffe*
Ultramontani nec inclinant cruci nec altari, allegantes illud: Simulacra gentium argentium et aurum etc.	If it be meant that God and stone are identical, it is heretical and to be denied.
(Tractatus de hereticis, p. 317)	(Wycliff, J. Miscellania philosophica. Vol. II. London, 1905, p. 104)

Persecution of New Testament usage in the vernacular

It is natural that this part should conclude with a comparison of the persecution, suffered by dualists for disseminating the New Testament in the vernacular, and the repression of Wycliffe's work on the translation of the New Testament.

Cathars	*John Wycliffe*
This is how the famous 14th century inquisitor, Bernard Gui, described the "forbidden" literary practice of the Cathars:	As Anne Hudson has mentioned in her Laicus literatus': the Paradox of Lollardy, "the Decree De heretico comburendo identifies the making of books as a typical activity of the heretics". In his Constitutions (1407), Archbishop Arundel forbade the use of Wycliffe's translations of the Bible without a special permission.
Item legunt de evangeliis et de epistolis in vulgari, applicando et exponendo pros se et contra statim Romane ecclesie.	
(Gui, B. Manuel de l'inquisiteur. T. I. Paris, 1926, p.26).	In 1412 the same cleric addressed a letter to the Pope accusing Wycliffe that "to fill up the measure of his malice, he devised the expedient of new translations of the Scriptures into the mother tongue".
	(Deanesly, M. The Lollard Bible, p. 238).

The specific New Testament vocabulary
of Wycliffite translations

Back again to the subject of New Testament translation, this proves rooted in John Wycliffe's dualistic philosophy. The measure of that involvement, however, is a much stronger and organic one and it found a peculiar linguistic expression in the translation of the New Testament. It turned out that the formula "ouer bread ouer othir substaunce" is accompanied by a certain vocabulary that carries traces of traditional Bogomil and Cathar interpretations of the Gospel. dualism is the philosophy that gave birth to the initiative of translating the New Testament into English, and the translation carries in itself the imprint of that philosophy. In other words, a mutual motivation that proceeds from the spirit of the "Bulgarian heresy". At that, we shall see that the Wycliffite approach to translation largely followed the Cyrillo-Methodian example. More specifically, we are speaking of daring coinage, of enriching and energising phrases, the latter distinction originating in the Greek phrase. In other words the literature of Bogomils, Cathars and Lollards rested on the cultural tradition of the Orthodox Church. What we have here is not heresy but a popularisation of the Holy Writ. It is this sense that Pope John Paul II discerned in the work of the Slav apostles, seeing in it "enculturation – the incarnation of the New Testament in local cultures – as well as their introduction to the life of the Church"[1]. The dualists did the same thing, too.

The opinion supported by Margaret Deanesly that the Wycliffite translation is "the most revised and idiomatic form of the Earlier Version"[2] indicates that Wycliffe's strong propensity for the vernacular is well known among the English authors. This author, however has assumed the even more radical view of the American researcher, Fred Robinson, who introduced the expression "the Lollards' Englishing of the Vulgate Bible"[3]. He pays special attention to the *General Prologue* included in nine Wycliffite copies, where ambition to render the Scriptures in the vernacular is declared, a proposition reinforced by the argument that such a translation would overcome some ambiguities in the Vulgate. The linguistic proce-

---

[1] Йоан-Павел II. Кирил и Методий (Благовестие и екуменизъм). София, 1966, с. 55.

[2] Deanesly, M. The Lollard Bible and other Medieval versions by Margaret Deanesly, M.A, Cambridge at the University press 1920/1966, p.VII.

[3] Robinson, F. Commentary. – In: Wycliffite Manuscript. The New Testament. England, 1400-1450. Ed. by Bridwell library/Dallas/ and Octavo corporation.CD.1999, p.4.

dures of the English translation are commended as being richer in a discussion on the importance of using Middle English as opposed to Latin word order in the translation[1].

Subsequently we shall quote some cases of intentional substitution of Latin words and roots for English ones, as well as impressive examples of creating new words, both of which indicate that John Wycliffe and his followers conceived and achieved a translation alternative to the Vulgate. Obviously, the wanted to render the Holy Writ into the spoken, vernacular language. Among other things, their achievement also differs from the biblical excerpts translated into Old English in terms of flexibility and lexical abundance.

To put it simply, the translation reveals a visible effort to replace the Latin for the Anglo-Saxon, i.e. the older and more widespread substratum of the English language. One example is a crucial notion and image, that of the resurrection of Christ. The word "възкресение", used in Bulgarian, was absolutely new and bore considerable poetic charge. It was not a direct translation of the Greek ἀνάστασις that means "getting up, rising". The Bulgarian word means rising from the Cross, ascension above the Cross. The great Bulgarian writer and medievalist Stefan Gechev assumed that the image originated among the earliest Slav converts to Christianity around Salonika and that the apostles of the Slavs, Cyril and Methodius, adopted quite a lot of that first Slavonic Christian popular vocabulary.

The Wycliffite translators repeatedly used the Latin term *resureccioun,* resurexioun of Christ (Acts 1:22). Thus they share a vocabulary with King James' version. (Please, see the Appendix). Nevertheless, they preferred a purely English term, **agenrysing,** and used it in the key phrase where Christ says: "I am **agenrysing** & lyf" (John 11:25). True, according to the OED this word was used in 1380 in a variant of the Catholic Credo, i.e. agenrysing of fleish[2]. Its introduction as New Testament lexis, however, was a feature of the Wycliffite version. The OED also mentions that Wycliffe used the same word in 1382[3]. At that, the word **agenrysing** appears on thirteen other occasions: in Luke 20:27; John 11:24-25; Ro-

---

[1] Robinson, F. Commentary. – In: Wycliffite Manuscript. The New Testament. England, 1400-1450. Ed. by Bridwell library/Dallas/ and Octavo corporation.CD.1999, p. 3.
[2] Oxford English Dictionary, 1989, V. I., p.241.
[3] Ibidem.

mans 1:4; I Corinthians 15:12-13; I Corinthians 15:42; Acts 4:33; Acts 17:18; Acts 23:6; Acts 24:15; Acts 24:21; Acts 26:23; I Peter 1:3 and Revelation 20:6. It would be interesting to note that one sometimes finds a certain similarity to this phrase in King James' version. In Romans 4:25 we have "was raised again", almost a complete coincidence with "roos agen" in the Wycliffite translation. The only difference is that passive voice was used in King James' version while the Wycliffite translation uses the active voice.

Wycliffe and his disciples did not achieve a richer image than that contained in the Bulgarian word "възкресение" (rise, ascend above the cross). With a similar desire to use their native language as much as possible, however, they achieved an expressive rendition of the Greek and Latin term into English. Instead of using Latinised lexis they created their own Christian vocabulary in English with the dedication and frequency the Slav apostles applied in creating its Slavonic equivalent.

John 11:25 "I am the resurrection, and the life"

Greek	Latin	Wycliffite	King James'
Ἐγώ ἐιμί ἡ ἀνάστασις καὶ ἡ ζωή.	Ego sum resurectio, et vita.	I am agenrysing & lyf .	Jesus said unto her, I am the resurrection, and the life.

Now here is yet another example in this respect. The Wycliffite translation uses the word **cristne**, i.e. christianise, instead of or parallel to baptise. Cristne is an old root in the English language. According to the OED, it was first mentioned back in 890 (cristenesta)[1] and Wycliffe obviously used it to increase the presence of English vocabulary in the translation of the New Testament. His use of **cristne**, by the way, is mentioned on the respective page of the OED that states Wycliffe used the word in 1380[2]. That, too, was the supposed date when the translation of the New Testament was begun, it being said in both the case of **agenrysing** and **cristne** that the words were used by Wycliffe himself.

---

[1] Oxford English Dictionary, 1989, V. I., p. 178.
[2] Ibidem.

Matthew 3:11-12

Greek	Latin	Wycliffe	King James'
Αὐτὸς ὑμᾶς	Ipse vos bapti-	He schal baptise	he shall baptize
βαπτίσει ἐν	zabit in Spiritu	or cristne you in	you with the
πνεύματι ἁγίωι	sancto, et igni	the Hooly Gost,	Holy Ghost, and
καὶ πυρί		& fier	with fire

Another example: 'Thanne Ihesus cam fro Galile into Iordan to Iohn, for to be **cristened** of hym. Sotheli Iohn forbeed hym & seide, I owe forto be **cristenid** of thee, & thou comest to me?" (Mt 3:13-14).

The desire to anglicise did not stop even at the titles of the chapters. Instead of Acts of the Apostles, as in King James's version where it originates directly from Actus Apostolorum in the Vulgate, the Wycliffite version offered **Dedis** of apostolis, using the Old English word of *ded*, *dæd*. This ambition even went to the point of detail. In the Lord's Prayer (Mt 6:13), the Wycliffite translation follows "amen" with its translation – that is **so be it**.

Now we come to the dualistic tones. One can discern a measure of dualistic interpretation in the case of the verb **waische** (to wash). On the one hand, the Wycliffite translation uses this verb in its traditional meaning of "to wash", a full coincidence with its meaning in the King James' version. This is what one finds in *Matthew 15:2*:

Wycliffe	King James
Whi brekenthi disciplis the tradi-	Why do thy disciples transgress the
ciouns of eldre men? For thei wais-	tradition of the elders? For they
chen not hondis, whanne thei eten	wash not their hands when they eat
breed.	bread.

When speaking of baptism, however, the stress lies on the fact that John the Baptist baptises with water, i.e. that what he did was rather a ritual cleansing for repentance and ablution than baptism, while true baptism according to Bogomils, Cathars and Lollards was in the Holy Spirit[1]. In

---

[1] This was how the inquisitor Bernard Gui recorded that fundamental Cathar tenet: "...confingentes loco baptismi facti in aqua baptismum alium spiritualem, que vocant consolamentum Spiritus sancti. Gui, B., op. cit., p.12. As to the view of the Lollards, cappelanus Robertus Cavell wrote the following in his confession: "Imprimis videlicet quod sacramentum Baptismi, factum in aqua secundum formam Ecclesia usitatam, modicum vel parum est ponderatum, quamcito anima infantis in utero matris est corpori unita, infuditur gracia Spiritus Sancti, per quam parvulus est sufficienter baptizatus." Tanner, N. Heresy Trials in the Diocese of Norwich 1428-31. London, 1977, 94-95.

other words, we have an absolutely free introduction of the verb **waische**. No similar term exists either in the Greek or the Latin text, nor can it be found in King James' version. Hence what we have here is dualistic re-editing.

Matthew 3:11-12

Greek	Latin	Wycliffe	King James'
Ἐγὼ μὲν ὑμᾶς	Ego quidem	I waische you in	I indeed baptize
βαπτίζω ἐν	baptizo vos in	watir; into	you with water
ὕδατι εἰς	aqua in poeni-	penaunce.	unto repentance
μετάνοιαν	tentiam		

One finds yet another usage of **waischun**, as a past participle, in order to underscore that John's baptism is "with water" (Mt 3:5):

Wycliffe	King James' version
Thanne Ierusalem wente out to hym & al Iudee, & al the cuntre aboute Iordan, & thei weren waischun of him in Iordan	Then went out to him Jerusalem, and all Judaea, and all the region round about Jordan. And were baptised of him in Jordan, confessing their sins.

Another dualistic accent in the Wycliffite translation, and in this case we are not talking of John Wycliffe's dualistic texts in general, but of a dualistic thesis in the translation of the New Testament, added as a commentary. This is an important thing to know because it leads to the thought that Wycliffe's translators could have used not the Vulgate as an original, but a version the dualists spread in Latin. The Prologue to St. John's Gospel mentions that he is more beloved of God than the other disciples (seid loued of God bifore othere disciplis). This is a familiar dualistic idea, directly embodied in the *Secret Book* of the Bogomils where John with head resting on the breast of Christ, receives Christ's explanation of the origin and structure of the universe. With this detail we already have two indirect quotations of the *Secret Book*. As we have mentioned already, John Wycliffe called upon ex fide scripture in his work *De compositione hominis* and mentioned that human souls are borrowed from angels.

From *haeresia Bulgarorum* to *exemplum Bulgaricum*

It is quite natural that we should answer yet another question. Considering such obvious typological similarity between the dualists and Wycliffe, could one find proof of a genetic link between the English reformer, his supporters and haeresia Bulgarorum, i.e. the Bogomil movement. The answer is in the positive and, although we have mainly indirect evidence so far, this is still something unique. In other words, the evidence points at a single interpretation and it is difficult to find another one that would refute it. For example, the fact of Wycliffe's dualistic, or geographically eastern, orientation is also supported by his special preference for Greek lexis. To the best of this author's knowledge, English scholars have not yet commented on it.

John Wycliffe had a penchant for Greek. We find three characters in conversation in his work *Trialogus*: Alithia, Phronesis and Pseudis. However, Alithia, Phronesis and Pseudis are Latinized Greek words that mean Truth, Reason and Fraud. A witness at the 1382 trial against Wycliffe reported that he considered antiquity as an authority and quoted names like Orpheus, Plato, Aristotle, Pythagoras, etc.[1] When he proposed the idea of an English Church independent of the Vatican, the reformer called upon the "Greek tradition" (more Graecorum), as it was usually called in the Middle Ages[2], i.e. the tradition of the Orthodox Church. When he argued against an opinion of Socrates Wycliffe relied on Aristotle[3].

What we have in this case is a scholar who, by his knowledge of Greek philosophy and the Greek original of the New Testament, overstepped the Latin linguistic restriction, imposed by the Catholic dictate over culture at that time. That, according to the British author F. Hearnshow, was the earliest humanistic sway in medieval England[4].

None of Wycliffe's biographers ever wrote he knew Greek, nor do his works (at least those this author has seen) feature quotations in Greek.

---

[1] Ingressus fratris Kynyngham Carmelitae contra Wicclyf – in: Fasciculi Zizaniorum, p.5.
[2] XXIV Conclusiones Wycclyf damnatae Londoniis in synodo – Fasculi Zizaniorum, p.279. A similar statement is also made on p.264: sicut Graecos.
[3] Wycliffe, J. Summa in theologia. Tractatus tertius. De civili domino. London. MDCCCXXV, p. 99.
[4] Hearnshow, F. Some Great Political Idealists of the Christian Era. London, Bombay, Sidney (s.a.), 44-45.

Then the use of Greek words could mean that he had an erudite friend who directed him towards the Greek cultural heritage. According to historians, quite a few of the "perfect" (that was what Bogomil and Cathar leaders were called) knew Greek besides their native language and Latin. We also know about Bogomil missions from Consantinople to Western Europe, quoted by Stephen Runciman. Therefore, such a man could possibly have been next to Wycliffe.

It is high time, though, to reveal the power and dynamics of the Wycliffite phrase, qualities that in a sense had a measure of Greek origin. Let us take the well-known place in Acts 26:23 "that Christ should suffer, and that he should be the first to rise from the dead", or "if Crist is to suffre, if he is the firste of agenrysing of deed men, that schal schewe light to the peple & to hethen men" in the Wycliffite version. While King James' version uses the verb "should suffer", the Wycliffite translation adopts an if-clause that is almost identical with the Greek original "ei protasis" form, "ei" or the Latin "si". The act of the resurrection expressed by the gerund (agenrysing of deed men), is more emotional and more lasting than in the case of the simpler verbal form of King James' version that promises but lacks the same emphasis – "he should be the first that should rise from the dead." Generally speaking, when one compares the Wycliffite and the King James' translation, one cannot but see that the former is a more masterly rendition of the Greek text. Last, but not least, the Wycliffite expression is more poetic and bears more sharing of the glory of the resurrection, while King James' version is a rational presentation of the final outcome.

Greek	Wycliffe	Latin	King James'
εἰ παθητὸς ὁ Χριστός, εἰ πρῶτοσ ἐξ ἀναστάσεως νεκρῶν	if Crist is to suffre, if he is the firste of agenrysing of deed men	si passibilis Christus, si primus ex resurrectione mortuorum	That Christ should suffer, and that he should be the first thats hould rise from the dead

These not only lexical but also stylistic and syntactic peculiarities were also noticed by some Western scholars. This was how, for example,

Fred Robinson characterised them: "The General prologue also defends a more flexile translation of Latin ablative constructions, of polysemous words, of present participles, etc."[1] This approach is quite close to the linguistic results that, according to A. Schlötser and P. Lavrov, were achieved in the translations of the Bible in Slavonic languages[2].

Translators from the Greek were forced to use "introductory sentences, ten different participles related to one another, rich resounding words", and so on[3]. In other words, this outlines a marked typology of translation characteristic of the Cyrillo-Methodian tradition. To put it more precisely, Greek has left the imprint of its system on the recipient languages. As we have already mentioned, C. Schmidt and Yordan Ivanov thought this typology was conveyed by the Cyrillo-Methodian copies that the Bogomils relayed to Western Europe. Of all British authors Bertrand Hamilton alone is interested in looking for such Greek reflections with a dualist flavour, and that in the sphere of lexis: 'A faint memory of such a process may be preserved in the gloss on the Lord's Prayer in the Cathar Rituel of Florence: '' Quoniam tuum est regnum" - hoc verbum dicitur esse in libris greccis vel hebraicis'(For thine is the kingdom' - this phrase is said to be in the Greek and Hebrew texts).' he wrote.[4]

Considering all this, one gets even more convinced that John Wycliffe and his adherents did not use the Vulgate as the source of their translation, but a Cyrillo-Methodian copy. The latter was most probably translated into Latin but it had preserved to some extent the freedom of translation achieved by St. Cyril, St. Methodius and their disciples. In the earliest Slavonic variant of the Lord's Prayer, dating from the 10th century and discovered by Trendafil Krustanov in the Vatican palimpsest (Codex Vaticano graeco No. 2502), Ana-Maria Totomanova deciphered the word "хлѣбъ нашь епноүснн", doubtless a direct borrowing from the

---

[1] Robinson, F. Commentary. – In: CD: Wycliffite Manuscript. The New Testament. England, 1400-1450. Ed. by Bridwell Library (Dallas) and Octavo Corporation, 1999, p. 4.

[2] Лавров, П. Материалы по истории возникновения древнейшей славянской письменности. Ленинград, 1930, с.VII.

[3] Ibidem

[4] Hamilton, B. Wisdom from the East: the Reception by the Cathars of Eastern Dualist Texts. – In: Heresy and Literacy. Cambridge, 1994/1996, p.51. By the way, in his article on the Lyonnaise Ritual Yordan Ivanov wrote that this peculiarity contained the Bogomil-Cathar (one could say the Greek) version of the Lord's Prayer. Иванов, Й., op. cit., p.112. See also p.p. 67-68 of this chapter.

Greek[1]. We know that this is not an isolated case: other Old Bulgarian translations of the New Testament have preserved "**єпноүснн**" in the Lord's Prayer.

However, one finds a preference for the term επιουσιον in John Wycliffe. At the synodal trial in 1382, Thomas Wyntirton tried to achieve a measure of condescension for Wycliffe because they were both members of the Augustinian order. Thus Wyntirton's treatise was called *Absolutio* and he polemicised with his opponent much more subtly and intelligently than the other accusers. Without entering into detail we shall only say that, according to Wyntirton, Wycliffe said "Panem dixit quidem, sed ephiusion 'hoc est supersubstantialem'"[2]. This evidence that Wycliffe used a Latinised form of the term επιουσιον, i.e. **ephiusion**, outlines a visible chain of conceptual and lexical transfer. The chain begins with the Bulgarian transcription **єпноүснн** in the Vatican Gospel (10th century) and ends with the Latin transcription of this term, ephiusion, in Wycliffe. This chain of transfer, the initial and final stage of which are clearly outlined at this point, lies in the context of Wycliffe's undoubted spiritual association with the dualists, as well as in the context of his marked interest in Greek culture.

Detailed restoration of the vocabulary and the environment of the Wycliffite translation of the New Testament, the clarification of dualistic elements in Wycliffe's theology allow one to draw the following general picture from the separate facts:

1. John Wycliffe was an adherent of Bogomil-Cathar dualism. He and his disciples introduced specific dualistic tones into the New Testament translation;

2. The Wycliffite translation reveals similarities with the Cyrillo-Methodian approach to the translation of the Scriptures, including coining new words and extracting lexical material from the mother tongue, dynamic phrase and a variety of participles;

3. Wycliffe had a visible penchant for Greek lexis and for Greek culture. Although it is not specified still, this Greek source is a reality that is liable to further investigation. At this point, the most acceptable assumption is that this could have been Bogomil "Perfecti" who came from Constantinople or Bulgaria;

---

[1] Кръстанов, Тр., А.-М. Тотоманова, И. Добрев. Ватикански палимпсест. София, 1997, c.101.

[2] Fasciculi Zizaniorum, p. 190.

4. These data allow one to endorse the hypothesis that the Wycliffite translation could have been made not from the Vulgate, but from a Cyrillo-Methodian version that was Latinised and transported by dualist Bogomils and Cathars. The least that can be said is that the Wycliffite translation was made with a knowledge of and a respect for the Greek version of the New Testament.

Thus, *haeresia Bulgarorum*, with its already proven Pan-European diffusion and footing in the cultural life of many countries like Italy, France – particularly Provence, Germany, Spain and Flanders, became the *exemplum Bulgaricum* of popular translations of the New Testament, bearing the freedom of direct communication with the Scriptures.

One should also look at this phenomenon from the aspect of social and cultural change. One could definitely claim that Wycliffe, his circle and the popular culture of the Lollards achieved a sort of renaissance of the English language. That liberated culture even created its own social type, the educated layman or, to borrow the term from Anne Hudson, *laicus literatus*[1]. What she had in mind was the investigation against the Lollard Walter Brut in the period between 1390 and 1393[2], opened by Bishop Trefnant of Hereford. The defendant Brut displayed broad culture, a knowledge of Latin and the ability to argue with the bishop's rather impressive team, including 15 officials, three masters and two bachelors of theology, and two doctors of civil and canon law. Although she still retained some doubts as to how widespread Brut was as a social phenomenon, Anne Hudson concluded that "Walter Brut may have been an extreme example of the Lollars *laicus literatus*, but he was far from the only one"[3]. To her comments she added the fact that "the Lollard heresy was learned, indeed academic", and that "the immediate source of the heresy was the thought of John Wycliffe"[4].

---

[1] Hudson, A. 'Laicus literatus': the Paradox of Lollardy. – In: Heresy and Literacy, 1000-1530. Cambridge, 1994/1996.

[2] Walter Brut's beliefs principally coincide with the Dualist views: "the eucharist was primarily a memorial, papal pretensions to powers of absolution, along pontiff's claims to temporalities, demonstrated his identity with antichrist, war and legal execution were against Christian insistence on charity, oaths were illegal...the just layman, more outrageously to his readers, the just laywoman was a priest...he/Brut/ wonders why canon law and the fathers quoted there so often base themselves on the Old Testament shadow of the Law and not on the light of Christ gospel." Ibidem, p.p.224-225.

[3] Ibidem, p. 223.

[4] Ibidem, p. 228

That cultural upsurge was in harmony with the brilliance of the Cathar civilisation in Provence, with the cultural and literary activity of the Bulgarian and Bosnian Bogomils. A phenomenon where evangelisation, that grew into self-evangelisation, developed into a national and popular self-education, into a proto-Renaissance.

Appendix

Why undertake this comparison between the Wycliffite translation and King James' version?

First, the Authorized version of the Bible is really the most popular variant in England and the USA that performs the prime prescription "appointed to be read in the Churches". The translation of the Bible, done by 54 learned men under the aegis of King James in the period between 1604 and 1611, was designed as an alternative of the Vulgate in order to achieve "a more exact Translation of the holy Scriptures into the English Tongue" by a fresh interpretation of Hebrew and Greek originals[1]. That initiative also aimed "to offer a palpable defence against the criticisms of "Popish Persones at home and abroad"[2]. The *Cambridge History of English and American Literature* in 18 Volumes specifies: "It is agreed on all hands that the English of the *Authorised Version* is, in essentials, that of Tindale"[3], who in 1525 made a translation of the New Testament from a Greek original. Other authors add that *Textus Receptus* by Erasmus was also considered when the version of King James was produced.

For our purpose, we ask what the degree of Anglicisation is when one compares the Wycliffite and the King James' version? Andrew Sanders sees "inaccuracies and Latinate rhythms of the Vulgate" in the Wycliffite result[4], meaning that King James' version is supposed to be more Anglicised. But when one undertakes a textological analysis one comes upon an opposite trend. The vocabulary of King James' version is more influenced by Latin than the Wycliffite one. Besides, the Wycliffite rhythm is more distant from the Latin that the former.

---

[1] Sanders, A. The Short Oxford History of English Literature. 1996, p.191
[2] Ibidem
[3] The Cambridge History of English and American Literature in 18 Volumes (1907–21). Volume IV. Prose and Poetry: Sir Thomas North to Michael Drayton, p.48
[4] Sanders, op. cit., p.51

Another fact supporting this observation. King James' version adopted the translation principle that "the old 'ecclesiastical words' (as 'church' for 'congregation' and 'charity' for 'love') were to be preserved"[1]. That meant substitution of the English word love (ME<lufu, akin to OHG luba, Goth lubo) for the Latin root charity (ME & Ofr charite <L caritas). Commenting on Tindale's work Bishop Stephen Gardiner of Winchester gave similar advice, i.e. "that certain 'ecclesiastical words' should be left as they appeared in the Vulgate, chief among them being *ecclesia, episcopus, caritas and gratia*"[2]. Thus, recurrent returns to Latin vocabulary is a practice in King James' version.

This author has no intention of implying some kind of rivalry when speaking of the Wycliffite and King James' version because both of them proclaim the defense and the development of the English language. This comparison is intended to reveal some visible specific features suggesting that Wycliffe and his followers may have used a Latin translation of the Cyrillo-Methodian version of the New Testament. A source more specific than the ''corrupt text of the Latin Vulgate''[3].

[1] Encyclopaedia Britannica vol.3. 1970, p.584

[2] Ibidem, p.583

[3] Sanders, A. op.cit., p.50

Chapter V. Dualist Ideas in the Works of Tyndale

Courage

A large white flower on its stalk
in the deserted garden
meets with the wind and has a talk.

Stefan Gechev

Tyndale – the covert dualist

Two centuries later, William Tyndale reiterates to some extent the historic cause of John Wycliffe, while voicing a great respect for his predecessor. Revealing such continuity entails many surprises. It is already the 21st century but new discoveries are still made in the history of the Middle Ages and sometimes established views are changed. William Tyndale is one such phenomenon the conception of which will seemingly become richer with time. The observation of David Daniell that "he has reached more people than even Shakespeare"[1], has good grounds considering the quantities in which the Authorised Version of the Bible, which is based on Tyndale's translation, has spread across the world. Tyndale's translations enriched the English language with the "sounds and rhythms" and he himself became a sculptor of the language, going on to create "unforgettable words, phrases, paragraphs and chapters"[2].

While supporting the opinion of David Daniel on principle, this author also naturally retains the right of his own concept of the issue with some nuances. It seems to me that the first quality level of the English language was created by the circle around John Wycliffe with the translation of the New Testament. William Langland's *Piers Plowman* (c. 1360, text *A*) is practically contemporary to that undertaking, sharing the philosophy of dualism and using its imagery. In other words, just as the foundations of a rich and expressive English language were laid in the

---

[1] Daniell, D. William Tyndale. A Biography. Ed. Yale University Press. New Haven&London, 2001, p.2.
[2] Ibidem.

Langland-Wycliffe period, to which one should add the brilliant contribution of Chaucer (particularly the 1392-1395 period when he wrote the main part of the *Canterbury Tales*)[1], the English literary language emerged in all its richness and glory in the Tyndale-Shakespeare period. Chaucer is no mechanical addition here. There are grounds to pay attention to the information indicating such sympathies in the founder of modern English literature for it is also known that he translated the *Roman de la Rose* in which Cathar moods are a proven presence. In addition we know what honour Chaucer paid to Pierce Plowman in his *Prologue* to *The Canterbury Tales*. Then again, should one turn back to the linguistic contribution of Wycliffe himself. One should quote Herbert Workman who wrote that "Wycliffe's Bible was one only, not by any means the most widely read, or the standpoint of influence on the English language, the most important"[2].

I should point out that this paper has a strictly specified subject, i.e. the presence of hitherto unstudied dualistic ideas in the work of Tyndale. In other words, this is not a biographical or critical literary study but an ideological and theological analysis or, more specifically, a case study of the history of ideas. Such analysis allows one to outline:
- the origin of certain ideas and images;
- their transfer from their place of origin to the host country, and
- their interpretation adequate to a certain age.

Then again Bogomilism with its West European branches of Patarenes, Cathars, Beguins and Lollards is probably the most outstanding example of transcontinental, Pan-European proliferation and interaction between cultures. It was for such an approach that Dimitri Obolensky appealed even in the first edition of his excellent book on the Bogomils: "the study of the Bogomil movement has its own, and by no means negligible, part to play in the investigation of the cultural and religious links between eastern and western Europe, the importance of which is increasingly perceived at the present time."[3]

So what is our starting point? A thesis that William Tyndale stepped on

---

[1] By the way, according to R. Vaughan, Chaucer adopted many of Wycliffe's doctrines. Vaughan, R. The life and the opinions of John de Wycliffe, D.D. London. MDCCCXXXI, v.II, p.437, see also v.I, p.137

[2] Workman, H. The Dawn of the Reformation. IV. The age of Wyclif, L., 1901, p.203.

[3] Obolensky, D. The Bogomils: a Study in Balkan Neo-Manichaeism. Cambridge. 1948, p.VII

Bogomil-Cathar philosophy in his motivation for the translation of the Scriptures, as well as in many of his interpretations of mainly *New Testament* material. Now let's move on to the facts. It is well known that Tyndale communicated with Luther, but in the thinking of the Englishman there is definitely something more specific than the influence of the head of the German Reformation. For example, one discerns Tyndale's own renditions in relation to the parable of the dishonest manager in St. Luke, which also impressed his authoritative biographer, David Daniell. Daniell compares Luther's famous *Ein Sermon dem unrechten Mammon Lu.XVI* with the manner in which Tyndale treats this parable in *The Wicked Mammon*. To quote David Daniell "Luther's printed sermon occupies only six leaves in quarto; Tyndale has six times as much...Moreover, Tyndale alone sets out the whole parable – Luther's text is only the final verse..."[1]

This preference turns one's attention to the fact that the same parable from St. Luke is an important part of *The Secret Book* of the Bogomils. It explains the beginning of Satan's treachery and the corruption of the angels who followed him. It explains how Satan became the impious lord of this world. In other words, for Tyndale this story acquired nearly the same importance it had in *The Secret Book* of the Bogomils.

Could this preference for the parable shared by Tyndale and the Bogomils be a coincidence, a mere chance? One can cast any doubts aside when one adds to the fact we are discussing a remarkable definition of Tyndale's whereby he exhorts the foundation of the Bogomil-Cathar teaching: "God and devil are two contrary fathers, two contrary fountains, and two contrary causes: the one of all goodness, the other of all evil"[2]. Now for comparison we shall give Bogomil and Cathar texts, which reveal complete cognitive and almost complete lexical correspondence:

Bogomils:	*Cathars:*
Against him who says and believes that there are two principles, a good one and a bad, one the creator of light, the other of darkness, one of	...I hereby wanted to speak of the two principles in honour of the Holy Father...

---

[1] Daniell, D. William Tyndale. A Biography, p. 161

[2] Expositions and Notes on Sundry Portions of the Holy Scriptures together with the Practice of Prelates by William Tyndale, Martyr 1536. Cambridge, M.DCCC.XLIX, p.190

men, the other of the angels and other living bodies, anathema.

(Theophyact Lecapenus writes to Tsar Peter of Bulgaria about Bogomils).[1]

(Liber de duobus principiis, end of the 13th century)[2]

One should mention here that such notable dualistic definitions are not an isolated phenomenon in English literature. When he wrote that he had called his *Cain* a mystery, Byron added that he had done so in accordance with the old "very profane" mysteries and moralité. And in *Cain* Lucifer reigns together with Jehovah:

• Lucifer: No we reign
   Together; but our dwellings are asunder."
• ...To the great double mysteries! The *two*
   Principles! (Byron's italics)[3].

It seems that dualism was a certain trend in English literature and since Byron himself confided from where he had borrowed the dualistic theme and imagery, it is our turn now to reveal how it is present in Tyndale and how he chanced upon it. The dualistic views of the reformer find an even more comprehensive expression when he voices another important idea of Bogomils and Cathars, i.e. that this world is the kingdom of the devil. Acknowledging the power and the great hold of the devil on people's souls, Catholics and Orthodox Christians adamantly define the world and the creatures as God's creation while the dualists regard it as the creation and kingdom of Satan. This, too, is why Presbyter Cosmas reproaches them: "They should also be condemned because they call the creator of the sky and the earth father, but regard his creation as one of the devil."[4] Now here

---

[1] Christian Dualist Heresies in the Byzantine World c.650-c.1405. Selected sources translated and annotated by Janet Hamilton and Bernard Hamilton. Manchester & New York.1998, p.100. The original reads: Ὁ δὺο ἀρχὰς λέγων καὶ πιστεύων εἶναι, ἀγαθήν τε καὶ κακὴν, καὶ ἄλλον φωτὸς ποιητὴν καὶ ἄλλον νυκτός, ἄλλον ἀν(θρώπ)ων καὶ ἄλλον ἀγγέλων καὶ τῶν λοιπῶν ζώων, ἀνάθεμα ἔστω. Theophylacti Constantinopolis patriarcha epistola – in: Гръцки извори за българската история. Т.V., София, 1964, с. 186.

[2] De duobus autem principiis ad honorem patris sanctissimi, volui inchoare...in: Livre des deux principes. Introduction, texte critique, traduction, notes et index de Christine Thouzhellier. Paris. 1973, p.160

[3] Byron, G. Complete Poetical Works. Oxford. 1970, p.p. 536, 537.

[4] Презвитер Козма. „Беседа против богомилите" – в: „Стара българска литература (2). Ораторска проза". София.1982, с.49

we find the same thinking expressed through the words of Tyndale: "Seeing we are conceived and born under the power of the devil, and we are hiss possession and *kingdom* (italics G.V.), his captives and bondmen..."[1] We shall recall here yet another element of harmony with the dualists in the above phrase: Tyndale obviously shared their opinion that conception as essential to the flesh is subordinate to the devil.

Of course, these dualistic definitions in the works of the reformer are not placed one next to the other, nor do they comprise a comprehensive and consistent exposé. It seems that, as he was aware the dualist philosophy should be concealed, Tyndale made a fragmentary intertextual presentation, making it accessible to insiders, to those who had previous knowledge about it or who spread it secretly amongst sympathisers. This, by the way, is an old Bogomil method to which Euthymius of the Periblepton (11th century) devoted plenty of space but before that was described by Presbyter Cosmas (10th century): "ostensibly they do everything to avoid being distinguished from orthodox Christians", which attracted people "to approach them" and to think that they are "orthodox and capable of guidance to salvation"[2]. The explanation is simple – on the one hand, as K. Radchenko has explained, it was an established Bogomil habit to mix canonical with non-canonical literature to enable the heretics to push their philosophy through without trouble. On the other, Bogomils and Cathars were communities of non-violence, they had no means to defend themselves and consequently used such mimicry. Tyndale himself said that "to lie also, and to dissemble is not always sin".[3]

Tyndale's method was so successful that not only his opponents but his researchers as well failed to discern the dualistic presence. Consequently, we shall hereafter bring these fragments to the fore and connect them in that comprehensive dualistic exposé they form. This will be accompanied by comparisons with well-known Bogomil and Cathar formulas in order to reveal to what extent they overlap with Tyndale's theses. For example, Tyndale repeatedly used the definition "good man", which what Bogomils and Cathars called their dualist leaders: "good men",

[1] Doctrinal Treatises and Introduction to Different Portions of the Holy Scriptures by William Tyndale, martyr, 1536. Cambridge. M.DCCC.XLVIII, p.47

[2] Презвитер Козма. „Беседа против богомилите", с.31

[3] Tyndale, W. An Exposition upon the V,VI, VII Chapters of Matthew, Antwerp, 1533, p.57.

"boni homines", "boni christiani", "perfecti". Now let us make the direct comparison we need. The Cathars said "and thus they call themselves good Christians, good men and holy".[1] Tyndale, in turn, used "good and learned man", "a Christian man is a spiritual thing and hath God's word in his heart"[2], "and God make thee a good man"[3]. On a single page of his Doctrinal Treatises he mentioned the root "perfect" four times exactly in the sense of achieving the dualist status of spiritual elevation: "For *perfecter* (italics G.V.) we be, the greater is our repentance, and the stronger is our faith. And thus, as the Spirit and doctrine on God's part, and repentance and faith on our part, beget anew in Christ, even so they make us grow, and wax *perfect*, and save us unto end, and never leave us until sin be put off, and we clean purified, and full formed, and fashioned after the similitude and likeness of the *perfectness* of our Saviour Jesus..."[4] One finds a constant usage of the same definition with the Lollards (good man, good woman, true man, homo fidelis, perfit man). According to studies of this author which carry abundant evidence the Lollard communities definitely professed the dualist philosophy. The scope of this chapter does not permit us to go into more detail so we shall give an unequivocal answer: yes, the Lollards were the last, most western branch of the Bogomil-Cathar heresy[5].

Just as Bogomils, Cathars and Lollards say that the state "good man" and "perfect" is acquired through the act of consolamentum, by the descent of the Holy Spirit on the ordained Tyndale describes the same sacrament as more powerful than papal ordination: "but prayer as when we say God make you good man, Christ put his spirit in thee..."[6]

---

[1] bene tamen se vocabant boni christiani, boni homines et sancti – in: Döllinger, Ign. v. Dokumente vornehmlich zur Geschichte der Valdesier und Katharer herausgegeben. t.II.München. 1890, p.195
[2] Tyndale, W. The Obedience of a Christian Man. London. 2001, p.118
[3] Ibidem, p.113, p.129
[4] Doctrinal Treatises and Introduction to different portions of the Holy Scriptures by William Tyndale, martyr, 1536. CUP. M.DCCC.XLVIII, p.27
[5] In Bulgarian: Василев, Г. Български богомилски и апокрифни представи в английската средновековна култура. София, 2001. See chapter I.
[6] In comparison we suggest the expression quod heretici vestiti essent Spiritus Sanctus from Döllinger, Ign. t.II, p.195 and Tyndale's expression in The Obedience..., p.113

Dualism as reformation potential

The next major chapter in the parallels between Bogomil-Cathar theology and Tyndale's interpretations pertains to the problems of direct communication between believers and God (respectively the Scriptures):

- on the denial of saints and icons
- on the denial of service
- on the denial of confession
- on the role of the priest

The Bogomil position regarding the saints is categorically negative, as Euthymius of the Periblepton put it succinctly: "The blasphemers say no one is or should be called holy; only God is holy".[1] Tyndale's opinion is equally unequivocal: "Take Christ from the saints and what are they? What is Paul without Christ?"[2] Or "...not the saints, but God only receiveth into eternal tabernacles, is so plain and evident, that is no to declare, or prove it."[3]

One should underscore here the complete coincidence between the Bogomils of Euthymius of the Periblepton and Tyndale. The former say "only God is holy" and five centuries later their British follower repeats "but God only receiveth into eternal tabernacles". The personal nuance with Tyndale is that he is inclined to a little concession: he is ready to take the saints for an example only[4], naturally not as mediators between God and believers. Once the cult of the saints is removed there is no longer need to revere their icons, or as Presbyter Cosmas wrote "the heretics do not revere the icons and call them idols".[5] Tyndale is a bearer of the same attitude, calling the reverence of icons "false faith, superstitiousness and idolatry and damnable sin".[6]

He enhances the reprimand, objecting in God's name against the depiction of God's images: "for nothing bringeth the wrath of God so soon and so sore on a man, as the idolatry of his own imagination".[7] By the

[1] Christian Dualist Heresies in the Byzantine World..., p.161. Greek source: Λέγουσιν οἱ ἀσεβεῖς, ὅτι ἅγιος οὔτε ἐστὶν οὔτε ὀφείλει λέγεσθαι, ἀλλά ἅγιος εἷς ἐστιν ὁ θεός (Ficker, G. Die Phundagiagiten. Leipzig. 1908, p.76)
[2] The Obedience, p.145
[3] The Parable of the Wicked Mammon. Antwerp.1528, p. 66
[4] The Obedience, p. 142
[5] Презвитер Козма. „Беседа против богомилите", с. 33
[6] The Obedience, p.143
[7] The Obedience, p.145

way, Bogomil-Cathar criticism of the icons and particularly Tyndale's last phrase are also in harmony with some texts in the New Testament "It is not as though Christ had entered a man-made sanctuary which was <u>only</u> modelled on the real one; but it was heaven itself, so that he could appear in the actual presence of God on our behalf." (Heb 9:24). He we encounter a tendency to which we shall return later in this study. Although they had a philosophy complicated by Manichaeism and Gnosticism, the dualists practically strove to identify themselves with the early Christian communities with evangelical type of conduct. And considering that the Bulgarian Bogomils and the Cathars, representatives of mitigated dualism, reinstated the reverence of the cross and called themselves fashioned after the manner of Christ, one can see that the activity and the spiritual efforts of these communities constituted a spontaneous return to the initial form of Christiantiy. This is essentially an example of reformation, of shedding the depravity amassed in the church as an institution.

Rejection of liturgies logically follows the rejection of icons. The Bogomils, as Presbyter Cosmas wrote, considered them "many worded" maintaining that it was not "the apostles who established liturgy and communion, but John Chrysostom."[1] One should recall here that the critical expression "many worded" corresponds to Matthew 6:7: "In your prayers do not babble as pagans do, for they think that by using many words they will make themselves heard." One finds similar views and definitions in Tyndale: "Subdeacon, deacon, priest, bishop, cardinal, patriarch and pope, be names of offices and services or should be, and not sacraments."[2]

In other words, the superfluous and profuse ecclesiastic bureaucracy was not in service of the sacraments, did not contribute to the spiritual development of the people, did not Christianise. William Tyndale pointed out that the hearing of mass, matins and evensongs, and receiving of holy water, holy bread and the bishop's blessing and so forth[3] did not make one love one's neighbour more, be more merciful or more thirsty for the spiritual. This seems to launch the thesis of the Bogomils (according to the letter of Euthymius of the Periblepton) "what is a priest"[4] some

---

[1] Презвитер Козма. „Беседа против богомилите", с.50, с.36
[2] The Obedience, p.110
[3] The Obedience, p.139
[4] Christian Dualist heresies…, p.161.

96

thing useless, but in this case developed in lengthier form. At this point, by the way, Tyndale added his own commentary, according to which the priest should be the elder and more experienced preacher, as it had been in early Christian communities, which in turn was also to be the image of contemporary church[1]. A definition in this sense Tyndale often makes in his *Table of the Book*: "in Greek called presbyter, in Latin senior, in English an elder" and "priest is to say an elder".[2]

To the Bogomils and the other dualists God is the sole recipient of personal confession. In this case, too, we have many observations to make. According to the 15th century *Summa contra haereticos*, Cod. Monac. Lat. 544, the dualists thought believers confessed their sins directly to God and received forgiveness from Him[3]. This, too, was the opinion of the Lollards, featured in the 15th century Norwich heresy trial records: "the same Margaret claims confession is made only before God and no other priests."[4] William Tyndale also literally rejected the opportunity for a priest to be "a mediator between God and us".[5]

One also finds the respective coincidence in the other, the public variant of dualist confession. We know that Bogomils and Cathars also practiced the so-called collective confession, a 14th century description of which we can again in Ign. Döllinger's collection of documents: "This confession is preferred in public where the prelate holds the Scriptures above his head while the rest lay their right hands with prayer".[6] Tyndale's definition of the two models of confession repeats the dualistic in both spirit and letter: "Confession, not in the priest's ear (for that is but man's invention), but to God in the heart and before all the congregation of God".[7]

The practice according to which the actual function of the priest is above all either in the sermon or in leading collective confession, or in

---

[1] The Obedience, p.111

[2] Priest is to say an elder – in: The Obedience, p.197

[3] Dicunt etiam haeretici: quod homo vadit ad confessionem, jam compunctus est et contritus pro peccatis suis et statim Deus dimissit ei peccata sua. in: Döllinger Ign., p.282.

[4] quod oraciones non sunt effundende ad sanctos sed ad solum Deum, qui solus audit orantes. – in: Tanner, N.(Ed.) Kent Heresy Proceedings 1511-12. Kent Archeological Society. 1997, p.2

[5] The Obedience, p.111

[6] Haec confession fit publice praelato tenenti librum evangeliorum super caput eius; reliqui dexteram apponunt cum orationibus – Cod. Alderspa.184.(membranac) – in: Döllinger Ign., p.295

[7] An Exposition upon the V, VI, VII Chapters of Matthew. Antwerp. 1533, p..477

spiritual guidance makes these activities also achievable by the ordinary but spiritually elevated man. This is the common stance of the Bulgarian and the European dualists, of the Lollards, Wycliffe and Tyndale, and it offered outlets for religious activity of women.

Our British colleague Margaret Aston has pointed out quite correctly that "in the fourteenth and fifteenth centuries, as earlier," Cathars, Waldenses and generally "unorthodoxy offered women outlets for religious activity that were not to be found in the established church."[1] Thus this tradition was introduced and spread by the Bogomils even in the 10th century, as Presbyter Cosmas wrote. The letter of Euthymius of the Periblepton mentions the heretic leader Churila who split with his wife because of the Bogomil requirement for abstinence from marriage and made her a "mock abbess".[2] When discussing the place of women in the Lollard community, Margaret Aston pointed out that there women used to study, read and preach the Scriptures and were some sort of evangelists, although she couldn't take it upon herself to say definitely whether women were given the role of priests[3].

It seems to this author, however, that we can rely on the records of the Heresy Trials in Norwich, where several heretics categorically stated that "every trewe man and woman being in charite is a priest".[4] Margaret Aston herself quoted the same thesis voiced by Wycliffe. Such categorical positions give grounds to assume that, although we do not know a name of a Lollard priestess to this day, such a document could be discovered one day, particularly as there are numerous recordings of the phenomenon of "perfect" Cathar women in Provence. In addition, Döllinger's collection features a 14th century document of the Inquisition in Provence, according to which "Perfect" Cathar women officiated at the supreme sacrament of the dualists, consolamentum, i.e. baptism in the name of the Holy Spirit[5].

Since precedents abound so much they could possibly have found their concrete expression somewhere in England too. In addition, one

---

[1] Aston, M. Lollards and the Reformers (Images and Literacy in Late Medieval Religion). London. 1984, p.49.
[2] Christian Dualist Heresies..., p.159. Greek text: τὴν γυναῖκα αὐτοῦ κατέλειπεν ποιήσας αὐτὴν ψευδαββαδίαν – in: Ficker, G. Die Phundagiagiten. Leipzig, 1908, p.66
[3] Aston, M., op. cit., p.49
[4] Tanner, T. Heresy Trials in the Diocese of Norwich, 1428-31. London,1977, p.57. And also: every good man and good woman is a prest. Ibidem, p.147
[5] Döllinger, Ign. op. cit, p.165

should not forget that preaching God's Word, public reading of the Scriptures in the native tongue and their explanation are the real priestly functions according to the dualists. In other words, the role of evangelist, which Margaret Ashton agrees was granted to Lollard women, means acting like a priest according to the dualists. The question is whether English women heretics had the right to give consolamentum, the supreme unction. The fact that this has not been recorded does not mean a negation in itself since the abundant archives on the Lollards to the best of this author's knowledge do not feature a description of consolamentum. The reason seems understandable – the Lollards hid their dualistic essence (and consolamentum was their supreme sacrament) and rather presented the structure and creed of their church, defending them as direct conformity to the Scriptures in order to generate respect in the official church. Nor did the Inquisition surmise that the English heretics were a continuation of the continental dualistic heresy.

About a century later Tyndale in turn placed the high sacrament "to bind and loose" (which according to the Catholic doctrine proceeds from the Pope) in the hands of "every man and woman that know Christ and his doctrine"[1] In other words, his continuity with the dualists is doubtless because he shared the then extremely unusual for Orthodoxy or Catholicism idea of female clergy, which today too bother the Orthodox and the Catholic churches.

As the reader can see for himself, nothing external has been introduced here and only thoughts and images of Tyndale have been used. One could, however, pose the question whether the stress is not laid extremely on some of his separate views and whether they actually have the weight they are allotted? Such focusing in our case is not only allowed, it is a necessary process as we can thereby reconstruct actual material which had the meaning of at least concealed narrative. Besides, although it is concealed, the narrative is of primary not secondary significance. Therefore to distinguish it – which has not been done so far – is an important academic task. As one can see, it bore the personal, confessional and functional philosophy of the reformer. Things become much clearer when the new narrative is related to two important religious discussions, which the British colleagues in most cases treat as a product of English national life. True, they are part of the cause of the national church, but in their

---

[1] Practice of Prelates by Wylliam Tyndale, martyr, 1536. CUP, M.DCCC.XLIX, p.284

foundation they were imported from the dualist movements in eastern and western Europe.

At places – for example in *The Obedience of a Christian Man* – Tyndale did not launch any sharp discussion involving transubstantiation obviously with the intention of concealing his negation. In his *Doctrinal Treatises* he compared various fundamental views on the issue ending exactly in the spirit of the dualists and directly expressing his negation. To him the idea of transubstantiation is false: "through the eyes and other senses perceive nothing but bread and wine…and thereof, no doubt, came up this transubstantiation through false understanding".[1]

And, of course, transubstantiation is defined as a papal mistake: "The pope confirming transubstantiation did purchase his own gain to the overthrow of the right use of Christ's sacrament."[2] In the place of the idea of transubstantiation Tyndale raised an extremely free interpretation of his. To him the cup of the New Testament should be understood as the cup holding the blood of Christ: "this cup is 'my blood of the New Testament'", or even more directly "my blood of the New Testament"[3]. This, however, is in harmony with the Bogomil metaphore recorded by Euthymius Zigabenus: "The 'new wine' they say is their teaching".[4]

One should also mention that Tyndale's refusal of Eucharist with "the blood of Christ" harks of the Bogomils' early objections to the cross, i.e. the memory of Christ's suffering cannot be accepted as His symbol. "Now the testament is, that is his blood was shed for our sins; but is impossible that the cup or his blood should be that promise," wrote Tyndale[5]. In essence he emulated the style and the words of the Bulgarian dualists: "But how can we bow to it? Because the Jews crucified His son on it the cross is most hated by God. That is why they teach their own to hate it, not to bow before it, saying thus: If anyone murdered the prince on a cross of wood could that wood be beloved of the king? The same is true of the cross and God."[6]

---

[1] Expositions and Notes on Sundry Portions of the Holy Scriptures together with the Practice of Prelates by William Tyndale, Martyr 1536. Cambridge, M.DCCC.XLIX, p.-p. 221-222

[2] Doctrinal Treatises and Introduction to different portions of the Holy Scriptures by William Tyndale, martyr, 1536. CUP. M.DCCC.XLVIII, p.373

[3] Ibidem, p.363

[4] Christian Dualist Heresies…, p.202. The original reads: Οἶνον μὲν καλοῦσι νέον τὴν διδασκαλίαν ἑαυτῶν – in Die Phundagiagiten, p.109

[5] Doctrinal treatises, p.379

[6] „Беседа против богомилите", с.34

One could also add another borrowing. The Bogomils and the Cathars were authors of a familiar in the Middle Ages sarcastic attitude against the Eastern Orthodox and Catholic belief that the body of Christ is in the Eucharist. Here we shall quote it according to Bernard Gui's 13th century *Manual of the Inquisitor*: "The body of Christ, they say, is not there (in the Eucharist – author's note), for if we assume it could be compared to the greatest mountain then the Christians would have eaten it all by now; the Eucharist is born of straw, passes through the tails of stallions or mares. In other words when the flour is cleansed of this filth through the sieve it goes down to the end of the stomach and excreted through the dirtiest organ. That is why it is impossible, they say, for God to be there."[1] Now here we have the similar phrase – and with the same image of the horse at that – pronounced by Tyndale on the same occasion: "If thou bring a bowl of blood and set it before God to flatter him, to stroke him and curry and claw him, as he were a horse, and imaginest that he had pleasure and delectation therein, what better makest thou of God than a butcher's dog?"[2] One should explain here that such detailed quotation does not aim to recall the emotions and the character of the discussion between the dualists and the Catholic Church. It provides two proofs on principle of the relation between the dualists and Tyndale not in ideas alone, but in imagery, style and sustainable individual vocabulary. In other words we have one and the same theology, born in Bulgaria and transferred to England, expressed in the 16th century with an almost identical vocabulary. The study of these details is a procedure of comparative analysis, whose evidential powers increase with the respect for detail, for cliché images and expressions. In the Middle Ages they were typological indicators, something akin to the fixed epithets in Bulgarian folk songs.

Here we shall quote a series of examples of traditional dualist criticism against the official church starting from the Bogomils, passing through the Cathars and Lollards, and preserving a very characteristic imagery also shared by Tyndale. This criticism pertains to:

---

[1] dicentes quod non sit ibi corpus Christi, quia si esset ita magnum sicut unus maximus mons, jam christiani comedissent totum: item, quod illa hostia nascitur de palea et quod transit per caudas equorum vel equarum, videlicet quando farina purgatory per sedatium; item, quod mittitur in latrinam ventris et emitter per turpissimum locum, quod non posset fieri, ut aiunt, si esset ibi Deus. – in: Gui, B., op. cit., p.26
[2] Expositions and Notes, p.215

- the church itself
- the liturgies and sacrifices.

One should also add here the enrichment of this criticism by the dualists in Western Europe during their battle with the Vatican. It contained the following new items:

- the pope was declared Anti-Christ and his prelates – servants of Satan
- the idea of Purgatory was rejected
- as was that of indulgences.

Now lets discuss these one by one, starting with the rejection of the official church.

The words with which Presbyter Cosmas said the Bogomils denied the official church were the following: "The churches they consider crossroads and the liturgies and other services in them – many words."[1] Euthymius Zigabenus added: "They think that Herod is our Church, which tries to murder the Word of truth born among them."[2] Because in the case of the Cathars the conflict with the Catholic Church was more severe and the persecutions more systematic, this negation was graded. On the one hand they declared their community the true and benign church "benignam, quam dicunt esse sectam suam", while the church of Rome was bad, the "mother of fornication, the great Babylon, mistress and basilica of the devil, synagogue of Satan".[3] The formulations of the Lollards were equally categorical and sometimes even more temperamental. The parchment maker John Godesell declared at the Heresy Trials in Norwich (1428-1431) that the Pope was "Anti-Christ and the head of the dragon mentioned in the Scriptures and that the bishops and other prelates of the church were followers of Anti-Christ, and the mendicant orders – the tail of the dragon."[4]

---

[1] Презвитер Кузма. „Беседа против богомилите", с.50

[2] Christian Dualist Heresies…, p.195. The original reads: Ἡρώδην δὲ νοοῦσι τὴν καθ' ἡμᾶς ἐκκλησίαν, πειρωμένην ἀνελεῖν τὸν παρ' αὐτοῖς γεννηθέντα λόγον τῆς ἀληθείας –in: (Euthymii Zigabeni de haeresi bogomilorum narration) Ficker, G. Leipzig.1906, p.103

[3] appellant matrem fornicationum, Babilonem magnam, meretricem et basilicam dyaboli et Sathane synagogam. – in: Gui, B. Manuel de l'inquisiteur. T.I. Paris, 1926, p.10

[4] papa est Antechristus et caput draconis de quo fit mencio in sacra Scriptura, et quod episcope et ecclesiam prelati sunt corpus draconis, et quod fratres mendicantes sunt cauda draconis, episcope ac alii ecclesiarum prelati sunt discipuli Antechristi. – in: Tanner, N. Heresy Trials in the Diocese of Norwich, 1428-31. London. 1977, p.61

Such, too, are Tyndale's position and language. At first he pointed out that preaching was the essence of the first Christian churches (the dualists practiced this extremely modest churchgoing without any special church building) and declared that the church is not material but spiritual: "The Churches at the beginning were ordained that the people should thither resort, to hear the word of God there preached only, and not for the use wherein there now are."[1] By the way this type of "internal worship" was expressed in another way by the well-known Bogomil instruction how to pray: 'When you pray, go into your room'. They say that the room is the mind...[2]

This Bogomil instruction was literally reproduced by Tyndale: "Of entering the chamber and shutting the door to... the meaning is, that we should avoid all worldly praise and profit, and pray with a single eye and true intent according to God's word."[3]

This is a paraphrase of Matthew 6: 6: "But when you pray, go to your private room and, when you have shut your door, pray to your Father who is in that secret place, and your Father who sees all that is done in secret will reward you." This is the "private" churchgoing of Bogomils, Cathars and Lollards and Tyndale actually followed the prescriptions of the Scriptures verbatim.

After he outlined the image of the true modest church of direct communication with God in the heart of man Tyndale took up the fiery criticism of the dualists against the Catholic Church. Even in the *Table of Contents* of his books one finds expressions like "Pope... a sure token that the pope is antichrist."[4] The quoted subtitle of Tyndale's *An Answer unto Sir Thomas More* is reproduced in nine variants bearing a similar antipapism. One even find the attack "the pope is the whore of Babylon"[5], which is yet another literal coincidence with the Cathar anti-Catholic speeches. The Catholic prelates are presented as a greedy group "whose God is their belly"[6], as "murderers" and "liars"[7]. Destitute of the

---

[1] The Parable of Wicked Mammon. Antwerp. 1528, p.106
[2] Christian Dualist Heresies..., p.199. Σὺ δὲ ὅταν προσεύχη φασὶν εἴσελθε εἰς τὸ ταμιεῖόν σου· ταμιεῖον λέγουσι τὸν νοῦν. - in: Phundagiagiten, p.107
[3] Expositions and Notes on Sundry Portions of the Holy Scriptures together with the Practice of Prelates by William Tyndale, Martyr 1536. Cambridge, M.DCCC.XLIX, p.79
[4] The Independent Works of William Tyndale. An answer unto sir Thomas More. Washington, 2000, p.100
[5] Expositions and notes, p.298
[6] The Obedience, p.144
[7] Expositions and notes, p.243, p.244

truth they corrupt minds. Tyndale used the vocabulary of the Cathars and Lollards to attack donations and indulgences: they "beguile God's word…to establish their wicked tradition"[1], "with such glosses corrupt they God's word, to sit in the consciences of the people, to lead them captive, and to make a prey of them: buying and selling their sins to satisfy their unsatiable covetousness"[2]. And that this truly was the language of Cathars and Lollards one can see from a quotation of the same polemic vocabulary set down in the minutes of the 15th century trials in Norwich. Margery Baxter, probably the most outstanding defendant at the trial, claimed that the bishop of Norwich and his ministers were "members of the devil who spread the false indulgences given them by the pope" and that indulgences taught the simple people "damnable idolatry"[3]. One could ask here whether similar rhetoric couldn't have been used in other circles. The answer is unequivocal: in the Middle Ages only the dualists took the liberty of polemicising temperamentally against the Catholic Church openly and consistently, in the course of several centuries. They always felt theirs was a separate large world, they had an idea of the scope of their presence, particularly as they saw it under God's direct guardianship. It is only in their case that such a line of conduct was amassed and passed down from generation to generation with the respective emotional vocabulary which, by the way, was also taken from critical New Testament passages against the heathens and the Pharisees. Thus it became a sort of auto-characteristic feature which can hardly be mistaken.

Naturally, one can sense the time and 'couleur locale'. In the case of the Bogomils it is clear even in their *Secret Book* that they regarded this world as Satan's creation and therefore as hell. In Western Europe, however, a new element entered this explanation: the Cathars and their affiliates were forced to give their own answer as to the location of Purgatory and what it was as Purgatory was invented by the Catholic Church.

---

[1] The Obedience, p.119

[2] The Obedience, p.p.119-120. And also: They compel us to hire friars, monks, nuns, canons, and priests, and to buy their abominable merits, and to hire the saints that are dead to pray for us… Ibidem, p.142

[3] Norwicensem episcopum, et eius ministros, qui sunt membra diaboli, ante istud tempus nisi papa transmisset ad istas partes illas falsas indulgencias…que indulgencia induxit populum simplicem ad ydolatriam maledictam. – in: Heresy Trials in the Diocese of Norwich, p.46. And here is Robert Harryson's position: Robert said of indulgences and pardons to be of noon effecte nor profit. – in: Kent Heresy proceedings…, p.4

The earliest answers belonged to Bosnian Patarenes since they were the first to have direct contact with Catholic influence: "they say there is no Purgatory"[1]. Similar opinion was recorded in the minutes of a 1387-1388 heresy trial in North Italy: "there is no other purgatory nor other hell but this world"[2]. This was also the opinion of the Lollards tried at Kent, with the added warning that "there was no purgatory but only in this world, and aftir that a man was decessid he shulde go straight to heven or to hell"[3].

And while the above-mentioned objections against purgatory seem rather doctrinal in the sense that the dualists who expressed them considered that this world was actually purgatory or declared it an unreal, made up construction that did not correspond to God's creation, two centuries later Tyndale denounced the avaricious aspect of purgatory. He described it as a zone invented as a result of the commercial and power-lusting ambitions of papacy: "but have created them a Purgatory, to reign also over the dead and to have one kingdom more than God himself hath"[4]. This artificial kingdom acted as a customs office for untold riches were collected through it from the relatives of the deceased who paid generous sums for the expurgation of the souls in Purgatory and their "ascent" to heaven[5]. There were also elements of "economic" or rather anti-corruption criticism of purgatory on the continent. Ign. Döllinger quoted a document, according to which, in addition to denying the existence of purgatory, the heretics claim donations are unclean, good only for the priests who ate them and lived in luxury[6].

Tyndale was nevertheless rather more global, closer to the idea of modern times and civic society: he rejected purgatory not so much with theological arguments as denouncing it as a totalitarian scheme, an open tool of unprecedented social dictum and manipulation, of economic exploitation through which the clergy take away "faith, hope, peace, unity,

---

[1] Item dicunt, non esse purgatorim. – in. Rački, Fr. Prilozi za povjest bosanskih patarena. Starine. U Zagrebu. 1869 (1), p.139

[2] ...non est purgatorium nec infernos nisi in hoc mundo – in: Döllinger, Ign., op. cit., p.267.)

[3] Kent Proceedings..., p.46

[4] The Obedience, p.91

[5] The Obedience, p.100)

[6] Purgatorim negant...omnia suffragia ecclesiae subsannant, dicentes quod oblations ad altare pro defunctis bonae sint, scil. ad pascendu sacerdotes ut eo lautius comedant at luxuriasius vivant. – in: (Incipit Summa de haeresibus) Döllinger, Ign. op. cit., p.298

love and concord then house and land, rent and fee, tower and town, goods and cattle, and the very meat out of men's mouths. All these (the clergy – author's note) live by Purgatory."[1] The pope and his pardons are grounded on Purgatory, Tyndale giving the cross of Christ as an alternative to that rapacious theology[2]. A powerful gesture indeed, which summed up Tyndale's idea of a national church where all could read the Lord's Prayer in their mother tongue; where all should know that churchgoing was above all preaching God's word spread by modest servants, a church whose sign Christ and the holy cross were. In fact this was the image of early Christian communities.

By returning to the cross Tyndale surpassed the tradition of clandestine heretical communities and offered an open, general national church reformed in the best of dualist spirit and practice. Although the example we have quoted are unequivocal evidence of Tyndale's predilection for dualist theology he wanted the edifice of his church to be one for all society, for the entire nation. The return to the cross, in fact, is a trend of internal evolution of Bogomilism and the Cathars, which was discerned by authors like A. Solovjev, Dmitri Obolensky, Rene Nelli and Stefan Lazarov, among others.

Tyndale's determination to elevate the significance of the cross corresponded to that trend, but it also emerges as his personal initiative in England when one recalls that the bulk of the Lollard defendants at Norwich (1428-1431), who were obvious staunch supporters of absolute dualism, rejected the cross. One can also discern Tyndale's new attitude to the cross in the fact that he used imagery and rhetoric whereby the Bogomils denied the cross but without the very act of rejection. Therefore Tyndale was also a reformer in the hard wing of dualist tradition, suggesting that it come out of its self-isolation and converge with the institutionally and historically established Christianity but yet to shed corruption and other deformities by reform. Considering that most of the texts used by Tyndale stem from the books and formulas of absolute dualists, his officially declared reverence for the cross overcomes some internal dualist dogmas, which sound like extreme speculation to the general public.

In this sense Tyndale's position was an expression of humanism, of liberation from the faith of dogma and ossified perception, of toning down

---

[1] The Obedience, p.155
[2] The Obedience, p.154

excess confrontation. This was a return of Christianity to its calling to be the moral and motivation of love open to all, to that divine bounty, which can be called individual emotional life and individual imagination in the perception of the Word.

At the same time the reproaches he levied against the Catholic Church were rather the result of doctrinal disagreement for he saw a tendency of dehumanism there although he did not use this term. Above all he claimed that by using a foreign language the church terminated the process of Christianisation, of spreading the teaching of Christ and familiarising people with it, which meant the introduction of love. Without the native tongue there was no connection to Christ or complete appreciation of His kindness: "How shall I prepare myself to God's commandments? How shall I be thankful to Christ for his kindness?"[1] In addition, by corruption the church underwent a process of mammonisation, which was an anti-pode of Christianisation, and introduced the fashion of greed[2]. As a type such criticism was a position modern for those times for Tyndale saw evil not only in the mythological figure of the Devil but also in socially removable roots like the implantation of greed, of the bad passion for plentiful, excessive wealth as an end in itself, of the easiest corruption of people. One could add that this view is topical today, for after the fall of the communist dictatorship consumption, i.e. the modern form of mammonisation, remains the main internal problem of western society.

The dualist influence in the two English translations of the Scriptures

Now that we have seen that the philosophy of William Tyndale shared fundamental Bogomil-Cathar doctrinal positions it is pertinent to ask how, by what ways the dualist philosophy actually reached him. On the one hand things are complicated because he lived in the 16th century, his connections with the familiar writings of dualist culture were indirect and he was, so to say, a third generation dualist. What we have in mind as the first generation of dualists on the Albion are the German-speaking heretics described by W. Novoburgensis who were branded in Oxford in 1166. To this author the second generation consisted of Wycliffe and the 14th

---

[1] The Obedience, p.90
[2] An Exposition upon the V,VI, VII Chapters of Matthew, Antwerp, 1533, p.104

century Lollards with their abundant literary work. Naturally such perio-
disation is conditional and can only be finalised with the addition of new
data. For example, Henry Knighton quoted Higden in his Chronicle and
wrote: "Mony of the heretikes Albigense, commyn into Ynglonde, were
brent in lyfe". It was difficult for this author to decipher the exact date of
this report precisely because it retold Higden and I based myself on the
context to date it in 1209[1].

On the other hand the high degree of presence of clearly defined dualist theses in Tyndale's works cannot be explained without systematic
contacts with the dualistic heritage in England or in Europe. I would like
to mention here four of the many cases on which this relation was discussed. In 1906 W. Summers saw undoubted continuity between the English Reformation and Wycliffe's work[2]. Eighty years later Charles Nauert
Jr. saw the possible relation between Tyndale and the Lollards as an occasion to underscore the national character of Tyndale's work and to ex-
tract him from the notion that he was "merely an English disciple of the
Saxon reformer"[3]. David Daniell also assumed such closeness stating
that "his memory was still green" at the time when Tyndale studied at
Oxford. Daniell added that in 1520 "Lutherans as well as Lollards were
now sought out for punishment"[4].

The conviction that Tyndale communicated with Wycliffe's work –
and that means with Lollard writings – is most powerful (and I thing
quite rightly so) in D. Smeeton[5]. In addition to the quantitative indicator,
Smeeton also discerned a visible conceptual continuity: "In view of the
recent availability of critical editions of certain Wycliffite writings, it is
possible to examine Tyndale's writings in light of parallel passages from

---

[1] Albigenses haeretici veneruunt in Angliam, quorum aliqui comburebantur vivi as well
as the English version: Mony of the heretikes Albigense, commyn into Ynglonde, were
brente in lyfe. – in: Chronicon Henrici Knighton vel Cnitthon Monachi Leycestrensis,
Ed. By J. R. Lumby, D.D. London. vol. I, 1889, p.p.190,191
[2] Summers, W.H. The Lollards of Chiltern Hills (Glimpses of English Dissent in the
Middle Ages). London.1906, p.28: "The Reformation of the sixteenth century was the
inevitable resultant of series of forces which had been at work a century and half before
in the life and teachings of John Wycliffe, for six years the rector of Buckinghamshire."
[3] Nauert, G. Jr. Editor's preface in: Lollard Themes in the Reformation Theology of
William Tyndale (Sixteenth Century Essays&Studies, vol.6), 1986, p.11
[4] Daniell, D., op. cit., p.31,94
[5] "Almost half a dozen times Tyndale likewise invoked the name of Wyclif always in a
positive reference." –in: Smeeton, D.D. Lollard Themes in the Reformation Theology
of William Tyndale (Sixteenth Century Essays&Studies, vol.6), 1986, p.75

Wycliffite literature. It would be difficult indeed to show that Tyndale used a particular version of a particular treatise, but compatibility, approach, language and general theological themes could certainly be indicated"[1].

In the opinion of this author, Tyndale was not only familiar with Wycliffe's writings and work, but he also melted it the significance of apostolic example, which he himself wanted to follow. In other words, he quoted Wycliffe as his predecessor in the national anti-Catholic cause: "Wycliffe preached repentance into our fathers not long since. They repented not, for their hearts were indurate, and their eyes blinded with their own pope-holy righteousness"[2]. The measure of Tyndale's commitment to Wycliffe was so great that he supported him where the attacks against Wycliffe were most severe. Tyndale rejected the accusations that the ideas of his predecessor were among the causes of the peasant revolts: "These hypocrites laid to Wycliffe's, and doyet that his doctrine caused insurrection."[3]. By the way, by using the word "doctrine" Tyndale indicates that he had comprehensive knowledge of Wycliffe's system of ideas.

One should suppose that a more detailed study of the sources Tyndale used to create his dualist philosophy will also reveal other connections, some of which might prove continental. Here we have to answer the next question: if Wycliffe's influence on Tyndale is visible how do we prove this was a dualist influence. Because of the limited scope of this study we cannot present the existing detailed evidence, we shall only say that the previous chapter clarifies the Bogomil-Cathar views of John Wycliffe[4]. Here we shall only mention as an indicative illustration Wycliffe's well-known thesis of *Deus debet obedire diabolo*[5], which is a rather precise translation of the Bogomil view that the devil is the impious steward of this world[6].

Naturally, as a thinker with an impressive individual presence already far beyond the initial substratum of ideas Tyndale had his own peculiar

---

[1] Ibidem, p. 34. Note: The term "Wycliffite literature" denotes texts created in the circle of Wycliffe's followers and disciples

[2] Doctrinal treatises and introductions to different portions of the holy scriptures by William Tyndale, Martyr 1536. Cambridge. M.DCCC.XLVIII, p.458

[3] Ibidem, p. 224

[4] See Chapter IV.

[5] XXIV conclusions Wycclyf damnatae Londoniis in synodo – in: Fasciculi Zizaniorum. London. 1858, p.278

[6] „Беседа против богомилите", с.43

features. Thus, although he repeatedly expressed a dualistic preference for the New Testament and although the examples in his works predominantly came from the New Testament, unlike the dualists he accepted the use of the Old Testament. Like the Bogomil-Cathar assertion that the God of the Old Testament was cruel and unjust, that that was Satan, Tyndale judged the Old Testament quite critically: "The old, cruel and fearful testament, which drew people away..."[1] Respectively, he expressed a strong preference for the New Testament: "but this new and gentle testament, which calleth again, and promised mercy to all that will amend..."[2] In his own interpretation Tyndale did not bring the contradictions between the two testaments to a break, but rather defined the Old Testament as a sort of antechamber to the New Testament. The Old Testament is a "covenant...made between God and the carnal children of Abraham, and Jacob, and otherwise called Israel", while the New Testament is "a new covenant...that Christ's blood is shed for our sins", i.e. this was a way for spiritual elevation of man. Thus we can also see that Tyndale adopted the official doctrine of redemption[3], while the Bogomils and Cathars did not.

The dualist theology is softened in yet another important case. Cathars, Bogomils and Lollards rejected the baptism with water, asserting that true baptism was with the Holy Ghost[4], with the Word, with Christ's passion and blood[5]. While placing baptism with the word higher Tyndale avoided rejection of baptism at the font and preserved its significance as preparatory to baptism with the Word: "The washing without the word helpeth not: but through the word it purifieth and cleanseth us". Of course, he did not forget to define baptism in Christ's blood as the true baptism: "The washing preacheth unto us, that we are cleansed with Christ's blood-shedding"[6]. Thus he did not engage in conflict with important items in the official church tradition but introduced his own additional interpretation instead.

Now we shall make an aside here to say that, regardless of his critical discussion with the Catholic Church and the perseverance with which he

---

[1] Doctrinal treatises, p.364

[2] Ibidem, p.455

[3] ...all good things are thine already purchased by Christ's blood. – in: The Wicked Mammon, p.64 Or: Christ's blood only putteth away all the sin that ever was... Ibidem, p.72

[4] infunditur gracia Spiritus Sancti...in: Heresy Trials, p.95

[5] baptized in the blood of Crist... Ibidem, p.146

[6] The Obedience, p.109

denied, for example, transubstantiation, Wycliffe also in other cases tended to take into account to some extent official rituals, for one can see from both his works and his conduct that his objective was to reform the church institution not to bring it down. He assumed images of God could be used providing it was known they were just images and not a presence of God in the material itself: "If it is said that God and the stone are one, then this is heresy and should be denied"[1]. Thus the occasion for magical devotion is taken away from the icon and it is interpreted as a symbol, which brings about contemplation of God. Such an interpretation made a contact between believers connected with the official church and those in the Lollard communities. Therefore, both Wycliffe and Tyndale, each by his own means, had the identical initiative to establish a national church with reformation material borrowed from the dualists.

Tyndale also modernised the term "perfect" which denoted the Bogomil leader. With the English the achievement of this state by the special ceremony of consolamentum becomes rather redundant, it being enough for one to devote oneself to spiritually elevating knowledge: "The principal of Scripture perfectly learned, all the rest is more easy"[2]. From initiation of the elect it becomes an appeal and way for spiritual growth achievable by man. Those were the changes of the time and thinking of Tyndale – some purely dogmatic points of dualist theology were left behind to pass to the idea for a more unencumbered development of personality, of individual thinking and expression achievable by the means of education, culture, literary work and discussion. In fact that was a sort of evangelical humanism, the beginning of a Christian renaissance. One should recall here that his criticism of purgatory featured a similar aspect: purgatory was a prejudice, a mystic invention and a usury system to the enlightened, the educated with a broad view of the universe. One can even discern traits of Erasmus' *Encomium moriae* in the satirical barbs levelled at purgatory.

One can also see the genetic link between Bogomil-Cathar tradition and Reformation noted by an author closer to our time. In 1879 L. P. Brockett of the American Baptist Church, who used the freshly accu-

---

[1] Est, ita quod sit sensus quod deus et lapis penitus et omnino sunt unum et idem, tunc est sensus hereticus..." in: Wyclif, J. Miscellanea Philosophica. vol.II. London. 1905, p.104

[2] Doctrinal Treatises, p.27. And also: ...a good and learned man. –in: The Obedience..., p.118

mulated research material on Bulgarian dualists with great insight, declared the Bogomils were forerunners of Protestantism in his brochure *The Bogomils of Bulgaria and Bosnia*[1]. But if such global thinking is difficult for a large portion of the present-day British colleagues there are certain obvious outlines that cannot be overlooked.

We shall take the liberty here to make the following conclusion: the two key translations of the Scriptures into the English language, the two momentous efforts to generate reform in the official church – that of Wycliffe in the 14th century and that of Tyndale in the 16th – were motivated by Bogomil-Cathar philosophy and were accompanied by the introduction of elements of its practice. As John Foxe beautifully put it "over England's long night of error and superstition and soul-crushing despotism God had said "Let there be light and there was light" with Tyndale's work"[2]. The Bulgarian example of direct communion with the New Testament lay at the root of that work, of that enlightenment.

I would like to say that further work on clarifying Tyndale's hidden theology will probably enriched the information presented here. It will also definitely introduce more nuances and precision in detail. For example, one can say that although the Wycliffe-Tyndale influence is clearly visible, in certain nuances it seems they are representatives of two different trends in dualist philosophy. According to hitherto studied material, Wycliffe rather leaned towards the ideas of the Bulgarian Bogomils who had "their own church of Bulgaria, believe in and preach a good omnipotent God without beginning (or end), who created the angels and the four elements. And they say that Lucifer and his accomplices sinned in the heavens"[3]. I would support this statement with Wycliffe's repeated quotation of the myth of Christ descending in hell and vanquishing it, a myth to which the Bogomils had a special predilection and which they borrowed from the *Nicodemus Gospel* included in the list of Bogomil literature. Tyndale's formulation in his *Expositions and Notes on Sundry Portions of the Holy Scriptures Together with the Practice of Prelates*:

---

[1] Brockett. L.P. The Bogomils of Bulgaria and Bosnia (The Early Protestants of the East. An Attempt to Restore Some Lost Leaves of Protestant History). Philadelphia, 1879

[2] Foxe's Christian Martyrs of the World. Westwood. New Jersey, 1985, p.358

[3] ...qui habent ordinem suum de Bulgaria, credunt i predicant tantum unum bonum deum omnipotentem sine principio, qui creavit angelos et IIIIor elementa. Et dicunt quod Lucifer et complices sui peccaverunt in celo. – in: Dondaine, A. Hiérarchie cathare d'Italie – in: Archivum fratrum Praedicatorum. Roma. XIX(1949), p.310

"God and devil are two contrary fathers, two contrary fountains, and two contrary causes: the one of all goodness, the other of all evil." overlaps with another tendency of dualism – that of absolute dualism preached by the Druguntia church, which reads "they believe and teach two gods, two lords without beginning or end, one good and one evil"[1]. At the same time it can be seen that Tyndale obviously read the *Homily of Epiphanius*, which also describes the scene of Christ's descent into hell, although Tyndale showed a preference for another equally impressive passage there and wrote: "Christ is in thee, and thou in him, knit together inseparably"[2]. This is an almost exact translation of the well-known phrase from the *Homily of Epiphanius*: "Thou art in me, as I am in thee – we are a primeval indelible face"[3].

One last professional requirement presupposes that we indicate the degree to which this subject has been studied so far. One can definitely say that, with the exception of some 19th century authors, the idea of the dualist heresy being transferred from the continent has not been raised among modern British medievalists. The philosophy and practice of the Cathars have been presented exceptionally well in Malcolm Lambert's *The Cathars*[4], one of the best works on this subject so far, although it does not outline a connection between the European proliferation of the Cathar movement and Britain. Dualist formulas sound strange and incomprehensible to our British colleagues. As the otherwise excellent scholar of the Lollards James Gairdner wrote about Wycliffe's fundamental dualist thesis "God, as he strangely put it, ought to obey the devil"[5] (i.e. the devil rules the earthly world". Some threads have been marked by the observant pioneer in this matter, W. Summers, who mentions Knyghton's information as well as one or two cases propitious for research[6]. These, however have been abandoned completely by present-day English medieval studies.

---

[1] …qui habent ordinem suum de drugonthia, credunt et predicant duos deos sive sine principio et sine fine, unum bonum et alterum malum penitus."Ibidem, p.309

[2] Doctrinal treatises, p.79

[3] Εὐ γὰρ ἐν ἐμοὶ κἀγὼ ἐν σοί, ἐν καὶ ἀδιαίρετον ὑπάρχομεν πρόσωπν. - in: L'Homélie d'Epiphane sur l'ensevelissement du Christ (édition par A. Vaillant). Radovi Staroslavenskog instituta. Zagreb, 1958, p.77

[4] Lambert, M. The Cathars. Oxford&Malden (USA),1998

[5] Gairdner, J. Lollardy and Reformation. v.I., L.1908, p.14.

[6] Summers, W. Our Lollard Ancestors. London. 1904, p.26. See also: Summers, W. The Lollards of Chiltern Hills (Glimpses of English Dissent in the Middle Ages). London.1906, p.9

Appendix

Finally, I should like to add another observation proving the salutary efforts of Tyndale Society to update the view on the reformer in a broader European circle. Commenting in the article The Authorised Version the translations of the Bible by the English reformers, including Tyndale's Bible (1525), *The Catholic Encyclopedia* summed it up: "That there was much good and patient work in them, none will deny; but they were marred by the perversion of many passages, due to the theological bias of the translators; and they were used on all sides to serve the cause of Protestantism"[1]. One could reply that this was written a century ago and one should not be so demanding. Regrettably, this text has been placed in the Online Edition www.newadvent.org/cathen/02141a.htm, copyright 1999 by Kevin Knight. To me as a witness on the side it is unacceptable for accusations of "profaned" Scriptures, rampant in such a benighted manner in the Middle Ages, to be transferred in the 21st century. Particularly as the translations of the Holy Writ are imposing, sometimes tragic national causes.

At that, emotions aside, one should recall the self-assessment of *The Catholic Encyclopedia* regarding the alternative to Reform Catholic English translation: "and although accurate, was sadly deficient in literary form". Or add the words of Yaroslav Pelikan describing the damages done by extreme reliance on the Latin version of the Bible and unfamiliarity with the Greek: "An inability to read Byzantine Christian writers (not to mention the New Testament) with any real expertness in the original language led Thomas Aquinas astray into a dependence on misinterpretation of Eastern Christian theology, and therefore into a distortion of the differences between it and the Western church on so fundamental point of dogma as the Filioque."[2] It seems to me that here a more adequate approach of the modern publishers of *The Catholic Encyclopaedia* would be to find a way to add the 2001 apology Pope John Paul II made to those persecuted with the fire and the sword by the Catholic Church.

---

[1] The Catholic Encyclopedia, Robert Appleton Company Volume II. 1907, p.141
[2] Pelikan, Y. with Valerie R. Hotchkiss and David Price. The Reformation of the Bible. The Bible of the Reformation. Yale University Press, New Haven and London, Bridwell Library, SMU, Dallas. 1996, p.7

114

Chapter VI. Bogomil-Cathar imagery and theology in *The Vision of Piers Plowman*

After having discerned how dualist concepts became an incentive for reformation, we enter literary horizons, where dualist theology gains majestic imagery. This applies to two giants of English literature - William Langland and John Milton, but a broader investigation of the subject would direct us to some other phenomena like the medieval miracle plays, very frequently featuring dualist apocryphal elements. It is assumed that William Langland's well-known poem, *The Vision of Piers Plowman*[1], was completed around the year 1370. This multi-plane work consists of 20 chapters containing some 6,500 unrhymed verses (B-text). The poem is, in fact, a comprehensive panel of 14th century reality in Britain, a valuable source of information about public and spiritual life in that age. Its main objective is to suggest a meaning for the existence of contemporaries from a Christian point of view. Unlike ecclesiastic homilies, however, in this case problems are posed for consideration before the individual and it is in this spirit that Langland expounds his deliberations and quests. In other words, we have a development of personal philosophy and position – a novelty in relation to medieval mass conscience. Quite a lot has been written about William Langland's poem, underscoring any number of aspects of its significance, be they historical, literary, socio-critical or religious. Two of these, however, have remained untouched. First, on many occasions *The Vision of Piers Plowman* sounds like a Bogomil-Cathar treatise in that it develops fundamental elements and images of Dualist philosophy. The second lies in the context of the first, the fact being that one finds it reproduces episodes from the Bulgarian *The Legend of the Tree*, or *The Tree of the Cross*, and from other Bogomil apocrypha like *The Secret Book* of the Bogomils as central elements of meaning and composition. It is the objective of this chapter to clarify these Bogomil-Cathar motifs, for they are a case of major cultural transfer, an interaction between geographically distant cultures in the Middle Ages that has become common cultural heritage. Or, to use a contemporary French term of sociology of culture and civilization, interculturalité médiévale.

---

[1] Langland, W. The Vision of Piers Plowman (A complete edition of the B-text/. London, Melbourne, Toronto, New York. 1978. A critical edition of the B-text based on Trinity Colledge Cambridge MS B.15.17 with selected variant readings, an Introduction, glosses, and textual and literary commentary by A.V.C. Schmidt

To ensure that our thesis is clear and convincing we shall use the most important of all comparative analysis means, i.e. direct text comparison. Then again, because of the limited scope of this chapter, we shall concentrate on the following major ideas and narrative elements in *Piers Plowman*:

– the fall of Lucifer and his angels;

– the descent of Christ into Hell and the liberation of all souls;

– Christ teaches Peter to plough and gives him a writ granting use of the land.

Now let us commence with the first scene. As we know, the Dualist myth begins with the legend of Lucifer's betrayal, his desire to place himself above the Lord, which ends with the banishment of Lucifer and those with him from the heavens and their descent into the void where they created the Earth as their own conception (not without help from God, of course). The classical narration of this legend is found in *The Secret Book* of Bogomils and a direct comparison reveals that the story retold by William Langland is very close to the original.

The fall of Lucifer

Piers Plowman

Lucifer with legions lerned it in hevene,/ And was the lovelokest to loke after Oure Lord {one}]/ Till he brak buxomnesse; his blisse gan he tyne, /And fel fro that felawshipe in a fendes liknesse/ Into a deep derk helle to dwelle there for evere./ And mo thousandes myd hym than man kouthe nombre/Lopen out with Lucifer in lothliche forme/ For thei leveden upon hym that lyed in this manere:/ Ponam pedemin aquilone, et similis ero Altissimo./

And alle that hoped it myghte be so, noon hevene myghte hem holde,/ But fellen out in fendes likness [ful] nyne days togideres,/ Til God of his goodnesse [garte the hevene to stekie/And gan stable it and stynte] and stonden in quiete.

Passus I, ll. 111-123

The Secret Book of Bogomils or Interrogatio Joannis (Carcassone Text):

...et traxit cum cauda tertiam partem angelorum Dei, et projectus est de sede Dei et de vilicatione coelorum. Et descendens Sathanas in firmamentum hoc, nullam requem potuit facere sibi nec iis qui cum eo errant.

(Иванов, Й. Богомилски книги и легенди. София. 1925, p.76)

...and with his tail he dragged away one-third of the angels of God, and he was banished from the throne of God and from the overlordship of the heavens. And Satan, descending to this firmament, was unable to find rest either for himself or for those who were with him.

(Translation Tom Butler. Monumenta bulgarica. Michigan Slavic Publications. 1996, p.193)

The reader may notice that this book more than once repeats quotations from Bogomil and Dualist scripts. These recurrences are a visible reality in different cultural monuments of the English Middle Ages. There is yet another peculiarity: the myth of Lucifer's fall is repeated in *Piers Plowman* at least three times whereby the Dualist thesis of Satan's overlordship on Earth becomes dominant in the poem. It is on that that the specification of Antichrist imposing his power in the Papal institution lies: "And thane shal Pride be Pope and prynce of Holy Chirche,/Covetise and Unkyndenesse Cardinals hym to lede."[1] And the consequence will be their power over secular authorities, for "false prophetes fele, flatereris and gloseries/ Shullen come and be curatours over kynges and erles".[2] In other words, Langland's well-known anti-clericalism is Dualistic. It is in synchrony with the Cathar thesis that "since the Pope, the bishops and the Catholic priests subordinate to the Church of Rome do not follow the holy faith and are hostile to their (the Cathars – author's note G.V.) holy faith, they have no power whatsoever to absolve anyone of their sins."[3] The English Lollards were no less temperamental and closer in their imagery to Langland when they declared the Pope in Rome Antichrist and all bishops, prelates, presbyters and men of the church – followers of Antichrist[4]. At the bottom of that anti-clericalism lay Bogomil criticism, which called Orthodox priests blind Pharisees and whose adepts offered a negation of the official world order (because this world was a Devil's construction) even more radical than Langland's: "they teach people to disobey their masters; they hate the king; they vilify elders and reproach the boyars…"[5]

Christ descends into Hell and sets all souls free

The motif of Christ setting human souls free from Hell was transferred to medieval Europe by two apocrypha, the *Gospel of Nicodemus*

---

[1] Ibidem, p. 242. Passus XIX, ll. 224-225

[2] Ibidem. Passus XIX, ll.222-223

[3] Sed papa, episcope, sacerdotes catholici vel ecclesiae Romanae, quia non tenebant sanctam fidem et errant inimici fidei eorum, non habebant potestatem aliquam absolvendi aliquem a peccatis . XIV век – in: Döllinger, Ign. v. Dokumente vornehmlich zur Geschichte der Valdesier und Katharer herausgegeben. t.II.München. 1890, p.p. 194 -195

[4] This is what we read in the confession of Johannes Reve de Becles at the well-known Norwich trial (1428-1431): "Item quod papa Romanus est Antechristus…Item quod omnes episcopi, prelati et presbiteri et viri ecclesiastici sunt discipuli Antechristi."(Tanner, T. Heresy Trials in the Diocese of Norwich, 1428-31. London. 1977 p.108)

[5] Презвитер Козма. „Беседа против богомилите" - in: „Стара българска литература 2. Ораторска проза". София. 1982, с.37, с.51

and the *Homily of Epiphanius*, their main distributors – particularly of the former – being Dualist: Bogomils and Cathars. British historians have accepted the presence of scenes from the *Gospel of Nicodemus* in the literature and art of medieval England, *Piers Plowman* included[1], but it seems the second aspect of the process, i.e. the fact of Dualist transfer, practically remains outside their field of vision. By comparison in the tables we shall prove that the scene from Passus XVIII coincides quite precisely with chapters XXIV and XXVI of the *Gospel of Nicodemus* from a copy taken to Ukraine by Bulgarian Bogomils. The compiler of the excellent anthology *"Апокріфі і легенди з українських рукописів"*, the poet Ivan Franko, was one of the first to point out that this story spread by the Bogomils penetrated into England[2]. He was outstripped only by M. Gaster, who spoke of the same transfer in 1887, without forgetting to point out its Bogomil context or the direct relation between the *Legend of the Cross* and the *Gospel of Nicodemus*: "The legend in its simplest form is part of the apocryphal *Gospel of Nicodemus*."[3] Some would object that, albeit on the extreme periphery, this scene was mentioned by medieval Catholic authors as adopted by the Orthodox Church. In the case of the Dualists, however, its means the complete destruction of Hell and the liberation of all souls - Ac alle that beth myne hole brethren, in blood and in baptisme,/Shul noght be dampned to the deeth that is withouten ende (Passus XVIII, ll. 377-378) – while the official churches admit only the liberation of Adam and Eve. (Please refer to the Appendix attached to this chapter.)

Passus XVIII	
(320-321)'Dukes of this dymne place, anoon undo thise yates,/that Crist may come in, the Kynges sone of Hevene!'	И каза Господ, простирайки ръката своя: елате при мен всички мои светии, защото вие имате подобие на моя образ, защото зарад делата на дървото на дявола – на смърт бяхте осъдени. Сега виждате: чрез дявол-

---

[1] In the notes to Passus XVIII of The Vision of Piers Plowman (A Complete Edition of the B-Text). London, Melbourne, Toronto, New York. 1978, A.V.C. Schmidt makes reference to the Gospel of Nicodemus (p.p.350-352). We find more detailed notes by J.F. Goodridge – cf. p.308 of the edition Langland, W. Piers the Ploughman translated into modern English with an introduction by J.F. Goodridge. New York etc.,1959/1977. But they pertain to separate details without interpreting the philosophy underlying the Gospel of Nicodemus and its perception by Langland.

[2] Франко, І. Апокріфі і легенди з українських рукописів. ІІ. Львів.1899, с.VII

[3] Gaster, M. Ilchester Lectures on Greeko-Slavonic Literature and its Relation to the Folklore of Europe During the Middle Ages. London. 1887, p.35

(324-325) Patriarkes and prophetes, *populus in tenebris,*/ Songen Seint Johanes song, '*Ecce Agnus Dei!*'
(356-361) Getest bi gile tho that God lovede;/And I, in liknesse of a leode, that Lord am of hevene,/ Graciousliche thi gile have quyt – to gile ayen gile!/And as Adam and alle thorugh a tree deyden/Adam and alle thorugh a tree shal turne to lyve;/And gile is bigiled, and gile fallen...
(372-373) That I drynke right ripe must, *resureccio mortuorum.*/And thane shal I come as a kyng, crowned, with aungeles,/And have out of helle alle mennes soules.
(376-379)Ac to be merciable to man thane, my kynde is asketh,/For we beth brethren of blood, but noght in baptisme alle./Ac alle that beth myne hole brethren, in blood and in baptisme,/Shul noght be dampned to the deeth that is withouten ende:/*Tibi soli peccavi&.*

ското дърво смъртта осъдих. И когато така каза, всички светии под ръката Господня бяха. И държейки Адам за десницата, Господ му каза: "Мир на теб с всичките ти чада"...
(And the Lord stretched His hand and said: "Come unto Me all My saints, for you have My likeness and were sentenced to death for the deeds of the Devil's tree. See now that I have judged death through the Devil's tree." And when He said this all saints were under the Lord's hand. And the Lord took Adam by the hand and said "Peace be with you and all your children...")
Така и всички светии, преклониха колени пред нозете Господни и в един глас казаха: "Дойде избавителят на вековете! Изпълни се казаното от пророците и от закона. Избави ни с животворният си кръст и чрез кръстната си смърт слезе при нас, и ни избави от адовата смърт с твоята сила, Господи. (Никодимово евангелие, глава XXIV, глава XXVI в Апокріфі і легенди з украіньских рукописів. т.II. Львів, 1899с.с.300-301; с.312/.
(And all saints kneeled before the Lord and said as one "The Savior of all ages has come! And the words of the prophets and the law have come to be. He saved us with his life-giving cross, came to us through His crucifixion and saves us from Hells' death by your power, oh Lord." Gospel of Nicodemus, Chapter XXIV, XXVI in Apocrypha and Legends in Ukraine Manuscripts. Vol. II. L'viv, 1899, pp. 300-301; p. 312.)

At that, Christ's descent into Hell and the salvation of Adam and Eve, along with numberless others[1], "out of helle alle mennes soules" is mentioned again in Passus XIX. There is the addition of a particularly important detail, signifying yet another element of Dualist character, i.e. that after that Lucifer is chained, which is a repetition of the same scene from *The Secret Book* of the Bogomils:

Piers Plowman Passus XIX, ll. 56-57	*The Secret Book* (Codex Carcassoniensis)
And took [Lucufer the lothly], that lord was of helle/ And bond [hym] as [he is bounde], with bondes of yrene.	... et claudet Diabolum ligans eum insolubilibus vinculis fortibus.[2] (...and he locked the Devil in powerful invincible chains.)

The Bulgarian image of Christ the Ploughman and Piers Plowman

There is only one image of Christ Ploughman in the world of apocryphal literature and that is the one in Father Jeremiah's *The Legend of the Cross*. This Old Bulgarian story from the last quarter of the 10th century features Christ teaching man to plough better, i.e. in both directions, whereas until then he would go to the end of one furrow and then, instead of turning the plough again in the field, would surround it and go back to square one from where he would start on the next furrow. Naturally, this is also an image of the sowing of Christian virtues. **Bulgarian popular theology thus created a new hypostasis of Christ – Christ the Ploughman** – probably just as widespread in the plains at the time as Christ Pantokrator was in official church icon painting. The tetraevangelion describes the life line of the Lord's Son in the direction from earth to heaven. Christ's Passion or the road to Calvary is respected by all believers and His self-sacrifice – an unsurpassed example. The people of the plains, however, did not want Christ to leave them, they wanted to see Him among themselves, to witness His deeds in everyday life, to regard Him as a wiser brother who taught them to work and live better. According to their thinking the outcome is the descent, the return of Christ from heaven to the earth, to the people. This

---

[1] The Vision of Piers Plowman (A complete edition of the B-text... Passus XIX, ll. 53-58: "And tho was the conquerour called out of quyke and dede,/ For yaf Adam and Eve and othere mo blisse/ that longe hadde yleyen before as Luciferis cherles.

[2] Иванов, Й. Богомилски книги и легенди. София. 1925, с. 86

great and appealing image took the road to Western Europe carried by the Bogomils, only to reach William Langland. What the possible ways of this transfer were we shall see a bit later.

In addition to the complete similarity of meaning and scenery in the episodes we have compared, readers cannot but notice some peculiarities of time and local custom. In Langland's case it is Grace, not Christ, who teaches Piers to plough – a process entirely metaphorical in the poem as the field of truth is ploughed, virtues are sown and the team of four oxen are the four evangelists. This difference, however is *licentia poetica*, the freedom to interpret the source apocrypha and the desire for personal expression in creativity – early tentative hits of the Renaissance in the age of Langland. Nevertheless, the links to Bogomil imagery and theology remain visible and are not lost.

Christ the Ploughman

Piers Plowman

Grace, the "Christes messeger", that comes "fro the grete God" gives Piers Plowman a team of four oxen to plough the field of Truth and sow there the seeds of the Spirit of Prudence, the Spirit of Moderation, the Spirit of Fortitude and the Spirit of Justice, to break the clods with the harrows of the Old and the New Testament:

Passus XIX, ll. 260-268

..'My prowor and plowman Piers shal ben on erthe,/And for tilie truthe a teeme shal he have.'/Grace gaf Piers a teeme – four grete oxen./ That oon was luk, a large beest and a lowe chered,/And Mark, and Mathew the thriddle – mighty beestes bothe;/And joined to them oon Johan, moost gentil of alle,/ The pris neet of Pires plow, passynge alle othere.

Повест за кръстното дърво

Един ден Исус отиваше във Витлеем и намери един човек, че оре и отхвърля на една страна пръстта и обикаля нивата. И видя Господ, че денят минава [напразно] и взе ралото, та изора три бразди, па обърна, даде му ралото и рече: "Сбогом, ори, брате!" ("Повест за кръстното дърво"- в: Стара българска литература. т.I, с.282)

"One day Jesus went to Bethlehem and saw a man who was ploughing and throwing the earth on one side, going round and round the field. And the Lord saw that the day was passing [fruitlessly] and took the plough in His hands, plough three furrows, then turned the plough, gave it to the man and said: "Fare thee well, brother, plough!" (Old Bulgarian Literature. 1. Apocrypha, Sofia, 1982, p. 282 - in Bulgarian).

The legend by which the land is given to Adam – to Piers Plowman in Langland's poem – is yet another fundamental Bogomil thesis that has found place in chapters XVIII and XIX of the poem. Christ makes Piers his spiritual ploughman on earth. This new covenant between the Lord and the Farmer runs in contradiction with the old agreement. According to the old obligation, featured in the apocryphal *"Слово за Адам и Ева от началото до свършека"* – Story of Adam and Eve from the Beginning till the End[1], the Devil urges Adam to give him a bill (запис), registering that he, Adam, and all his progeny will belong to him. That is because Adam has been given the right to till the land belonging to the Devil, for don't the Bogomils say that the earth is created by the Devil. The same paragraph, however, also features "but Adam knew that the Lord would descend on earth in human form and would vanquish the Devil." That Bogomil imagery was followed can also be seen in Langland's usage of the verb "register" to underscore his closeness to his source. In other words, Langland continues his dialogue with apocryphal legend. He presents the new convention by which Grace gives the land to Piers Plowman, a situation promised by the above mentioned apocryphal phrase: "but Adam knew that the Lord would descend on earth in human form and would vanquish the Devil."

Christ's register

Piers Plowman Passus XIX, ll.260-263
'For I make Piers the Plowman my procuratour. and my reve,/ And register to *receyve redde quod debes*. /My prowor and my plowman Piers shal ben on erthe,/ And for to

"Слово за Адам и Ева от началото до свършека"
И тъй Адам улови воловете и започна да оре, за да изкара прехраната си. Тогава дяволът дойде, застана [пред] воловете и не даде на Адам да работи. Рече му: "Моя е земята, а божии са небесата и раят! Ако искаш да си мой, обработвай земята, ако ли пък искаш да

---

[1] As Donka Petkanova has clarified, the origin of the apocrypha indicates the Book of Jubilees written about 140-100 BC. There is an independent version in Greek literature or else it is part of The Apocalypsis of Moses. The Bulgarian translation was made around the 10th century, the motif of Adam's writ being absent from the Greek version, in other words making it a Bulgarian Bogomil addition. Стара българска литература. Т. I Апокрифи. София. 1982, с.348

tilie truthe a theeme shal
he have.'

си бога, върви в рая." Адам каза:"Небесата, земята и раят, и цялата вселена са
на бога." Дяволът му рече: "Не ти поз-
волявам да ореш земята, ако не ми да-
деш запис,че си мой." Тогава Адам от-
говори: "Който е господар на земята,
негов ще бъда аз и моята челяд." Дяволът се зарадва. Адам обаче знаеше, че
Господ ще слезе на земята, ще се облече
в човешки образ и ще смаже дявола."
*Стара българска литература. Т.I Апо-
крифи.* София.1982, с.39)

*Story of Adam and Eve from the Begin-
ning till the End*

And thus Adam caught the oxen and began to plough for his living. Then the Devil
came, stood [before] the oxen and stopped
Adam from work. And he said to Adam "Mine
is the earth and the heavens and Eden are the
Lord's! If you want to be mine, till the earth,
but if you want to be with God – go to Eden."
And Adam said "The heavens, the earth and
Eden and all the universe are the Lord's." Then
the Devil spake: "Thou shalt not plough if thou
does not give me a writ that thou art mine."
Adam then answered "He who is lord of the
earth – his will be I and mine." The Devil re-
joiced. But Adam knew that the Lord would
descend on earth, would take human form and
destroy the Devil."

(Old Bulgarian Literature. Vol. 1. Apocrypha. Sofia, 1982, c. 39 - in Bulgarian)

One should note here that the quoted cases of borrowings from Bulgarian apocryphal literature are part of a much more comprehensive presence of Bogomil influence in the poem, but we do not have the opportunity to expound on it further here. Rather, we shall pass on to the next

important issue, i.e. in what way were these fundamental Bogomil and apocryphal myths taken to England? Although such a connection might seem nearly improbable to contemporary scholars there are nevertheless 19th and 20th century authors who have noted it. As we have already mentioned, such a transfer of Bogomil apocrypha to medieval England was discussed by M. Gaster, Alexander Vesselovsky and Ivan Franko.

A case in point regarding results of the transfer of variants of the *Legend of the Tree* to England was that they were noted by the prominent French expert on English literature Jean Jules Jusserand, although he did not note the Bulgarian origin of the apocrypha or their Dualist involvement. This he did in his *Histoire littéraire du peuple anglais*, the first volume of which was published in France in 1895, a work that was rounded off to three volumes in 1909.[1] Thus, without indicating the peculiarities of the apocrypha, Jusserand nevertheless gave a remarkably comprehensive description of variants of the *Legend of the Tree*, existing in England in: *Ayenbite of Inwit or Remorse of Conscience*, L., 1886; *Legends of the Holy Rood, Symbols of the Passion and Cross poems in Old English of the XI, XIV and XV centuries*. L., 1871; *An old English Miscellany, containing a Bestiary, Kenton sermons, proverbs of Alfred and religious poems of the XIII century*. L., 1872; *The religious poems of William de Shoreham*. L., 1842 (about the Holy Sacraments, orders, deadly sins, etc. – first half of the 19th century); *Cursor mundi, the Cursor of the World*. L., 1874-1893 (seven parts compiled c. 1300.)

In other words, Jusserand perceptively identified the story typologically without going on to clarify its genesis or its dualistic characteristics. Nevertheless, this was an achievement, which surpassed the efforts of his 20th century English colleagues. It is because of the same lack of time that we shall dwell here on only three cases of distinct transfer amidst the bountiful stream of manuscripts that were discovered:

– *La Légende de l'Arbre de Paradis ou «bois de la croix»* (poème anglo-normand du XIIIe siècle et sa source latine, d'après le Ms. 66 Corpus Christi College. Cambridge. Inédit – in Zeitschrift fur Romanische Philologie, 1960 (76)

---

[1] The bibliographic reference this author made indicates the following edition of the same story in English, the translation belonging to Jusserand himself: A literary history of the English people: from the origins to the end of the Middle Ages, 1926 3rd ed., New York. In our case, we have used the Russian edition of 1898 - История англійскаго народа въ его литературе. С. Петербургъ, 1898.

– *Cursor mundi* (transferred from France and translated in Northern England c. 1325-1330): *Cursor mundi*. Ed. by R. Morris. Four versions: British museum Ms Cotton Vespasian A.III; Bodlean Ms Fairfax 14; Goettingen University Library Ms. Theol. 107; Trinity College Cambridge Ms. R. 3.8. Seven parts. London, 1874/1961.

– and, above all, the famous series of 14th century ceramic tiles from the no longer existing church in Tring, Hertfordshire, with scenes from the apocryphal Infancy Gospel.

The above order of presentation has a significance of its own. The publication of the first manuscript provides information about the widespread presence of *The Legend* in the whole of medieval Europe, England included. *Cursor Mundi* is a case of permanent popularization of the manuscript in England, while the Tring tiles represent the very scene of Christ Ploughman reproduced in Britain.

Now let us consider them one by one.

M. Lazar, who published *The Legend about the Tree of Paradise or the Tree of the Cross*, an Anglo-Norman poem, kept at Corpus Christi College, Cambridge, laid the stress on "the great popularity of the legend in the Middle Ages" and one that had "countless adaptations of different names in many languages".[1]

Cursor Mundi is an enormous poem of some 30,000 verses, about which there are only a few British studies, none of which touches upon the problem of the manuscript's origin.[2] *Cursor Mundi* comes from France (just like *The Legend about the Tree of Paradise or the Tree of the Cross*), so to say an apocryphal miscellany of second generation. It is a mixture/contamination of several dualistic texts, the compositional axle being *The Legend of the Tree*. It could be compared to the Bulgarian apocrypha *Orafione of St. John Chrysostom on How Michael Vanquished Satanael*, classified by Anissava Miltenova as one "of the more general type Bogomil works intended for the general public". It was then, at the end of the 12th and the beginning of the 13th century, that the practice of compiling miscellanies of separate apocrypha originated in Bulgaria, in this case including parts of the *Secret Book*, the *Tiberiad Sea*, the *Dispute between*

---

[1] Lazar, M. La Légende de "l'Arbre de Paradis" ou "bois de la croix"(poème anglo-normand du XIIIe siècle et sa source latine, d'après le Ms.66. Corpus Christi College. Cambridge.(Inédit). - in: Zeitschrift fur Romanishe Philologie, 1960 (76), p.34

[2] The only more serious, albeit rather short analysis we have found belongs to Cl. Tomson, Ch. XIV. Later Transition English I. Legendaries and Chroniclers – in: Cambridge History of English Literature. V.II. CUP. 1933.

Our Lord Jesus Christ and Antichrist, the *Book of Enoch* and the *Apocalypse of St. John*, among others[1].

One should, however, note that although *The Legend of the Tree* and *Cursor Mundi* contain variants of the Bulgarian *Legend of Holy Rood* they do not feature the Christ Ploughman scene. Nevertheless this image appears in a sort of resurrection in the series of ceramic tiles from the no longer existent church in Tring, Hertfordshire, 14th century. The series constitute episodes from the *Infancy Gospel*, but following the above-mentioned practice of re-editing and mixing different apocrypha it also includes the episode in which Christ teaches the ploughman to plough correctly. In other words, an episode of *The Legend of the Tree* is incorporated in the *Infancy Gospel*. By the way, this type of mixing, incorporation and editing we call a "Bulgarian alteration" since it is one of the earliest registered in Europe peculiar types of creative freedom in unhesitant reworking of existent texts and resources. As *The Legend of the Tree* was itself created in such a way, we shall date the "Bulgarian edition" or the Bulgarian type of work with apocrypha around the end of the 10th century. A variety of this, by the way, shall be mentioned shortly.

Now let us look at the illustrations – two scenes, of which we shall first discuss the one to the right, **Fig. B. (Scene 28, D.2)**, Christ teaches the ploughman the right way to plough while the latter regards Him in amazement and gratitude.

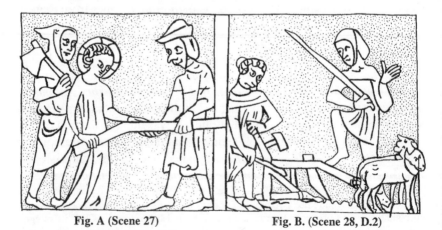

Fig. A (Scene 27)   Fig. B. (Scene 28, D.2)

---

[1] Милтенова, А. Бележки в: Българската литература и книжнина през XIII век. София. 1987, с.251

126

Without any doubt the scene reproduces a fundamental episode from Father Jeremiah's *The Legend of the Tree*. The text goes: "One day Jesus went to Bethlehem and saw a man who was ploughing and throwing the earth on one side, going round and round the field. And the Lord saw that the day was passing [fruitlessly] and took the plough in His hands, ploughed three furrows, then turned the plough, gave it to the man and said: "Fare thee well, brother, plough!" (Old Bulgarian Literature. 1. Apocrypha, Sofia, 1982, p. 282 -in Bulgarian). The eminent British medievalist M. R. James (1923) failed to understand the contents of this scene. "In D.2 is a scene of ploughing," he wrote. "A ploughman guides the plough, which is drawn by a yoke of oxen. A man with a goad, probably the master, seems surprised."[1]

The scene on the tiles coincides with the episode in *The Legend of the Tree* even in detail. One should add here, that the ploughman really does hold a goad. The very same goad, which made Father Jeremiah exclaim: "Oh, blessed tree, that the Lord took in His hands! Oh, blessed plough and blessed goad!". (Old Bulgarian Literature. 1. Apocrypha, Sofia, 1982, p. 282 -in Bulgarian).

Now we come to the Bulgarian correction or alteration we find in **Fig. A (Scene 27)**. Here Christ, as E. Eames wrote, "straightens the beam of a plough"[2]. M. R. James, whom she quoted, added that he also failed to find such an episode in *Evangelium Thomae Infantiae*[3] (or Infancy Gospel), and that "the scene was either altered or not understood"[4]. In this way, however, without knowing it himself, the British scholar has indicated the **Bulgarian alteration** in this version of *Evangelium Thomae Infantiae*, which consists of the following: **"in Latin is a grabatum that has to be made: here it is a plough,"** M. R. James comments[5]. It is true, that in the traditional version of *Evangelium Thomae Infantiae* Christ extends a plank for a simple, low-lying bed (grabatum), while in the Tring tile series Christ extends a plough beam. In other words, the idea of a plough has prevailed and substituted the low-lying bed (grabatum) in the

---

[1] James, M.R. Rare Medieval Tiles and Their Story with a note by R.L. Hobson – in: The Burlington Magazine for Connoisseurs. London. Vol. XLII, Jan-Jun. 1923, p.34.

[2] Eames, E. Medieval Lead-glazed Earthenware Tiles in the Department of Medieval and Later Antiquities, British Museum. Text and Catalogue. British Museum Publications. London. 1980, p.58

[3] Tischendorf, K. Evangelia apocrypha. Leipzig. 1852

[4] James, M.R., op.cit., p.34.

[5] Ibidem

traditional version of *Evangelium Thomae Infantiae* in the contamination of the *Infancy Gospel* and *The Tree of the Cross* that the Tring tiles constitute. The same Bulgarian alteration – extension of a plough beam, not of *grabatum* is found in the already familiar *Cursor mundi*[1], as well as in the Anglo-Norman variants of the *Infancy Gospel*, published in 1985 in a monograph by Maureen Boulton. It says there that that the father of Jesus, Jospeh, is told to make a plough "Ço ke a charue duit aver."[2]

One should note here that since all medieval manuscripts here have been registered as brought from France[3] we can also see the outline of familiar transfer of Bogomil literature, i.e. from Bulgarian to France, with the added link of England.

In conclusion, one could add to the quite apt observation of the well-known British literary historians, W. L. Renwick and H.Orton, who noted that in the early Middle Ages English literature featured "three traditions, three bodies of thought and imagination articulate and inarticulate, each possessing its own appropriate matter, language, and technique: the Latin, the French, and the English."[4] But since this chapter indicates a solid transfer and influence of fundamental Bogomil motifs and manuscripts in England, we should add yet another element – the Bulgarian one. In spite of the barriers, the isolation, lack of culture and dominant dogmatism, medieval Europe nevertheless had its zones of active cross-border communication, which in many cases became incorporated and stimulated the development of national literary processes. As Dimitri Obolensky has noted, the Bogomil-Cathar cultural milieu was exactly such a case of most intensive exchange, which lay in the bed of millennial transcontinental communication between the East and the West.[5]

---

[1] Cursor mundi, ll. 12387-12414

[2] Les enfaunces de Jesu Christ. Edited by M. Boulton. London. Published and distributed by Anglo-Norman text society. 1985, p.73

[3] Judging by the sgraffito used in the Tring tiles E. Eames assumed they were made in France. Op. cit., p.23

[4] Renwick, W. and H. Orton. The beginnings of English Literature to Skelton 1509. London. 1939/1952. V.I., p.33

[5] Obolensky, D.The Bogomils: a Study in Balkan Neo-Manichaeism. Cambridge University Press 1948, p.VII

Appendix: delivering the souls

To illustrate the difference between the Cathars position and that of the official church we shall quote two authoritative opinions on the mater – those of the Catholic and the Orthodox church.

The Catholic viewpoint is revealed in the words of St. Thomas Aquinas (13th century). After indirect and very well mannered polemics with St. Augustine, in his capital work *Summa Theologica* (Third Part, Question 52) he came to the conclusion that Christ gave grace – delivery from hell – only to some, at which they were released from Purgatory, not Hell: already cleansed sufficiently (qui jam sufficienter purgati errant). Aquinas yet again specifies that what is meant is selection and delivery, and that from Purgatory, not Hell. Consequently, it does not follow of necessity that all were delivered from Purgatory by Christ's descent into hell (et ideo non oportet, quod per descensum Christi ad inferos omnes fuerint a purgatorio liberati).[1] In other words, the conditions of delivery are complicated, it is practically very partial and that not from Hell but from Purgatory (the median zone the Catholic Church located between Heaven and Hell).

So to his own questions: Articulus V: Whether Christ descending into hell delivered the holy Fathers from thence?(Utrum Christus descendens ad inferos Sanctos patres inde liberaverit); Articulus VI: Whether Christ delivered any of the lost from hell? (Utrum Christus aliquos damnatos ab inferno liberaverit?); Articulus VII: Whether the children who died in original sin were delivered by Christ? (Utrum pueri qui cum originali peccato decesserant, fuerint a Christo liberati?) Thomas Aquinas gives a negative response.

The Orthodox interpretation is rather more comprehensive. Primarily, the descent into Hell in the time between the death of Christ and His Resurrection is perceived as completion of His work of redemption and a need of His human nature. The descent into Hell is also regarded as bringing the blessed news (annunciation), of the Gospel, to eternal darkness, thereby destroying its eternal power and "associating the entire pre-Christian world with redemption". Nevertheless, when the delivery from Hell is meant, it is assumed that those were mainly "Old Testament innocents".[2]

---

[1] Thomae Aquinatis Summa Theologica. Romae. Ex Typographia Forzani et S. M DCCCXCIV. Pars Tertia, Quaestio LII, Articulus VIII, p.448
[2] Православная богословская энциклопедія или богословскій энциклопедіческій словарь. Т.I. Петроградъ. 1900, с.821

The Bogomil-Cathar delivery is for all souls. The 13th century Inquisitor Rainier Sacconi presented the Cathar thesis that "Christ descended in that Hell to help them [the souls – author's note G.V.]…(et ad hunc infernum descendit Christus, ut auxiliaretur eis)[1]. This is what else was put down in the records of the Inquisition in Languedoc in the 14th century – "after Christ was resurrected He descended into Hell body and soul and took out from there all human souls, be they sinners or not, with the exception of Judas Iscariot…" (postquam Christus resurrexerat, descendit ad inferos in corpore et anima, ed de inde extraxit animas omnium hominium, tam peccatorum, quae ibie errant, excepta animae Judae Scariot…)[2].

(Some Cathar branches deny the descent into hell outright, because according to them this world created by the devil is hell. Then, for example, the birth of Christ in such a world would have the significance of a descent into hell. These dogmatic details were not so widespread and were related mainly to absolute Dualism.)

One should add yet another important point. Christ also delivers all souls from Hell in some early English manuscripts like the *Exeter Book*: "The exiles came crowding, trying which of them might see the victorious Son – Adam and Abraham, Isaac and Jacob, many of dauntless men, Moses and David, Isaiah and Zacharias, patriarchs, likewise too a concourse of men, a host of prophets, a throng of women and many virgins, a numberless tally people."[3] This complete salvation is a trace of Bogomils and Cathars. That is why the assumption of Renwick and Orton[4], as well as that the poem *The Descent into Hell* from the same manuscript was compiled around the year 800 seems unconvincing, for the *Gospel of Nicodemus*, which they quote as a second possible source (and it definitely is the first) was transferred in Latin translation to Western Europe not earlier than the end of the 10th – the beginning of the 11th century. The more probable specification of time would be their dating of the entire *Exeter Book* – c. 1072 - when the transfer of Dualist manuscripts from Bulgaria and the Balkans to Western Europe began. A more precise dating of the *Exeter* manuscript should at least take into consideration the already mentioned pro-dualist delivery of all souls.

---

[1] Sacconi, R. Summa de catharis par Fr. Sanjek O.P. – in: Archivum fratruam praedicatorum. Vol. XLIV. Roma. 1974, p.57.

[2] Döllinger, Ign. v., Op. cit., p.p.193-194.

[3] Anglo-Saxon Poetry. An Anthology of Old English poems in Prose Translation (with an Introduction and Headnotes by S.A. Bradley). London, Melbourne, Toronto. 1982, p.393.

[4] Renwick, W. and H. Orton, op. cit., p.198.

Chapter VII. The Spiritual Kinship between *Paradise Lost* and the *Secret Book* of the Bogomils

Speculation and Miltonian self-identification

The scope of action in Milton where man tackles evil on a cosmic or universal plane – and that from the position of fundamental Christian tenets – has made scholars use definitions like "Christian heroism"[1]. This, however, is followed by a question that has been the object of much effort, which has failed to result in sufficient clarity, i.e. the character of the imagery used. According to the author of the expression "Christian heroism", B. Kurth, what we have there is a Biblical epic[2], in other words the imagery is biblical. Alexander Shourbanov holds a similar point of view, stating that Milton sensed that old European mythologies had already been used in new European literature, that a new fund of imagery was necessary and consequently came to the choice of "a biblical theme for the new epic"[3]. A more careful perusal of the material, however, gives rise to objections to those authors who define biblical background as being fundamental for Milton. True we have the foundations of Christian faith, complete with its great moral objectives, we have the Father, the Son, archangel Michael and the heavenly army, as well as their antagonists Satan and the rebellious angels. But it is exactly with the fall of Satan and the angels on the very first page of *Paradise Lost* that we come across plots and images absent in both the Old and the New Testament. These are borrowed from apocrypha, at that apocrypha of a certain type, spread by medieval heretics like Bogomils, Cathars, Lollards and partly Waldenses.

Some of the literary critics had the idea or the intuition to relate this to dualistic tradition, albeit without naming it directly. This happened as early as the 19th century when S. Gurteen published *The Epic of the Fall of Man* (A comparative study on Cædmon, Dante and Milton)[4]. Hugh White supported the thesis of Arthur Lovejoy propounded in an article

---

[1] Kurth, B. Milton and Christian Heroism. Berkeley and Los Angeles. 1959.
[2] Ibidem, p. 9.
[3] Шурбанов, А. Светотворчеството на Милтън. – In: Изгубеният рай. София, 1981, с. 29. (Translated by Alexander Shourbanov.)
[4] Gurteen, S. H. The Epic of the Fall of Man. (A comparative study on Caedmon, Dante and Milton.) New York. 1896.

published some fifty years ago, *Milton and the Paradox of the Fortunate Fall* (1937), and speaking of "Milton's participation in an ancient tradition which understands the Fall as *felix culpa*, an ultimately happy event, giving rise to more good than would have been without it"[1]. This "ancient tradition", however, remains unexplained. Hugh White points out that although *Pierce Plowman* and *Paradise Lost* are different worlds altogether they presuppose comparison as major religious poems gauging the secrets of sin and divine love. In this case, too White's intuition was quite correct as the two works are related by dualistic philosophy.

The *Anglo-Saxon Poetry* compiled by S. Bradley finds "broad similarities between parts of *Genesis* and of *Paradise Lost*"[2], without this typologically correct assumption, however, being bases on the dualistic foundations of the two works. The same relation was underscored earlier and more definitely by Marco Mincoff when he discussed the beginning of *Paradise Lost* and more specifically the fall of Satan and his angels. According to him, "it is probable that Milton knew the Cadmonic poem, a Latin translation of which had been published by Junius in 1655"[3]. E. Legouis, who assumed that the friendship between Milton and Junius could have helped inspire the former, also launched a similar thesis by the old poem[4]. The poem *Genesis* is part of the *Junius XI* manuscript also known as the *Cædmon* manuscript. British colleagues date it in the 8th-9th century, although it would seem more realistic to assume it came from the continent in the 12th century. It begins with the dualistic episode of the revolt and fall of the angels with Lucifer at their head. One could also add that the lament (of the fallen Satan from another dualistic text in the same manuscript, *Christ and Satan*) is very similar to the scene in *Paradise Lost* where Lucifer tries to raise the spirit of his fallen army.

The associations described so far seek plot similarities or precedents, they are occasional. In our time there is an energetic trend, which tries to formulate the spirit of concealed philosophy in the poet. The first propo-

[1] White, H. Langland, Milton and felix culpa. – In: The Review of English Studies. 1994. V. 45, No. 179, p. 336.

[1] Anglo-Saxon Poetry. An anthology of Old English poems in prose translation with introduction and headnotes by S. A. J. Bradley. London, Melbourne, Toronto. 1982, p. 12.

[3] Mincoff, M. A History of English Literature. Part I: From the Beginnings to 1700. Sofia, 1970, pp. 528-529.

[4] Legouis, E. A History of English Literature. 1The Middle Ages and the Renaissance. Modern Times by L. Cazamian. Revised edition. London. 1957, p. 40.

nents of a more comprehensive position of heresy in Milton were Maurice Kelley, one of the most prominent Miltonian scholars of the 20th century and publisher of *De Doctrina Christiana*, and Barbara Lewalski[1]. One of the most recent publications belongs to A. Nuttall who discovered Gnostic heresy in Milton and entitled his book *The Alternative Trinity: Gnostic Heresy in Marlowe, Milton and Blake*. There one finds the assertion that "Milton's thought is quasi-Gnostic"[2] and we know that in the Middle Ages Gnosticism spread through Bogomilism and its derivative trends. The same year saw the publishing of a collection with a similar compelling title, *Milton and Heresy*, by Stephen P. Dobranski and John P. Rumrich[3]. There, according to Stephen Fallan, instead of gnosticism Milton bore a combination of "unmistakable Armianism... complicated by Calvinist vestiges"[4]. In his review W. Walker has summed up the discussion as a question whether Milton was a heretical theologian or it would be more correct to interpret him as an orthodox Christian[5]. Maybe the most challenging title in this regard is Neil Forsyth's, *The Satanic Epic* (2002).[6]

But wouldn't it be better to substitute this intuitive quest for Milton's "invisible" heresy for the answers to two concrete questions:

– What are the historical sources of that heresy or nonconformity, and

– What can be quoted as its direct expression?

Such an approach is more successful, for it leaves behind general assumptions and steps on established facts and sociologically precise work with them. Here are two examples when the logic of general position does not lead in a sufficiently productive direction. Emil Legouis declares that Milton was the only poet who identified himself with Puritanism[7]. But why then do scholars admit they find it so difficult to gauge the true philosophy of the poet? In addition, Dobranski, Rumrich and

---

[1] Referential quotation: Studies in English Literature (Vol. 32, Winter 1992), articles by Barbara Lewalski, Christopher Hill, Maurice Kelley.

[2] Nuttall, A. The Alternative Trinity: Gnostic Heresy in Marlowe, Milton and Blake. Oxford, 1998, p. 127.

[3] Milton and Heresy. Cambridge, NY, CUP. 1998.

[4] Ibidem, p. 4, p. 14.

[5] Walker, W. Review of Stephen P. Dobranski and John P. Rumrich.eds. Milton and Heresy. – In: Early Modern Literary Studies 7.1. Special Issue 8 (May, 2001).

[6] Forsyth, N. The Satanic Epic. Princeton University Press. 2002.

[7] A History of English Literature, p. 567.

other authors in the above-mentioned volume tend to regard Milton's theological treatise, *De Doctrina Christiana*, as an expression of his deviation from orthodoxy. The fact is, however, that it does not feature Milton's fundamental theological theses, which we find in *Areopagitica* (1644) and *Eikonoklastes* (1649). Besides, one should add that *De Doctrina Christiana* is a text discovered as late as 1823 and belongs with the *dubia*, i.e. works of dubious authorship. To this day scholars argue whether it was truly written by Milton, a discussion which was renewed in 1991. It is because of this controversy that *De Doctrina Christiana* will not be included in the evidential part of this study. True, one can find there positions Milton himself defined as common with the Protestant church (cum universa Protestantium ecclesia)[1], as for example the denial of all who place themselves above the Holy Writ, the Scriptures being declared the sole authority (De me, libris tantummodo sacris adhaeresco...)[2].

These, however, are quite bland formulations, while in *Eikonoklastes* and *Areopagitica* Milton proclaimed the episcopal institution superfluous and proclaimed his spiritual appreciation of the Waldensian and Cathar heretical churches: "I add that many Western Churches Eminent for their Faith and good Works, and settl'd above four hundred Years ago in France, in Piemont and Bohemia, hath both taught and practis'd the same Doctrine, and not admitted of Episcopacy among them. And if we may believe what the Papists themselves have Written of these Churches, which they call Waldenses, I found in a Book Written almost four hundred Years since, and set forth in the Bohemian History, that those Churches in Piemont have held the same Doctrine and Government, since the time that Constantine with his mischievous Donations poyson'd Silvester and the whole Church."[3]

This passage shows that John Milton worked with heretical manuscripts and was familiar with the history of heretical churches from such documents. Then, although he mentioned the Waldensian church by name, he also mentioned a church in France, i.e. the Cathars, as well as the

---

[1] Milton, J. Latin Writings. A Selection. Van Gorgum, Assen MRTS, Tempre, AZ, 1998, p. 216. English version: A Treatise of Christian Doctrine Completed from the Holy Scriptures Alone. – In: The Prose Works of John Milton. Vol. V. 1883.

[2] As for me, I keep the sacred writings alone. – in: Latin Writings, p.217

[3] Milton, J. ΕΊΚΟΝΟΚΛΑΣΤΗΣ in Answer to a Book Intitul'd ΕΊΚΩΝΒΑΣΙΛΙΚΗ, the Portracture of His Sacred Majesty King Charles the First in His Solitudes and Sufferings. Amsterdam. 1690, p. 136.

Bohemian, i.e. Hussite church. In fact, he mentioned the Waldenses from Lyons and Languedoc as the first Protestant churches[1] and therefore proclaimed a continuity between English Reformation and the Waldenses from Lyons, while the mentioning of Languedoc can be assumed to speak of the Cathar community. Milton regarded them as having the same doctrine and practice, thus showing himself as a historian who established at the earliest hour the link between Cathars, Waldenses and Hussites. A global historical view, which quite a few modern medievalists are still unable to adopt. This reveals a new image of Milton before us; the image of a historian with knowledge topical even today, with concrete quotations and correct conclusions one can also encounter in his assessment of Wycliffe's work.

By expressing particular respect for John Wycliffe, Milton indicated he had another important ideological resource. By the way, he also thus integrated in one spiritual context Cathars, Waldenses, Hussites and Wycliffe (and that means Lollards). The affinity for the reformist spirit and work of Wycliffe is expressed on several occasions. The *Areopagitica* quotes Wycliffe and Huss as authors of the first significant conflict between reform and papacy[2]. Milton placed Wycliffe at the basis of English reform, which was developing in his own time. This was a declaration of continuity, a statement that outlined the transfer inside England itself: "although indeed our Wicliff's preaching at which all the succeeding reformers more effectually lighted their tapers."[3]

Milton complemented his apology of Wycliffe by placing him in the beginning of European Reformation, by considering that if his work had been successful on the Albion, England would have achieved international fame and recognition, would have been the centre of European Reformation: "And had it not bin this obstinate perverseness of our Prelates against the divine and admirable spirit of Wiclef, to suppress him as

---

[1] The Tenure of Kings and Magistrates. – In: Prose Works of John Milton. Vol. II. 1883, p. 27.
[2] ...for about that time Wiclef and Husse growing terrible, were they who first drove the Papal court in a stricter policy of prohibition - in: Areopagitica; A Speech of Mr. John Milton for the Liberty and Vnlicenc'd Printing, to the Parliament of England. London. 1644, p.7
[3] Of the Reformation in England and the Causes That Hitherto Have Hindered it. In Two Books. – In: Areopagitica and Other Prose Works of John Milton. London, New York, Toronto. 1927, p.58.

an schismatic and innovator, perhaps neither the Bohemian Husse and Jerom, no, or the name of Luther, or Calvin had bin ever known: the glory of reforming all our neighbours had been completely ours".[1]

The expression *quod erat demonstrandum* (QED) is a bit difficult to use in social sciences but in this case we can say QED, for we see Milton's self-identification with the spirit of heretical churches four centuries previously, with the ideological heritage of Wycliffe. And that what self-identification: Milton's definition of Wycliffe – "the divine and admirable spirit of Wiclef" – is one of the highest praises the poet ever gave to a compatriot of his. Therefore, the Milton-Wycliffe connection that only W. Summers mentioned categorically is actually a continuity declared by Milton himself, one which sheds light on the roots of his theology[2].

Doctrinal expressions

This is the place to add yet another indicative proof of John Milton's emotional involvement with the work of the heretics. During one of the Catholic purges of Waldenses in 1655, the poet denounced that crime with a poem entitled *On the Late Massacre in Piedmont* and written in the same year:

> *On the Late Massacre in Piedmont*
> *Avenge O lord thy slaughter'd saints, whose bones*
> *Lie scatter'd on the Alpine mountains cold*
> *Ev'n them who kept thy truth so pure of old*
> *When all our fathers worshipp'd stok and stones*
> *Forget not: in thy book record their groans...*[3]

Some experts on medieval heresies could object that the victims of

---

[1] Areopagitica: A Speech of Mr. John Milton for the Liberty and Unlicenc'd Printing to the Parliament of England. London. 1644, p. 31. Naturally, he recognised the influence of European reformers in England: "we have looked so long upon the blaze that Zuinglius and Calvin hat beaconed up to us, that we are stark blind." Areopagitica, p.31.

[2] Summers, W. Our Lollard Ancestors. London. MCMIV-1904, p. 29. Compared to Summers, the other assumptions this author has encountered were much more hesitant. In 1977 A. L. Rowse mentioned a possible Wyclifitte influence in his book titled *Milton the Puritan. Portrait of a Mind* (University Press of America).

[3] Milton, J. On the Late Massacre in Piedmont. – In: Selected Shorter Poems and Prose. London, New York, 1988/9.

the massacre in Piedmont were Waldenses and the poet should therefore be considered a friend of their church, which was not dualistic. Things take a different aspect, however, should one return to the facts. Milton had a clear idea of both the Waldenses and the dualists. He categorically approved the idea of a reformed church, common to both Cathars and Waldenses, in which the Word of God was preached in the language of the people, the Gospel was placed right in the hands of ordinary man and in which there was no place for institutions like the episcopate. By the way, in this the Cathars held priority, for they translated the New Testament into Provençal before Valdo who borrowed the model of his organisation from them. This is, so to say, the socio-reformist element common to Cathars and Waldenses, which subsequently became a sort of axis in the history of English Reformation and designated the line of Wycliffe (and the Lollards), Tyndale, Milton and so on. In addition to that, however, Milton constantly perused dualistic writings and borrowed from their imagery with both hands, proof of which shall be provided in abundance later. In the poem about the massacre in Piedmont quoted above he used the expression "When all our fathers worshipp'd stok and stones" and that is one, by which the English dualists, the Lollards, following Bogomil-Cathar theology denounced icons as "stokks and stonys"[1]. In addition, he propounded the fundamental dualistic idea quite directly: "Good and evil we know in the field of this world grow up together almost inseparably; and the knowledge of good is so involved and interwoven with the knowledge of evil, and so many cunning resemblances hardly to be discerned...that *the knowledge of good and evil, as two twins cleaving together* (the italics mine – G. V.), leaped forth into the world"[2]. This formulation is in harmony with the fundamental dualistic thesis, recorded as it was by the well-known 14th century inquisitor Bernard Gui: "The Manichaean sect and heresy recognise and preach two Gods or two Fathers, one benign God and one malign God"[3]. The difference is

---

[1] An expression recorded on August 8, 1511 at the trial of the Lollards in Kent. Kent Heresy Proceedings 1511-12. Edited by N. Tanner. Kent. 1997, p. 85. On the basis of factological material presented in Chapter I, I consider the connection between Bogomils, Cathars and Lollards sufficiently well outlined.

[2] Areopagitica and other Prose Works by John Milton. London, New York. 1927, p. 13.

[3] Manicheorum itaque secta et heresies et ejus devii sectatores duos Deos aut duos Dominos asserunt and fatentur, benignum Deum videlicet et malignum... - In: Gui, B. Manuel de l'inquisiteur. T.I. Paris, 1926. p.10

that Milton speaks of good and evil instead of God and the devil, and here we should take at good faith the pertinent observation of C. Vaughan explaining that, in Milton's case, the religious fervor of the reformers and the Puritans was already touched by the intellectual currents of the Renaissance[1]. In other words, the religious personification of good and evil was complemented with more abstract categories.

Nevertheless, the other theological views of the poet, which we shall quote hereafter, were not much influenced by the time, lacked such abstract complements and were presented almost as doctrinal expressions. The principal occasion for Milton to express his views was his polemic with the defenders of the Episcopal church: he defended the simple evangelical practice of the Presbyterian church. With his temperamental accusation that his opponents reproduced the vices of the Catholic Church (i.e. that although they had rejected papacy they had, in fact, embraced its practice and had distributed the power between themselves[2]) Milton actually built a comprehensive imputation against the history of deformation and repression of the Catholic Church. And that was done in the language of Cathars and Lollards – in other words, his treatises can be regarded a speech of historical retribution against the time-honoured persecutor of the dualists.

The <u>refutation of icons and the cross</u> is a traditional dualist characteristic. Evidence of this has been recorded in the oldest documents on the Bogomils. This was what Euthymius Zigabenus wrote in his 11th century *Panoplia dogmatica*: "They also despise the holy icons and call them heathen idols, silver and gold, made by human hand."[3] The formula "made with many hands" was documented among the English Lollard at the trial in Kent in 1511-1512[4]. Milton also repeatedly attacked icons, declaring them images and idols[5] and said their veneration was a deviation

[1] Vaughan, C. Introduction. – In: Areopagitica and other Prose Works by John Milton. London, New York. 1927, p. XIII.

[2] This historical aspect was noted by John Toland who saw its beginnings even in the time of Henry VIII. It was also confirmed by the publisher of Milton's prose, J. John, in 1883-1884. Editor's preliminary remarks in The Prose Works of John Milton. II. London, 1883, p. 363.

[3] Euthymii Zigabeni de haeresi bogomilorum narratio. – In: Ficker, G. Die Phundagiagiten. Leipzig.1908, p. 97.

[4] Kent Heresy Proceedings 1511-12, p. 85.

[5] Of the Reformation in England and the Causes That Hitherto Have Hindered It. In Two Books. – In: Areopagitica and Other Prose Works of John Milton. London, New York, Toronto. 1927, p.91.

from true Christian duty: "stones, and pillars and crucifixes, have now the honour and the alms due to Christ's living members."[1] To him the laudation of Christ on icons was both unacceptable and superfluous, as He was "pageanted about like a dreadful idol."[2]

It is interesting to see that, here too, Milton revealed how broad his historical culture was when he supported the iconoclastic feelings he shared with the dualists by giving examples with the actions of the iconoclastic emperors Leo III, who ruled from 717 to 741, and Constantine V Copronymus, who ruled from 741 to 775. This is an ability to draw a line of rationalism in the history of the church itself, respectively to present the veneration of images, cumbersome liturgies and complicated rites as a deviation from the early life of Christ's church, which consisted of communion with the Word (Christ) and following His example, as well as individual spiritual life following His precepts. It seems that to some degree discussion returned within the limits of official church tradition, but nevertheless expressions became quite temperamental, with Milton speaking of how those Byzantine emperors "broke all superstitious images to pieces"[3].

The trace of dualistic attitude is also visible in Milton when he speaks of the cross. The Bogomil objection to the cross is quite well known, as one can see from the following quotation from Presbyter Cosmas: "And they delude themselves and speak thus of the Holy Cross: How could we bow to it? It was on it that the Jews crucified the Son of God and the cross is consequently most abhorred by Him."[4] One should note that English Lollards also took up this early Bogomil objection - at the proceedings in Norwich in 1430 the tailor William Hardy of Mundham gave the following explanation: "and no more worship ne reverence oweth be do to the crosee than oweth be do to the galwes whiche men be hanged on."[5] Presbyter Cosmas also pointed out that "the heretics cut down the crosses and make weapons of them".[6] Once again Milton demonstrated historical

---

[1] Ibidem, p. 66.

[2] Ibidem, p. 57.

[3] ΕΊΚΟΝΟΚΛΑΣΤΗΣ ..., p. 135.

[4] „Себе си заблуждавайки, така говорят за Господния кръст: Как да му се кланяме? Понеже евреите разпънаха на него Божия син, затова кръстът е най-омразен Богу." Презвитер Козма. „Беседа против богомилите". – in: „Стара българска литература. 2. Ораторска проза". София. 1982, с.34.

[5] Tanner, N. Heresy Trials in the Diocese of Norwich, 1428-31. London.1977, p.154.

[6] "еретиците секат кръстовете и си правят от тях оръдия" – in: „Беседа против богомилите", p.33.

knowledge, presenting an analogy of such extremism by mentioning he knew of such "enormities" in England[1]. These, by the way, are known as moods amidst some Lollards. The information found in Milton is among the oldest found in English literature and it is confirmed by the minutes of the trials against the Lollards in Norwich published by Norman Tanner. This is what one of them says: "all ymages owyn to be destroyed and do away"[2]. In his subsequent comments the poet distanced himself from the above-quoted extremes with the rationalistic objection that official pre-Reformation practice had made idols out of crucifixes. He also warned that "extreme veneration" of the cross could bring about prejudice[3] and quoted cases of fetishism of the cross in Christian tradition when nails from the cross, found by Constantine and his mother Helena, were put in helmets as protective amulets or were attached to reins of mounts[4]. In the long run, one can discern a certain distance from the cross in his words, as he obviously did not think Constantine and Helena had made a feat by discovering the cross, adding that if that had been so important it would have been done by the disciples of Christ themselves[5].

We are also familiar with the Bogomil and Cathar conclusion that, with their predilection for icons and rituals, the official clergy were bearers of idolatry and that "all church fathers" were idolators[6]. The Bogomils considered "the churches as crossroads and the liturgies and other services conducted therein – as superfluous wordiness"[7]. These motifs have their place in Lollard texts which ridicule the rituals with wine, bread, wax, oil and incense of the Catholic Church as *vera practica necromantiae.*[8] They are repeated with a similar vocabulary in John Milton's polemic prose. He ridiculed the clergy that they dressed in "de-

---

[1] ΕΊΚΟΝΟΚΛ'ΑΣΤΗΣ, p.153.
[2] Heresy Trials in the Diocese of Norwich, p.86.
[3] Of the Reformation in England, p.69.
[4] Ibidem.
[5] Ibidem.
[6] Euthymii Zigabeni de haeresi bogomilorum narration - in: Ficker, G. Die Phundagiagiten. Leipzig, 1908, p. 99.
[7] „църквите смятат за кръстопътища, а литургиите и другите служби, които се извършват в църквите за многодумие" – in: „Беседа против богомилите", с.50.
[8] Fasciculi Zizaniorum magistri Johannis Wyclif cum tritico. Ed. by Walter W. Shirley. London. 1858, p. 362. English version: "Þat exorcismis and halwinge made in þe chirche of wyn, bred and wax, water, and oyle and encens…" - in: Hudson, A. Selections from English Wycliffite Writings. CUP. London, New York, Melbourne.1978, p.25.

formed and fantastic dresses, in palls and mitres, gold, gewgaws fetched from Aarons's old wardrobe" which made them neither heavenly nor spiritual[1]. The same biting phrases as "popery and idolatry" and "true heresy"[2] characteristic of dualistic language. The same conviction of Bogomils, Cathars and Lollards that "but to the gospel each person is left voluntary, called only, as a son, by the preaching of the word"[3].

The traditional dualistic objection to baptism with water was also expressed, albeit in an implied manner: "Then the baptism changed into a kind of exorcism, and water sanctified by Christ institute, thought little enough to wash off the original spot..."[4] This to some extent echoes the Bogomil-Cathar-Lollard belief that "baptism with water does not contribute to salvation in any way", for true baptism to dualists was that with the Holy Spirit, i.e. consolamentum[5]. Another case of Bogomil-Cathar influence is the expression "good men", which is found frequently in Milton's prose and which reproduces the appellation "good men", "good Christians" given to dualistic leaders, the so-called Perfects. They had exceptional prestige amongst their flock for it was known that the dualistic leaders were extremely pure, dignified people and legend had it they were beloved by God[6]. Thus in the 14th century Cathar movement followers in southern France still believed in "good men" and that where there were "two good men, God stands between them"[7]. The laudation of good men called *bougres* (i.e. Bulgarians) in southern France came to the point where, as it is recorded in the Doat collection, t. XXV, F° 216 v°, they by God's grace could stop lighting with books they had in Bulgaria. This information dates from 1275 and, by the way, the heretic who, ac-

---

[1] Of the Reformation in England..., p.56.

[2] Milton, J. A Treatise of Civil Power in Ecclesiastical Causes. – In: Milton's Prose. Oxford, London, New York, Toronto. 1925/1949, p. 426.

[3] Ibidem, p. 439.

[4] Of the Reformation in England..., p. 57.

[5] ...dicunt, quod baptismus aquae nihil facit ad salvationem. Cod. Cassamat. A IV.49, p. 322. – In: Döllinger, Ign. v. Dokumente vornehmlich zur Geschichte der Valdesier und Katharer herausgegeben. t. II. München. 1890, p. 322.

[6] Patarini, qui se dicunt bonos hominess et sine peccato. – In: Döllinger, Ign., op. cit., p. 376.

[7] Ibidem, p.241 Confessio Guillelmi Bavili de Monte Alione: Sibila credidit haeriticos esse bonos homines in eo quod faciebant multas abstinentias et quod non accipiebant aliquid de alieno nec reddebant malum pro malo et quia etiam servebant castitatem; p.250: qui bonos homines in domos suas recipiebant, quia ubicunque duo de bonis hominibus errant, in medio eorum erat Deus.

cording to the witness Petrus Perrini de Podio Laurentia, had voiced such an opinion was an Englishwoman (Anglesiam)[1]. This is the oldest, positive connotation of the word *bougre*, which reached England as "bugger", already loaded with extremely negative connotations by Catholic propaganda[2].

The Lollards defined themselves as being true to Christ and pure in an English version of the *Twelve Conclusions of the Lollards* in Anne Hudson's volume *Selections from English Wycliffite Writings*: "we pore men, tresories of Cryst and his apostlis"[3]. In many preserved documents, by the way, the Lollards call themselves "good men" and "true men".

Milton, too, speaks of "good men", more particularly of "good men and Saints"[4] and "thousands of good men"[5]. At the same time, in order to place good men under protection, he declared: "And this all Christians ought to know, that the title of Clergy St. Peter gave to all God's people." According to Milton, the deformation had set in when "pope Higinus and the succeeding Prelates took it from them, appropriating that name to themselves and their Priests only."[6] We know that the dualists denied the existence of saints, but in this case Milton obviously resorted to dualistic mimicry, i.e. to the skill of defending heresy with a Christian precedent, with the names of the apostles of Christ presented as the first "good men". Thus he tells us that Apostle Paul "made himself servant to all"[7], in other words communion meant to serve people humbly. At the same time it was easy for the poet to make the radical opposition between the "good men" and episcopacy, an echo of the Cathar custom to call themselves

---

[1] …quod audivit Anglesiam, uxorem quondam Petri Raterii, que fuit combusta propter heresim, dicentem quod heretici habebant quondam librum quem respiciebant quando videbant tale tempus, et hoc in Bulgaria – in: Duvernoy, J. Météorologie et Bulgarie – under press in Bulgarian Historical Review 1-2/2003, p. 255.

[2] On this matter see Chapter I. Nikolai Osokin correctly pointed out that the Albigensians were subject to the same type of maligning that „the first Christians also fell victim to". Осокин, Н. История альбигойцев и их времени. Москва. 2000, с.170. First edition in 1869, Казань.

[3] Hudson, A., op. cit., p. 24.

[4] The Reason of Church Government Urged against Prelaty – in: Milton Prose. Oxford, London, New York, Toronto. 1931/1949, p.108

[5] Ibidem, p. 97.

[6] Ibidem, p. 127.

[7] A Treatise of Civil Power in Ecclesiastical Causes, p. 439.

the "good church" and the "church of Christ", and the Roman church – "bad" and "mother of adultery"[1].

Several centuries later, Milton's language still applied the same style: "They are not bishops, God and all good men know they are not, they have filled this land with late confusion and violence, but a tyrannical crew and corporation of impostors, that have blinded and abused the world so long under that name."[2] Experts commenting Milton's prose have also noticed that he did not include bishops among the good men[3].

In a next step related to the above topic John Milton reproduced yet another dualistic theme related to the idea of "good men" as he actually explained their spiritual form. This was the idea of "internal man" quoted by Bernard Gui: "They (the Cathars – *author's note*) deny the future resurrection of human bodies and instead invent some spiritual bodies and an internal man; thus, they say, the future resurrection should be understood."[4] On one page of Milton's *The Reason of Church Government Urged against Prelaty* (1641) "the inner man" and the "internal man" is mentioned twice in opposition to "external man"[5]. Then again, in his *Treatise of Civil Power in Ecclesiatical Causes* we find a repeated use of the term "inward man" on three pages, developed in the definition that "the inward man is nothing else but inward part of man"[6]. One also encounters a description of the qualities of inward man[7], with a calling for inward religion, as well as an explanation how Christ reaches conscience and inward man by the spiritual power with which He rules the church. Milton tried to legalise the dualistic theme of internal man by quoting the Scriptures. To both Bogomils and Cathars "internal man" called for a doctrinal specification of resurrection, i.e. that not physical bodies (which

---

[1] Item duas, confingunt esse ecclesias, unam benignam, quam dicunt esse secta suam, eaamque asserunt Ihesu Christi; aliam vero ecclesiam vocant malignam, quod dicunt esse Romanam ecclesiam... appellant matrem fornicationem – in: Gui, B. Manuel de l'inquisiteur. Tom I. Paris. 1926, p.10

[2] Of the Reformation in England..., p. 62.

[3] As for the bishops, many of whom he denies not have been good men". Vaughan, C. – Introduction to Of Reformation in England..., p. 54.

[4] Item, resurrectionem corporum humanorum futuram negant, loco ejus configentes quedam spiritualia corpora et quedam interiorem hominem, in quibus et qualibus dicunt resurrectionem futuram esse intelligendam. – in: Manuel de l'inquisiteur, p.14. Nikolai Osokin also speaks of "internal man" as a familiar Cathars one.

[5] The Reason of Church Government..., p. 126.

[6] A Treatise of Civil Power..., p. 427, p. 428, p. 429.

[7] Ibidem, p. 428:...flow of faculties of the inward man... inward religion.

will drop off like clothes) would be resurrected but spiritual essences would return to the Good Father. It seems that Milton sensed he had placed a visible dualistic accent by using the expression that Christ deals only with the inward man[1] and safeguarded himself by adding text from the New Testament, more specifically the familiar flesh-spirituality opposition of Matthew and Paul: "Jesus replied, 'Simon son of Jonah, you are a happy man! Because it was not flesh and blood that revealed this to you but my Father in heaven" (Mt 16:17). And also "We live in the flesh, of course, but the muscles that we fight with are not flesh" (2 Co 10:3).

One also encounters another familiar dualistic tendency: Milton lent a ear to the preference for the New Testament and the rejection of the Old Testament as the law of violence and the kingdom of Satan. The poet supported his views with examples from the New Testament and the figure of Christ, while the Old Testament was used mainly for negative examples. The above-mentioned "fantastic dresses" and "gold and gewgaws" of churchmen were taken "from Aaron's wardrobe"[2], i.e. the founder of Old Testament priesthood. In addition, one finds challenges to the Old Testament characteristics of God, Jehovah's face of dispenser of justice and punishment as well as denial of the "perishable rites" of the Old Testament[3]. God is presented as the Bogomil God – a Good Father with a more merciful, human and New Testament face: "God being no more a judge after the sentence of the Law, nor as it were a schoolmaster of perishable rites, but the most indulgent father governing his Church as a family of sons of their discreet age..."[4] Naturally, one should also pay attention to human inconsistency, frequently found in great writers, too. Regardless of the fact that he declared a preference for the humane and gentle spirit of the New Testament, Milton supported the beheading of Charles I in the spirit of the Old Testament...

So far, colleagues and readers have been presented with examples of John Milton's consanguinity with the dualistic doctrine passing from direct self-definition to cases presupposing some more interpretation. Our trip to Milton's *philosophia arcana*, however, does not end here. The time has come for the most temperamental and comprehensively expressed pro-heretical theses of Milton; his polemics against the so-called "dona-

---

[1] A Treatise of Civil Power..., p.429
[2] Of the Reformation in England..., p. 56.
[3] The Reason of Church Government..., p. 126.
[4] Ibidem.

tion of Constantine", *donatio Constantini ad Sylvestrem I papam*. What we have in mind here is the legend according to which Constantine the Great (306-337) granted provinces, places and towns (*provincias, loca et civitates*) to Pope Sylvester I[1]. In western Europe both the Cathars and the Waldenses rejected the legend of such a donation for they considered it the start of corruption in the church. From a spiritual community striving after the kingdom of heaven it not only became a secular proprietor but also thus found itself secured in the earthly kingdom of Satan. It is interesting to note that *donatio Constantini* is not mentioned in the Bogomil manuscripts or the historical documents related to them. This thesis is an important complement to the history of dualism introduced by the Cathars and spread by anti-clerical movements closely related to them.

Now in Milton one finds not one but repeated quotations of the problem, developed in one of the themes of his treatise *Of Reformation in England and the Causes that Hitherto Have Hindered It*. One should not forget the context of the then ongoing controversy between the Episcopal and the Presbyterian church in England. For Milton, an adversary of prelatism and an adherent to the reformist idea of a "priesthood of all believers", the discussion gave him occasion to accuse his opponents from the Episcopal church that they had inherited the Vatican's worst feature, ingrained corruption. On this occasion he gave in to the passion with which medieval evangelical teachings had denounced the root of that corruption – Constantine's donation. Milton declared that Christian times were spiritually unadulterated from the times of Christ until Constantine[2], after which he described the corruption stemming from *donatio Constantini*, which meant the influx of pride and lawlessness[3]. On every subsequent mentioning of the subject Milton levied biting words against various aspects of that corruption, sometimes even to the point of a vocabu-

---

[1] In actual fact there was no such donation. Constantine, who paid a lot of attention to the theocratic reconstruction of the empire, tried to mobilise all regions to that end, including by giving quite a number of rights to the Christian church. Thus it enjoyed equal privileges with the pagan temples and its clerics were exempt from taxes; a special form of liberating slaves through the church was introduced and it was permitted to receive donations from believers and to inherit property. This last fact evolved into a legend about which some clerics from the Catholic Church created a false document in the 8th or the 9th century, one that is placed in the collection of the so-called False Decretals.

[2] Of the Reformation in England..., p. 68.

[3] Ibidem, p. 72.

lary coinciding with that of the heretics. For the two main trends in medieval heresy, Cathars and Waldenses, the donation in question was equal to pouring poison in the bosom of the Church: "poison has diffused in the church today"[1]. The expression used by Milton was exactly the same: "since Constantine with his mischievous Donation poyson'd Silvester and the whole Church"[2].

And here we come to a culmination of European proportions: John Milton proved that the critical position against *donatio Constantini* was visible in the work of Dante (1265-1321), Petrarch (1304-1374) and Ariosto (1474-1533). Here we shall quote the proof he gave in full measure, for this was a case of conscious borrowing from the Italian humanists as well as one of interaction between the peaks of two cultures. By that Milton achieved two things. First, he proved that the dualistic motif of anti-clerical criticism was present in works of the most outstanding figures of Italian Pre-Renaissance and Renaissance and was therefore an important expression of European cultural history. His second visible ambition was to place himself as an heir to that trend, as its representative in England: yet another self-characteristic of Milton's "heresy".

Anti-clericalism was internationalised as a condition for the complete expression of Renaissance and the new times which, according to Milton, would come when the corruption and perversion amassed in Europe's church history were revealed in full and rejected. In this sense the names of the great Italians were quoted as an example and a precedent to be followed, one that became a measure of the freedom of speech, of human choice and human thought.

To Dante – and to Petrarch to a considerable extent – criticism of the Catholic Church was a matter of personal fate. Dante's treatise *De monarchia*, in which the poet placed the supremacy of the empire (i.e. the state) above the church, was pronounced a heretical work by Pope John XXII in 1329. In turn, Petrarch received minor orders at the papal court in Avignon in 1362, communicated with the Franciscans, the order of anti-corruption leanings in the Catholic Church, and denounced that corruption in his writings. To this line Milton actually added the epic of liberation of the English language from Catholic latinisation, of man's rise to free communication with the Scriptures. Milton quoted Wycliffe as the forerunner and the time between Wycliffe's 14th century and Mil-

---

[1] hodie diffusum est venenum in ecclesia Dei. - In: Döllinger, Ign., Op. cit., p. 356.
[2] ЕΊΚΟΝΟΚΛΑΣΤΗΣ..., p.136

ton's 17th was marked by the efforts for emancipation made by the Lollards and Tyndale.

In order to support the cause he defended with the Italian example already accepted as the leading cultural horizon in Europe Milton himself translated into English the fragment from Canto 19 of the *Inferno*, quoted in his work *Of the Reformation in England*:

> *Ah Constantine! Of how much ill cause,*
> *Not thy conversion, but those rich domains*
> *That the first wealthy pope receiv'd of thee![1]*

And here is the original text in Italian:

> *115 Ahi, Constantin, di quanto mal fu matre,*
> *116 non la tua conversion, ma quella dote*
> *117 che da te presse il primo ricco patre![2]*

Milton mentioned that Dante also expressed a similar position in Canto 20 of the *Paradiso*[3], as well as the objection against Constantine's mistaken move in Sonnet 108 of Petrarch. There, Milton wrote, the poet spoke of the "Roman antichrist as merely bred up by Constantine", nor did he fail to mention that the same sonnet was "wiped out by the inquisitors in some editions"[4]:

> *Founded in chaste and humble poverty,*
> *'Gainst them that rais'd thee dost thou lift thy horn,*
> *Impudent whore, where hast thou plac'd thy hope?*
> *In thy adulteres, or thy ill-got wealth?*
> *Another Constantine comes not in haste.[5]*

---

[1] Of the Reformation in England and the Causes That Hitherto Have Hindered It. In Two Books. – In: Areopagitica and Other Prose Works of John Milton. London, New York, Toronto. 1927, p. 71.

[2] Dante, A. La Divina Commedia. Le rime, i versi della vita nuova e le canzoni del convivo. G. Einaudi editore.1954, p.122.

[3] Dante, A., op. cit., p.588:
   (55) L'altro che segue, con le leggi e meco,
   (56) sotto buona intenzion che fe'mal frutto
   (57) per cedere al pastor si fece greco...

[4] Reformation in England..., p.71.

[5] Ibidem.

An 1832 edition of Petrarch features the sonnet under number XVIII in the section entitled *Sonnets and Songs by Petrarch on Various Subjects*, the following being the respective part of the sonnet in Italian:

> *Fondata in casta ed umil povertate,*
> *Contra tuoi fondatori alzi le corna,*
> *Putta sfacciata: e dov' hai posto spene?*
> *Negli adulteri tuoi, nelle mal nate*
> *Richezze tante? Or Constantin non torna:*
> *Ma tolga il mondo tristo, che'l sostiene.*[1]

Milton also discovered similar passages in Ariosto, more precisely at the meeting between the English knight Astolfo and St. John, Canto 34:

> *And, to be short, at last his guide him brings*
> *Into a goodly valley, where he sees*
> *A mighty mass of things strangely confus'd*
> *Things that on earth were lost, or were abus'd.*

When this author read the above-mentioned canto in Ariosto's poem he was unable to find verse exactly corresponding to Milton's translation. Couplet 73 does feature lines of a certain similarity[2], but one way or another neither Milton's text nor the quotation of couplet 73 could be accepted as sufficiently obvious criticism of Vatican sins. Milton was more precise in his translation of part of couplet 80 of the same canto:

> *Then pass'd he to a flowery mountain green,*
> *Which once smelt sweet, now stinks as odiously:*

[1] Le Rime del Petrarca. Tomo secondo. Firenze. M.DCCCXXXII, p.327
According to the commentary to this edition, the last sentence, particularly the expression "Or Constantin non torna" was an obscure passage (passo oscuro), p.327. The same commentary stated that pessimism stemmed from the fact that Constantine did not return to take back the ill-spent wealth. Milton, however, did not hold back from giving his own, quite free translation in the form of "Another Constantine comes not in haste."
[2] Ariosto, L. Orlando furioso. Firenze. 1957, p.469:
> *Da l'Apostolo santo fu condutto*
> *In un vallon fra due montagne istretto,*
> *Ove mirabilmente era ridutto,*
> *Ciò che si o per nostro diffeto,*
> *O per colpa di tempo o di Fortuna...*

This was that gift (if you the truth will have)
That Constantine to good Sylvestro gave.

And here is the Italian original:

Di varii fiori ad un gran monte passa,
Ch'ebbe già buono odore, or putia forte.
Questo era il dono (se però dir lece)
Che Constantino al buon Silvestro fece.[1]

After he had created a uniform all-European context of anti-Catholic and anti-clerical criticism, one of contact and interaction of literatures, Milton also found an opportunity to bring England to the fore. What he did was to indicate that Chaucer's Ploughman in England made the same objection against Constantine's donation even before Ariosto had been born[2].

It is surprising that Milton failed to notice the preceding passage in the same couplet 80, Canto 34 of Ariosto's poem, which contains traditional Bogomil-Cathar ridicule of the superfluous church services for the dead:

Di versate minestre una gran massa
Vede, e domanda al suo Dottor, ch'importe
L'elemosina è (dice) che si lassa
Alcun che fatta sia dopo la morte[3]

And what he saw was soup spil't aplenty
And he asked his Doctor what that meant.
The alms someone leaves here, he responded,
As is customary after death.

(Translation into English – B. Roushkova.)

The ironic attitude to wakes and masses for dead souls demonstrated by the image of low quality or foul food can also be found in a work of English literature marked by dualistic influence, i.e. William Langland's *The Vision of Piers Plowman*:

---

[1] Ariosto, L., op. cit., p. 470.
[2] Reformation in England…, p. 72.
[3] Orlando furioso, p. 470.

Ac hir sauce was over sour and unsaourly grounde
In a morter, Post mortem, of many bitter peyne...[1]
(But their sauce was too tart, four it was
pounded into acrid mess in a mortar called <u>*Post-mortem*</u>*)*[2]

This slightly breathless selection and translation of Italian quotations indicates that Milton could have made it with an Italian friend of his during his trip to Italy. We know that he had contacts with whom he discussed Italian language and literature. For example, in a letter to Benedetto Buonmattai written in Florence on September 10, 1638, Milton shared his pleasure in enjoying the works of Dante, Petrarch and many others[3].

Nor should one overlook yet another issue. Why did Milton, highly educated as he was and a close observer of the events and ideological life in Europe who was capable of historical comparisons dating right to the iconoclastic period in Byzantium, accept Constantine's donation as a historical fact. Hadn't the Italian humanist Lorenzo Valla proved the spuriousness of this myth in his well-known treatise of 1440 entitled *De falso credita et eminenta Constantini donatione declamatio* (On the False Credit Accorded to the Invented Donation of Constantine). This work of Valla's was published for the first time in 1517 by the German humanist and critic of papism, Ulrich von Hutten, i.e. it had become known in the circle of the enlightened. Now two assumptions can be made in this case. One, that this information in some way failed to reach Milton. The other – that he followed Ariosto's example who, although probably familiar with Lorenzo Valla's work[4], preferred to express his criticism of corruption in the official church by using the legend of Constantine's donation

---

[1] Langland, W. The Vision of Piers Plowman. Ed. By A.V.C. Schmidt, London, Melbourne and Toronto.1978. Passus XIII, 1.44 One finds a Lollard theological objection on principle against memorial services in the twelve conclusions of the Lollards of 1395 – "the special prayers for the dead in our church... are a false foundation for charity" (speciales orationas pro animabus mortuorum factae in ecclesia nostra...est falsum fundamentum eleemosynae) - in: Fasciculi Zizaniorum, p.363

[2] Modern English version: Langland, W. Piers the Ploughman. Penguin Books. 1966, p. 152.

[3] "I sometimes retire with avidity and delight to feast on Dante, Petrarch, and many others." – In: To Benedetto Buonmattai, The Prose Works of John Milton. Vol. III. London. 1883, p.497.

[4] Such an assumption is expressed in the commentary on verse 80 of Canto 34 in Orlando furioso. Orlando furioso, p. 470.

as an already well-known and widespread metaphor of the problem, as an opportunity to quote Dante's criticism[1]. By the way, Petrarch also reproduced Dante's criticism to some degree in his sonnet[2], in other words Milton aptly relied on an organic line of ideas and imagery in Italian literature. The facts are, therefore, beyond any doubt. What remains to be revealed are rather some connections, relations and personal line in these facts.

Bogomil imagery

After devoting sufficient space to theological views propounded by John Milton himself we can now turn to the philosophy of his imagery. As it was pointed out in the beginning of this chapter, that philosophy still remains a mystery to scholars who sense its powerful covert presence but find it difficult to explain. Marco Mincoff, for one, discerned a peculiar concern in Milton's early poem *Lycidas* - "he had been disturbed by the way in which God cuts off the deserving and allowed the vicious to flourish"[3]. In fact it is in this work that one can first discern feelings of the poet similar to the Bogomil-Cathar objections to the arrangements on the earthly world. According to them, this world was "an inferno, fire and ice, and evil of every kind"[4] as it was created by Satan, an unjust and cruel world. Marco Mincoff took yet another step in the correct direction by establishing a relation between the opening of *Paradise Lost* and the Old English *Genesis*. As we have already mentioned, Mincoff assumed the possibility of Milton's being acquainted with the Cadmonic poem, a Latin translation of which had been published by Junius in 1655[5]. Hesitant as our British colleagues might be when they date this poem and speculate as regards its origin, there is a fundamental historical situation

---

[1] A small correction is in order here: this edition quotes the source "anti-donation" statement of Dante's as being in Paradiso, Canto 19, line 115. There is no such thing there, however, the one meant probably being Paradiso, Canto 20, line 56: "sotto buona intenzion che fe' mal frutto"
[2] Sonetti e canzoni di Francesco Petrarca…, p. 327.
[3] Mincoff, M. A History of English Literature. Part I. From the Beginning to 1700. Sofia, 1970, p. 522.
[4] …in hoc mundum inferno esse, i.e. hic esse ignim et frigum et omne malum –in Döllinger, Ign., op. cit. (Das Buch Supra Stella von Salvus Burche zu Piacenza aus dem J.1235 (Florenz) über Cathari, Albanenses et Concorricii), p. 58.
[5] Mincoff, M., op. cit., pp. 528-529.

that can neither be overlooked nor rewritten. That is that Bogomils and Cathars introduced the dualistic plot of the fall of Satan who rebelled against God to medieval Europe. Milton himself confirmed his penchant for dualistic imagery, for to the already-mentioned theme, present on the very first page of *Paradise Lost*, he added Satan's interest in God's second creation according to an ancient Prophesie or report in Heaven. And the so-called "second creation" was one of the main features of Bogomil myth. To add more clarity to our observations we shall compare directly fundamental dualistic texts and passages from *Paradise Lost* and *Paradise Regained*. The first table that follows reveals an unquestionable coincidence between the episode with Satan's fall from heaven on the first page of Paradise Lost and that in *The Secret Book of Bogomils*. Further on, other dualistic theses will join this one.

VISIBLE DUALISTIC THEMES IN JOHN MILTON'S *PARADISE LOST*

Motif one: Satan's revolt against God and his fall from heaven

Paradise Lost, Book I, The Argument
The Serpent, or rather Satan in Serpent; who revolting from God, and drawing to his side many Legions of Angels, was by the command of God driven out of heaven with all his crew into the great Deep.[1]

Paradise Lost, Book I; verses 34-44:
…what time his Pride/Had cast him out from Heav'n, with all his Host/ Of Rebel Angels, by whose aid aspiring/To set himself in Glory above his Peers,/He trusted to have equal'd the most High,/If he oppos'd; and with ambitious aim/Against the

The Secret Book of Bogomils or Interrogatio Joannis: (Carcassone Text)
…et traxit cum cauda tertiam partem angelorum Dei, et projectus est de sede Dei et de vilicatione coelorum. Et descendens Sathanas in firmamentum hoc, nullam requem potuit facere sibi nec iis qui cum eo errant. (Иванов, Й. Богомилски книги и легенди. София. 1925, c.76)
…and with his tail he dragged away one-third of the angels of God, and he was banished from the throne of God and from the overlordship of the heavens. And Satan, descend-

---

[1] The quotations are after The Poetical Works of John Milton. London, Oxford University Press, NY, Toronto. 1958.

Throne and Monarchy of God? Rais'd impiousWarr in Heav'n and Battel proud/With vain attempt. Him the Almighty Power/ Hurld headlong flaming from th' Ethereal Skie/ With hideous ruin and combustion down/To bottomless perdition... ing to this firmament, was unable to find rest either for himself or for those who were with him. (Translation Tom Butler. Monumenta bulgarica. Michigan Slavic Publications. 1996, p.193)

And yet another occasion on which the same myth is mentioned: Book VII, verses 130-133:

> *Know then, that after Lucifer from Heav'n*
> *(So call him, brighter once amidst the Host*
> *Of Angels, then that Starr the Starrs among)*
> *Fell with his flaming Legions through the Deep*

The same obvious coincidence can be seen in the second table comparing the scene of the final victory over Satan from *The Secret Book* in which he was chained in indestructible chains (*insolubilus vinculus fortibus*) and thrown in a "lake of fire" (*in lacum ignis*), and, respectively, Satan's being hurled to dwell "in adamantine chains and penal fire" in Book I of *Paradise Lost*.

Motif two: the chaining of Satan in hell's lake of fire:

Paradise Lost, Book I, verses 45-49
what time his Pride
Hurld headlong flaming from th' Ethereal Skie
With hideous ruine and combustion down
To bottomless perdition, there to dwell
In Adamantine Chains and penal Fire,
Who durst defie th' Omnipotent to Arms.

The Secret Book of Bogomils or Interrogatio Joannis: (Carcassone Text) Et tunc ligabitur Sathans et omnis militia eius, et mittetur in lacum ignis. Et deambulabit Filius Dei cum electis suis de super firmamentum, et claudet Diabolum ligans eum insolubilibus vinculis fortibus.

And then Satan and all his army shall be chained and thrown in a lake of fire. And the Son and His elect shall walk on the firmament and shall imprison the Devil, locking him in chains indestructible and strong.

The third table shows a Bogomil myth retold by Milton, the one according to which after the creation of man part of mankind would return to the heavens to fill in the place of the fallen angels. We recalled that the second creation formula (after the Lord's) of "this visible Creation" of Satan is a familiar characteristic of dualism. For doesn't *The Secret Book* say that man was created by Satan and similar information about the said Bogomil belief was provided by Euthymius Zigabenus (12th century)[1]. In our case, however, Milton chose an interpretation that was a step back from classical dualism. Milton's view of a second creation ran in harmony not with the traditional variant of *The Secret Book* (end 11th- early 12th century), according to which Adam and Eve were created by Satan, but rather with the 13th century apocryphal *oratione* of St. John Chrysostom on how Michael the archangel defeated Satan[2]. Here we come to an important peculiarity of the Bulgarian Bogomil church, which constantly enhanced the role of the Father and the Son in its development. Thus, in the case of the above apocrypha, the subsequent consequence was a blending of the orthodox Christian idea of God as a creator of all creatures and all worlds. That is why the teaching of this church is called mitigated dualism unlike the absolute dualism of the Paulicians preserving the equal positions of God and Satan. At the end of this chapter we shall return to this Bulgarian element for it conditioned the poet's own outlook as regards the dualistic heritage. Thus we now come to

---

[1] Die Phundagiagiten, p. 98.

[2] Слово на Йоан Златоуст за това как Михаил победи Сатанаил. – In: „Българската литература и книжнина през XIII век". София. 1987, pp. 156. A publication of this text under the title „Слово за лъжливия антихрист, безбожния Сатанаил, как го плени архангел Михаил, воевода на всички ангели" was previously made by Donka Petkanova in Петканова, Д. Стара българска литература.1. Апокрифи. София.1982, pp. 41-48.

Motif three: after the creation of the human race part of it will return to the heavens to fill in the place of the fallen angels.

Paradise Lost, Book 1. The Argument To these Satan directs his Speech, comforts them with hope yet of regaining Heaven, but tells them lastly of a new World and new kind of Creature to be created, according to an ancient Prophesie or report in Heaven; for that Angels were long before this visible Creation, was the opinion of many ancient Fathers.

Paradise Lost, Book VII, verses 151-160
Already done, to have dispeopl'd Heav'n
My damage fondly deem'd, I can repaire
That detriment, if such it be to lose
Self-lost, and in a moment will create
Another World, out of one man a Race
Of men innumerable, there to dwell,
Not here, till by degrees of merit rais'd
They open to themselves at length the way
Up hither, under long obedience tri'd,
And Earth be chang'd to Heav'n,
& Heav'n to Earth,
One Kingdom, Joy and Union without end.

Апокриф "Слово на Йоан Златоуст за това как Михаил победи Сатанаил"

И рече им Господ: "Узнахте ли, мои ангели, как избяга прелукавият Сатанаил и как прелъсти множество ангели; аз ги сътворих със Свети дух, имах ги за свое небесно войнство, а той ги съблазни и заведе във външната тъмнина. Аз отново ще ги сътворя – човеци ще бъда избрани да изпълняват волята ми – апостоли, пророци, мъченици; и те ще ми бъдат като ангели. И стократно ще умножа ангелското си воинство вместо ангелите, отпадналите от небесата." ("Българска литература и книжнина през XIII век", с. 151)

(Oratione of St. John Chrysostom: "And God said unto them: 'Did you, my angels, see how evil Satan fled and lured away many angels; I created them with the Holy Spirit and saw them as my celestial army but he seduced them and took them to the darkness outside. I shall create them again and men shall be elected to do My will, be they apostles, prophets or martyrs, and they shall be like angels to Me. And my army of angels shall exceed a hundredfold the angels who fell from heaven.)

At the same time, the poet's preference for some elements of Bogomil theology does not preclude obvious cases of lexical similarity between Milton and traditional dualistic theology. Thus, although the poet returned to the orthodox idea of God as the author of all things created, we can see how the expression "this visible Creation" (*Paradise Lost*, Book I. The Argument) repeats for a moment the fundamental Bogomil-Cathar thesis that "all other things visible were created by the devil who fell from the heavens"[1]. It is interesting to note, as it has been quoted in the right column of the table, that Dante also paid attention to this dualistic myth in his *Il Convivio*[2]. The reader should bear in mind that exactly because they passed from theological canon to literature Bogomil-Cathar writings developed many nuances, which could be in doctrinal contradiction but remain united by the impressive beauty of their imagery, the poetics of wisdom, compassion and moral endeavour.

Thus Milton too freely borrowed ideas and concepts not from one, say *The Secret Book*, but from different dualistic apocrypha. Although he endowed Satan with the modern skill of building machines, the next episode actually reproduces the battle of Michael with Satan in the already mentioned *oratione* of St. John Chrysostom (and possibly from *The Tiberiad Sea*, which contains the same motif), with Michael coming out victorious with God's intervention. Milton created his own variant of the counterattack against the devil as a triumphant march of the Messiah, i.e. Christ.

---

[1] ...et omnia alia visibilia a diabolo, qui cecidit de coelo, erant creata et facta – in: Processus contra Valdenses, Pauperes de Lugduno, aliosque haereticos, Fraticellos, etc. – In: Döllinger Ign., p. 266.

[2] Dante, Il Convivio. Trat. II, cap. VI.– In: Dantis Alagherii Opera Omnia II. Leipzig. 1921, pp.113-114: Dico che di tutti questi ordini si perdereno alquanti tosto che furono create forse in numero della decima parte, alla quale restaurare fu l'umana natura poi creata.

Motif four: Michael, sent forth by God, defeats the Devil in a dramatic battle:

Paradise Lost, Book VI.

The Argument

Raphael continues to relate how Michael and Gabriel were sent forth to battel against Satan and his Angels. The first Fight describ'd: Satan and his Powers retire under Night: He calls a Councel, invents devilish Engines, which in the second dayes Fight put Michael and his Angels to some disorder; But, they at length pulling up Mountains overwhelm'd both the force and Machins of Satan: Yet the Tumult not so ending, God on the third day sends Messiah his Son, for whom he had reserv'd the glory of that Victory: Hee in the Power of his Father coming to the place, and causing all his Legions to stand still on either side, with his Chariot and Thunder driving into the midst of his Enemies, pursues them unable to resist towards the wall of Heaven; which opening, they leap down with horrour and confusion into the place of punishment prepar'd for them in the Deep: Messiah returns with triumph to his Father.

Апокриф "Слово на Йоан Златоуст за това как Михаил победил Сатанаил", с.151

След като Гавраил се побоява да се срази със Сатанаил, "Владетелят (тоест Бог, б.Г.В.) прости на Гавриил и отново рече на архангел Михаил: "Ти беше първи в царството на моя единороден син, на теб прилича, казвам, днес да слезеш при долния мъчител антихриста, за да вземеш от него боготъканата премяна, богоплетения венец, скиптъра на ангелските чинове, които ми открадна. Отними му красотата и славата, както прилича, та да познаят неговите слуги кой е Господ."

(*Apocryphal oratione of St. John Chrysostom*. After Gabriel fails to sum up courage to fight with Satan "The Lord forgave Gabriel and again said unto Michael: 'You were first in the kingdom of my Son, who proceedeth from me, and it is thine today to go down to that vile antichrist and take from him the heavenly mantle, the crown and the sceptre of angelic orders, which he stole from Me. And divest him of his beauty and glory so that his servants see who the Father is.")

Апокриф "За Тивериадското море", с.32

И изпрати Господ Михаил при Сатанаила. Михаил отиде, но бе опален от Сатанаила и се върна при

Господа: "Направих това, което ми заповяда, но огън от Сатаната ме обгори."...

...Архангел Михаил дойде, удари със скиптъра сатаната и го захвърли на земята с цялото войнство. И падаха три дни и три нощи като капки дъждовни." (*The Tiberiad Sea.* "And God sent Michael to Satan. And Michael went but was scorched by Satan and returned to God and said 'I did what You sent me to do but the fire of Satan fell unto me.'... And Michael came and struck Satan with the sceptre and threw him down with all his army. And they fell three days and three nights like drops of rain.")

The Tiberiad Sea also includes the particularly important dualistic story, according to which Satan allows Adam to plough the earth, which belongs to the devil, under the condition that Adam and his offspring would go to Hell after their death. Or, as the apocrypha explains "the Devil received and sent to Hell both the godly and the sinners."[1] This accretion is made to enable us to bring to the fore a Bogomil association, which is implied in *Paradise Regained*: after the injustice of the devil taking all human souls in bondage and locking them in Hell before the coming of Christ has been done, there comes the understandably noble gesture of Christ (an episode in the *Epiphanius Homily* and the *Gospel of Nicodemus*) who goes down to Hell to free the imprisoned.

The following fundamental Bogomil-Cathar motifs are outlined in *Paradise Regained*: Satan and the rebel angels are driven from heaven; the devil, enraged by yet another spiritual feat performed by Christ, i.e. his fast, flies to the desert to tempt Him; a description of the devil as the lord and master of this world; the devil threatens Christ; Christ descends into hell and sets the souls imprisoned there free; the victory of Christ over the devil in the two versions of hanging him head down from the

---

[1] Стара българска литература. 1. Апокрифи..., p. 34.

clouds and being trodden down. All of these, with the exception of the beautiful myth of the human souls being set free from hell by Christ, are contained in some brief form in the well-known apocryphal *Dispute between Christ and the Devil*[1]. In other words, the apocrypha can be defined as the core of ideas and imagery in *Paradise Regained*, and there is also some similarity in composition. Donka Petkanova assumes that the *Dispute* was generated in dualistic circles[2]. Milton himself indicated the apocryphal literature he used in Paradise Regained with the words that he would laud feats of Christ that were "in secret done" and "unrecorded left through many an age"[3]. In fact, the texts on Christ being tempted by the Devil in the New Testament cover only 11 lines in Matthew (4: 1-11) and 13 lines in Luke (4:1-13) but they nevertheless do not contain the episodes in *Paradise Regained*. Volume has also been added in relation to the source apocryphal *Dispute*, which consists of several pages while the poem contains more than 2,000 verses.

To add conviction to such an assertion we shall again resort to direct comparison between passages in *Paradise Regained* and the dualistic apocrypha. Once again we come to the episode of Satan being driven from heaven with which the dualistic mythology begins and which we repeatedly encountered in *Paradise Lost*. This practically divides the world into two: the realm of God in the heavens and that of the devil on earth[4].

---

[1] Прение на антихрист с Господа наш Исус Христос – In: Стара българска литература. 1. Апокрифи, с.с. 173-175.

[2] Ibidem, p.380.

[3] Paradise Regained, Book I, verses 14-17:

> *...to tell deeds*
> *Above heroic, though in secret done,*
> *And unrecorded left through many an age,*
> *Worthy to have no remained so long unsung.*

[4] The contemporary scholar René Weis has given an example of such a definition of the essence of Cathar belief when he wrote "These were known as Cathars, and they believed that the devil was co-eternal with God and that the material world and the flesh were his evil creation." – In: The Yellow Cross. The Story of the Last Cathars' Rebellion against the Inquisition 1290-1329. New York. 2002, p.XXI.

VISIBLE DUALISTIC THEMES
IN JOHN MILTON'S *PARADISE REGAINED*
Motif one: Satan is cast from heaven

Paradise Regained[1]
Paradise Regained, Book I, verses 356-361
Is true, am that spirit unfortunate/ Who, leagued with millions more in rash revolt/ Kept no my happy station, but was driven/ With them from the bliss to the bottomless deep...

Paradise Regained, Book II, verse 150:
Belial, the dissolutest spirit that fell...

Paradise Regained, Book IV, verses 602-608:
The Son of God, with godlike force endued
Against the attempter of thy Father's throne
And thief of Paradise, him long of old
Thou didst debel, and down from heaven cast
With all his army; now thou hast avenged
Supplanted Adam, and, by vanquishing
Temptation, has lost Paradise.

Dualistic apocrypha
The Secret Book or Interrogatio Joannis (Carcassone text):
...and with his tail he dragged away one-third of the angels of God, and he was banished from the throne of God and from the overlordship of the heavens. And Satan, descending to this firmament, was unable to find rest either for himself or for those who were with him. (Translation Tom Butler. Monumenta bulgarica. Michigan Slavic Publications. 1996, p.193)

The next episode in *Paradise Regained*, given here as motif two, is an inception of all subsequent action, just as it is in the apocryphal *Dispute*.

Motif two: enraged by the fasting of Christ the devil flies to the desert to tempt Him

Paradise Regained, Book II, verses 241-244
Then to the desert takes with these his flight/ Where still, from shade to shade, the Son of

Прение..., с. 173
Дойде Господ на Маслинената планина и каза на своите ученици: "Да постим 40 дни!" И започна Исус да пости 40 дни със своите ученици, за да надвие в спор дявола. И като чу, че Исус пости, дя-

---

[1] The quotations after Milton, J. Complete English Poems, Of Education, Areopagitica. London. 1909/1990.

God,/ after forty days' fasting, had remained,/ Now hungering first, and to himself thus said

волът много се разгневи и се яви гневен пред Исуса.

(*Dispute*, p. 173 "And the Lord came to the mountain and said unto his disciples "now let us fast 40 days!' and Christ began to fast with his disciples to overcome the devil in dispute. And when he heard of Christ's fast the devil was enraged and stood before Him in his anger.)

Tempting Christ with the earthly pictures and visions of this world the devil feels like a lord, the "master of this world" as the Bogomils used to say. Once again we have obvious lexical proximity with Milton calling him the "supreme of earth" and the Cathars, according to Bernard Gui, the *princeps hujus mundi*.

Motif three: the devil described as the master of the world

Paradise Regained, Book I, verses 99-100
Ere in the head of nations he appear,
Their king, their leader, and supreme of earth.

Синодик на цар Борил, - in: Държава и църква през XIII век. София.1999, с.76:
На онези, които казват, че дяволът е владетел на света – анатема трижди. (1211)
(*Synodicon* of Boril: "And thrice accursed those who say the devil is the master of the world. [1211]")
Gui, B. Manuel de l'inquisiteur. T.I. Paris. 1926, p.10: quia ipsum vocant Deum malignum et Deum hujus seculi et principem hujus mundi. (1322)

The envy and open malice of the devil in the *Dispute* are developed in a more rhetorical manner in *Paradise Regained*, but this is one and the same threat of the evil one to use his earthly power against Christ.

Motif four: the devil threatens Christ

Paradise Regained, Book IV, verses 386-388
Sorrows and labours, opposition, hate,

"Прение...", с.175
Дяволът каза: "Ако не се преборя с тебе, няма да бъда равен с Вишния. Аз влязох в сърцето на Каяфа еврейски, да те

Attends thee; scorns, reproaches, injuries, Violences and stripes, and, lastly, cruel death...	мъчат, да те разпънат и да те умъртвят". (*Dispute*, "And the devil said: 'If I do not prevail over thee I shall not be equal to the Lord. And I made me a nest in the heart of Caiaphas, the Jew to make them torture you, crucify you and bring about your death.")

The humanity and completeness of Christ's victory are expressed by the great gesture in which the gates of hell are destroyed and the human souls – set free. This scene was borrowed from the *Gospel of Nicodemus* spread by Bogomils and Cathars.

Motif five: Christ descends into hell and sets the souls imprisoned there free

Paradise Regained, Book I, verses 153-155 All his vast force (Christ – author's note G.V), and drive him back to hell/ Winning by conquest what the first man lost/ By fallacy surprised.	*"Никодимово евангелие", гл. XIV,* Апокріфі і легенди з украінских рукописів.II. Львів. 1899, с.300: "И каза Господ, простирайки ръката своя: елате при мен всички мои светии, защото вие имате подобие на моя образ, защото зарад делата на дървото на дялова – на смърт бяхте осъдени." (*Gospel of Nicodemus*, "And the Lord said with hand extended 'Come to me all my saints, for you have a likeness of My image, for you were sentenced to death for the deeds of the devil's tree.")

The note on which the *Dispute* and *Paradise Regained* end draws an exceptionally impressive, irreversible victory over the devil. The unequivocal tone of the *Dispute* was probably the reason why Milton chose to base himself on the apocrypha which begins with Christ promising to defeat the devil with the words "And the Lord said 'I have come to erase thee from the face of the earth" and ends with another promise of His to deal once and for all with the enemy of man at a place called Chise – "And there, oh devil, shall I destroy you!"

162

Motif six: Christ finally defeats the devil by casting him from heaven, hanging him from the clouds or treading him underfoot

Paradise Regained, Book IV, verses 618-621:
But thou, infernal serpent, shalt not long Rule in the clouds; like an autumnal star, Or lightning, thou shalt fall from heaven, trod down Under his feet (of Jesus Christ – author's note G.V.)...

Прение на антихрист с Господа наш Исус Христос
с.174 Щом каза това Петър, Господ заповяда на облака да слезе от небето като мълния, да върже дявола и да го обеси за петите с главата надолу между небесните облаци.
с.175...защото Исус Христос обеси нашия княз в облаците небесни.
(*Dispute* , p. 174, "And when Peter said that the Lord ordered the cloud to descend from the sky like lightning, to tie the devil and hang him down amidst the heavens."
p. 175 "...for Jesus Christ hath hung our master in the heavenly clouds.")

Thus the two Bogomil myths:
• of Satan's revolt and his respective casting from heaven
• of the final victory of Christ over the devil described in detail, seem to leap forth as a global frame of the two poems, this being particularly obvious in *Paradise Regained*. And inside that frame there is an abundance of images and interpretations borrowed from a whole set of dualistic apocrypha.

In other words, dualistic imagery is the principal structure and it is that which determines the stream of thoughts and ideas. Nowhere else in world literature has Bogomil-Cathar philosophy enjoyed such comprehensive – and obviously magnificent – reproduction, not even in the Bulgarian one, even though the teaching was born in Bulgaria.

Therefore, if we sum up the apocryphal material used we could say that images, fragments and sometimes vocabulary from *The Secret Book*, the *Dispute*, *Gospel of Nicodemus*, the *Oratione of St. John Chrysostom*[1]

---

[1] It is about this apocrypha that Anissava Miltenova has made the following important observation: „There is no known Greek source of this apocrypha so far. This gives us grounds to assume that the oratione dedicated to Michael's victory over Satan was an original Bulgarian work, the chronology of which is determined by the already existent

and possibly the *Tiberiad Sea*[1] can be discerned in the two poems. This author has so far failed to encounter a scholar to have remarked on this peculiarity or to have mentioned the presence of apocryphal influences in these two great poems. With the exception of some cases when they were mentioned in passing by names like Marco Mincoff or Emile Legouis, medieval apocrypha are absent from the analyses of Milton experts. What we have at best are attempts at vague definitions. Emile Legouis called *Paradise Lost* the most Hebraic of great English poems[2], obviously because he failed to discern the apocryphal material. True, apocrypha frequently include Hebraic motifs, but after all starting with *The Secret Book* and ending with the *Dispute*, all dualistic apocrypha, whose influence is revealed in this paper, retold a pre-history stemming not from the Old but from the New Testament. There the figure of Christ is a leading one in terms of expectation, appearance, accomplishment and final victory.

This is where we should comment on an opinion shared by some of the Miltonian scholars. According to Emile Legouis, in spite of himself Milton was in deep sympathy with Satan, the great rebel of Heaven and enemy of God[3], but it seems to me that things are a bit more complicated. Should one look carefully at *Paradise Lost* one would see that this epic poem was not completed and it is even difficult to say to what extent the planned plot was fulfilled. This incompleteness or deficiency[4] was probably due to the fact that the poet may have overestimated his powers, for he fell short of both the time and energy to cover more comprehensively the panorama of the universal battle between God and Satan. And when he realised that his lifespan was running short, that his human and poetic potential was restricted, he decided to present the final victory of Christ over the devil in an unquestionable way. That was why he wrote *Para-*

---

and spread Bogomil apocrypha used in its compilation: *The Secret Book, The Tiberiad Sea, A Dispute between Christ and the Devil,* the *Book of Enoch* and the *Revelation,* among others. It is assumed that the compilation of this apocrypha can be dated in the end of the 12th or the 13th century. – In: Българската литература и книжнина през XIII век, p.251. This scholar has outlined a set of Bogomil literature, which obviously travelled in time and space and reached Milton at one point.

[1] Стара българска литература. 1. Апокрифи, p.380.

[2] Legouis, E., op. cit., p. 580.

[3] Legouis, E., op. cit., p. 581.

[4] Such incompleteness was discerned by Kurth, B., op. cit., p. 7: the Fall should be viewed as the beginning of a larger action rather than the end of a tragedy.

dise Regained relying on a time-honoured formula – an apocrypha presenting precisely the defeat of the enemy of God and man.

Although he expressed himself in the medieval style of the apocrypha Milton laid the stress not so much on the divine as an the human nature of Christ, thus allowing man not only to bow before Christ's passion but to take up directly, to follow the example of His battle and overcome the demon on his own[1]. Albeit in much more succinct form than in *Paradise Lost*, the poet carried out his personal covenant, which was a double victory of Christ and of man over the devil.

And the victory of man is in some respects a modern solution, for it represents spiritual struggle, a struggle not of power, but of character. In this struggle Satan tries to denigrate light, Christ and man and to lead him astray with temptations such as today consumer society offers in abundance. The answer is practically imperative: spiritual elevation is the destiny of Christ and man who follows the road of emulation of the Son. This can neither be eroded nor misled. Thus man is given the meaning of his existence against the backdrop of the entire universe.

Naturally, the specifics of the genre have registered their influence. Even formally *Paradise Regained* strives after connection with the Gospel, with the devil and the demons being driven in the herd of swine, just as in the New Testament parable. There is also dogmatic intonation. The rigorist characteristics of the Christian apocrypha *A Dispute between Christ and the Devil*, chosen as the direct model of *Paradise Regained*, resound for example in the surprising denigration of antiquity as a "temptation". The same Milton who bore a love of ancient Greek literature repeatedly expressed in his essays and with a presence of its own in the numerous gods and heroes of antiquity in *Paradise Lost*, reached the point in *Paradise Regained* where, obsessed with the idea of complete supremacy of Christ as the "light from above, from fountain regained"[2], he disqualified that culture as "but dreams/Conjectures, Fancies, built on nothing firm"[3]. Thus the poet paid certain due to his vacillation among genres because of his human failure to harmonise the beauty of ancient

---

[1] His intention was discerned by an excellent French expert on English literature, Jacques Jusserand, who wrote that with his resistance to the demon Christ saved the mankind woman had brought down by giving in to the snake. In: Jusserand, J. Histoire abrégée de la littérature anglaise. Paris. 1896, p.153.

[2] Paradise Regained, Book IV, verse 289.

[3] Ibidem, verses 291-292.

sensitivity and Christian feelings. When he chose poetic pathos with complete freedom of imagination and artistic temperament he seemed to fall a bit short of the Christian finality he would have wanted to see in his work. When he related categorically the triumph of Christ it turned out he had taken up the objections of many Christian theoreticians against the "pagan" Greek antiquity. By the way, the presentation of Christ's victory over the devil in Milton's poem and the apocryphal *Dispute* was a task exceeding classical Christian teaching, for such a victory is not described but expected through the New Testament. The task Milton set before himself was supra-human, it was a task of the Divine Plan.

Dante was a bit more merciful towards Greek and Roman antiquity by placing their personages in purgatory and giving Vergil the freedom to be a guide in the journey between the worlds. This heritage of unresolved contradiction between Christ as a noble ideal but one that imposes a strict, icon-like type of conduct, and the increasing freedom of human enterprise from the Renaissance onwards was carried over time right to the literature of the 20th century. What is probably its most original solution can be found in the plays of the writer and thinker Stefan Gechev titled *The Case of the Disappearance of the Body of Jesus of Nazareth*[1] and *Barabbas' Calvary*[2]. In both of these Christ is actually absent from the stage – He is called upon as a memory, as an idea to enable the remaining mortal protagonists to carry out their idea of Christ with the complete freedom of the best they carry and can find in themselves.

17th century Waldensian translocations

Now where could Milton's association with apocrypha come from? The Puritans, the main ideological trend in the English bourgeois revolution, are known to have sympathized with the Waldenses, the last surviving continental heresy. The 17th century saw the translocation of Waldensian literature from the valleys of Piedmont to England. One of the earliest comments on the significance of that translocation was made by the

---

[1] Гечев, Ст. Голготата на Варава. София.1999. Presented in Columbia Arts Center, Washington, 1994. Reviewed in *The Washington Times* (June 1, 1994) and in *The Washington* Post (June 6, 1994; June 16, 1994)
[2] Гечев, Ст. Голготата на Варава. Пиеси. София.1999.

19th century prominent Russian scholar of the Cathar movement Nikolai Osokin: "When the persecution of Waldenses was renewed in the 17th century and they felt threatened by extermination the most important manuscripts were transported to England – and Cromwell – who was then considered to be the head and protector of Protestantism, or *capo et protettore* to quote Venetian relations. They have been kept at the library of Cambridge since 1658. These are numerous pieces of theological, edifying, historical, ritualistic or *purely poetic character* "(the italics mine – G. V.)[1]. The same author has added the important for us information that the said literature was included in the following publications: Jean Paul Perrin, *Histoire des Vaudois* and *Histoire des Chrestiens albigeois* (Genève, 1618) and J. Léger, *Histoire des Eglises Evangéliques des vallées de Piémont* (Leiden, 1669). According to Osokin, Jean Perrin made no difference between Cathars and Waldenses[2], which indicates that Waldensian and Cathar literature already constituted a mixed fund.

Anne Brenon, a contemporary scholar of the Cathar movement of note, has made several publications confirming this information since the 1970s. She quoted the evidence of Jean Léger, a pastor in the valley of Lucerne and moderator of the Piedmont valley churches, that he personally gave six manuscripts "into the hands of Mr. Morland, special commissioner of milord Oliver Cromwell, Protector of Great Britain"[3]. In turn, Samuel Morland presented the manuscripts to the university in Cambridge and published in London the *History of Evangelical Churches in Piedmont* in 1658.

Another group of texts in 12 volumes, collected by the erudite Archbishop of Armagh, James Ussher (1581-1656), arrived in a similar albeit slightly more roundabout way in Dublin and finally Trinity College. It is assumed that he bought all or at least eight of them from a French jurisconsult, Perrin being the initial starting point. After Ussher's death his library, including the above-mentioned collection, was added to that of Trinity College.

According to Anne Brenon, Waldensian manuscript collections usually contain biblical texts and liturgical sermons, moral and theological

---

[1] Осокин, Н. История альбигойцев и их времени. Москва. 2000, p.183.
[2] Осокин, Н., op. cit., p. 815.
[3] Brenon, A. Localisation des manuscripts vaudois. Centro studi piemontesi. Torino. 1978, p.196.

treatises[1]. She has provided a rather more comprehensive description of the manuscripts in Dublin in another paper, published in 1973, in which she pointed out that MS Du10, which probably dates from the end of the 14th century, "is not Waldensian but Cathar and contains only two treatises"[2]. In fact, she leads us on to the important discovery of the Belgian philologist Théo Venckeleer of 1960-1961[3], who made a detailed study of the manuscript previously known as A.6.10 and today as MS 269, which has conditionally been accepted to have been copied from an unknown original around 1375-1376. According to Théo Venckeleer, the said manuscript A.6.10. in the Dublin collection of Waldensian manuscripts was a "Cathar document"[4] of French Provençal origin, the first part presenting the basic tenets of the Cathar church and the second – a gloss of the principal Cathar prayer *Pater noster*. As we cannot quote them all here we shall dwell on the following basic points:

1. The main Bogomil sacrament, baptism with the Holy Spirit, is described in the first part of the manuscript: "lo saint baptism sperital, ço es lo enposament de las mans, per lo cal es donat lo Saint Sperit"[5].

2. The well-known Bogomil-Cathar view on the expression "panem nostrum supersubstantialem" in *Pater noster* is quoted in the second part of the manuscript as "suprasubstantial bread", i.e. spiritual food intended not for the body but for the human soul. As even Euthymius Zigabenus wrote, the Bogomils "say that Jesus fed them with the Word"[6]. With John Wycliffe the same thing is underscored very strongly as the reformer

---

[1] Jolliot, A. Les communautés vaudoises des Hautes Vallées alpines aux XVe et XVIe siècles. Fédération historique du Languédoc méditerranéen et du Roussillon. XLIVe Congrès (Privas, 22-23 mai 1971). Université Paul Valéry – Montpellier. 1972, p.189.

[2] Jolliot, A. Les livres des Vaudois. Catalogue. Ecole pratiques des hautes études. Ve section – sciences religieuses. Annuiare. Tomes LXXX-LXXXI. Extraits du fascicule II, p. 71.

[3] Venckeleer, T. Un recueil cathare: le manuscript A.6.10 de Dublin. Une apologie. – In: Revue Belge de Philologie et d'Histoire. t.38. 1960, pp. 815-834; Une Glose sur le Pater. – In: Revue Belge de Philologie et d'Histoire. t. 39. 1961, pp. 759-762.

[4] Venckeleer, T. Un recueil cathare: le manuscript A.6.10 de Dublin. Une apologie. – In: Revue Belge de Philologie et d'Histoire. t. 38. 1960, p. 816.

[5] Ibidem, p. 829. In comparison we shall quote the same ritual described by Salve Burce in his anti-heretical treatise *Supra stella* (1235): "Dicunt Albanenses et Concorricii, quod homines per impositionem manuum accipiunt Spiritum sanctum et fiunt salvi." – In: Döllinger, Ign., op. cit., p. 61.

[6] ...ὅτι ἐνεβρωμάτισεν αὐτοῖς ὁ Ἰησοῦς λόγον – in: Ficker, G. Die Phundagiagiten. Leipzig. 1908, p.110.

translated *panem nostrum supersubstantialem as oure breed ouer other substaunce*[1] in English and explained that daily bread should be understood as spiritual, that this is a divine precept[2]. By the way, such a translation is closer to the Greek original τον αρτον ημων τον επιουσιον than the daily bread in the Authorized edition and, respectively the widely adopted in Catholic services *panem nostrum quotidianum* from Luke in the Vulgate. This is so because επιουσιον means *suprasubstantial*, without the dualistic stress on word as spiritual bread being incorporated in the Orthodox one. The non-material aspect has also been brought to the fore in an unquestionable manner in the Dublin manuscript, but in this case it is the love of Jesus Christ not the word that is the spiritual bread: *ço es lo sobre substantial, ço es la la carita; car la carita per ço es apela pan sobre sustancial car es sobre totas las aotras sustancias*[3].

3. In the gloss the *Pater noster* ends with the expression "for thine is the kingdom and the virtue and the glory" - *quoniam tuum est regnum et virtus et gloria*. This expression is absent from the Vulgate as well as from King James's Bible but it is present in the Greek text of the Orthodox Bible: διότι σοῦ εἶναι ἡ βασιλεία καὶ ἡ δύναμις καὶ ἡ δόξα εἰσ τοῦς αἰῶνας. For Théo Venckeleer this is a sure sign of Greek origin[4]. And this Greek trace – as Nikolai Osokin assumed nearly 150 years ago and as Ch. Schmidt confidently stated before him – is a sign that the Cathars borrowed the *Pater noster* from the Cyrillo-Methodian version (i.e. on the basis of the Greek Orthodox Bible), which the Bogomils took west[5].

In addition to the evidence of the Cathar character of the manuscript quoted here it turned out that this was not an isolated phenomenon. Théo Venckeleer accorded it a key position in Cathar literature, considering it the third authentic Cathar manuscript after *Le rituel provençal* (published

---

[1] The Holy Bible, Made from Latin Vulgate by John Wyccliffe and his Followers. v.IV. Oxford. M.DCCCL, p. 18.
[2] Restat igitur ut panem cotidianum accipiamus spiritualem, precepta scilicet divina, que cotidie oportet meditari et operari. - In: Wyclif, J. Opus Evangelicum. Vols. I and II. London. 1895, p. 285.
[3] Une Glose sur le Pater…, p. 774.
[4] Ibidem, p. 760.
[5] Осокин, Н. История альбигойцев и их времени. Москва. 2000, с.143. First edition 1869. Schmidt, Ch. Histoire et doctrine de la secte des Cathares ou Albigeois. Paris-Genève. t.II. 1849, p. 271.

by Cunitz for the first time in 1852 and again by L. Clédat in 1887) and the *Liber de Duobus Principiis*, published by R. P. A. Dondaine in 1939. The unquestionable Cathar spirit is also confirmed by the fact that, according to Venckeleer, chapters I and II of the Dublin manuscript almost coincide textually with *Le rituel provençal* (ff. 237^{ra-vb}, resp. 329^{ra-vb})[1].

The documents we have quoted allow the conclusion that the 17th century witnessed repeated heretical transfers containing Cathar texts to England. How this "fine example of heretical syncretism"[2], to use the apt definition of Anne Brenon, actually occurred is a question answered even by Nikolai Osokin. He noted that after the Cathars were subdued in the beginning of the 13th century the Waldenses were joined by all sects of purely evangelical teaching[3]. According to Anne Brenon herself, regardless of the controversies between Cathars and Waldenses, the Cathar euchologion was adopted in the said set of Waldensian literature for the treatise on the church of God it contains has a purely evangelical intonation, one that was shared by those pre-Reformation movements. The scholar of the first third of the 20th century Leo Seifert wrote about the conviction of later heretics (meaning the Hussites and the Bohemian Brethren) that Wycliffe originated from the Waldenses, under which name they understood the whole group of sects based on dualism[4].

We shall expand the review of Waldensian literature with obvious Cathar faith admixtures by mentioning two earlier cases, respectively dating from the 12th and the 14th century. The first was indicated by Jean Duvernoy when he wrote that dualistic opinions on creation and a negation of purgatory were noticed at a disputation between Catholic clerics and Waldenses in southern France (chaired, by the way, by the English priest Raimond of Daventry)[5]. The second case harks from North Italy. The records of a trial held in 1387-1388 note that the defendants were Waldenses, poor men of Lyons and other heretics, fraticelli. It is exactly the documents of that trial, however, that on several occasions feature

---

[1] Une Glose sur le Pater…, p. 833.

[2] Brenon, A. Les archipels cathares. Dissidence chrétienne dans l'Europe médievale. Cahors. 2000, p. 109.

[3] Осокин, Н., op. cit., p. 183.

[4] Зайферт, Л. Световните революционери (от Богомил през Хус до Ленин). София. 1994, p. 50. Original title: Seifert, J.L. Die Welterevolutionäre. Von Bogomil über Hus zu Lenine. Wien,. 1931

[5] Duvernoy, J. Les origines du movement Vaudois. – In: Heresis N13 et 14. 1990, p. 184.

fundamental dualistic theses[1] and, what is more, information that Italian Cathars communicated with "Bogoleni" (i.e. Bogomils) of the Ecclesia Sclavoniae, the Bosnian Bogomil church related in terms of ideas to the Bulgarian one[2].

Conclusion

We are at the end of this chapter, but before that let see:

– whether even more detailed specification of Milton's dualistic views is possible;

– why the case of Milton's affiliation to the philosophy of dualism remains unrevealed to this day, just as the genetic link between the Lollards and continental heresies remains for British medievalists.

Now in answer to the first question, for example, we can try to specify for which trend of dualism he had a preference. Which of the two main dualistic churches transferred to Western Europe did he choose as his source? The church of absolute dualism, for which the Good and the Bad God were equal without beginning or end, or the Bulgarian church of moderated dualism, according to which the Good God would after all prevail and Satan would be shamed and conquered. The *Areopagitica* features the following assertion: "Good and evil we know in the field of this world grow up together almost inseparably; and the knowledge of good is so involved and interwoven with the knowledge of evil, and so many cunning resemblances hardly to be discerned...that *the knowledge of good and evil, as two twins cleaving together* (italics mine – G.V.), leaped forth into the world."[3] It seems that we are faced with a definition of absolute dualism, but Milton did not leave it to remain all-powerful. He found that the painfully potent power of evil on earth was **temporary**, to become a test for virtue in which virtue would learn to discern good from evil by itself and, on the basis of that bitter experience, would no longer let itself be misled or deceived. As Milton further on explained, in that way Adam's fall **meant to know good by evil**[4]. This intepretation of

---

[1] Processus contra Valdenses, Pauperes de Lugduno, aliosque haereticos, Fraticellos etc.: Et docuerunt primo, quod deberet credere, quod Deus non creavit seu fecit aliquam rem visbilem, sed mundus iste et omnia alia visibilia a diabolo qui cecidit de coelo, errant create et facta. – In: Döllinger, Ign., op. cit., p. 266.

[2] Ibidem, p. 255: veniendo successive de loco Machiarum versus Bogolenum..., loco Bogoleni, ...dicti Sclavoni.

[3] Areopagitica and Other Prose Works of John Milton. London, New York. 1927, p. 13.

[4] Ibidem.

his is an answer to the hypothesis of Arthur Lovejoy and Hugh White of the *felix culpa*, of the fall with a supreme meaning. It is in this spirit, but against the backdrop of modern historical experience, that Stefan Gechev updated the meaning of Bogomil philosophy as an idea whether mankind could leave evil at all: "But I think that there is something very important with Bulgarian Bogomilism as the Bogomils asked a question crucial to mankind, i.e. could there be God without there being a devil. In other words, could there be good without there being evil?"[1] This is a dramatic question left to us, for we enter into so many conflicts in the new millennium while having sufficient knowledge and means to avoid them. Theoretically man is now stronger than evil and is familiar with its faces and temptations from past experience. Therefore man has to make his choice of good on his own and thus prove himself as a power of goodness.

Milton's painfully achieved optimism is in harmony with the reasoning of the Bulgarian Bogomil church, for don't we see the ultimate victory of Christ over the devil categorically stated in *Paradise Regained*. It rings closely to both the Bogomil apocrypha model of the poem, the *Dispute between Christ and the Devil*, and to information from records of the Inquisition regarding "the beliefs of the Cathars from Bagnolo and Concorreggio, who received their faith from Sclavonia, i.e. Bosnia" (which adopted the Bulgarian Bogomil church): "These others from Bulgaria believe in one omnipotent God without beginning…"[2] Then we have grounds to note that Milton not only sympathized with the theology of the Bulgarian Bogomil church but also gauged the tendency towards internal evolution in it – the hope that the Good God would prevail.

By the way, this essentially monotheistic position converges with another important intention of Milton's. Like Wycliffe and Tyndale he did not set himself the task of creating a separate dualistic zone in English society but to carry out a radical reform in the English church with the spiritual material and the evangelical example of the dualists.

It seems that the same reasons, i.e. a necessary compromise with widely established orthodox beliefs, made Milton acknowledge the Blessed

---

[1] Interview in the Novo Slovo newspaper, Sofia. November 26, 1994.

[2] Quidam alii de Bulgaria credunt tantum unum Deum omnipotentum sine principio – in: Döllinger, Ign., p. 612. This information could be dated around the middle or the end of the 13th century for it mentions heretical communities in northern Italy described in "Summa Fratris Raynerii de Ordine Fratrum Predicatorum de Catharis et Leonistis seu Pauperibus de Lugduno" (1250).

Virgin's immaculate conception and declare John the Baptist the forerunner of Christ at whose hands He was baptised, just as the gospels say. Now let us recall that the dualists allotted John the Baptist a place among the devil's entourage in the Old Testament. And another example: while Bogomils, Cathars and Lollards denied the saints and acknowledged only Jesus Christ and the Father, the saints in Book VI of *Paradise Lost* fight the devil as champions of Christ[1]. Milton's desire to preserve the reformed church as a national institution and to complete the reformation in it is also quite obvious in his polemics with the adherents of the episcopal church, not to mention the fact that he considered the church necessary for the establishment of the republic, of civic society. That was why he also considered the prospects of its unification in spite of his polemic opinions.

On the other hand, when church controversy entered political life Milton, who was a Puritan of exceptional note involved directly in Cromwell's politics, discarded the spirit of peace and the dualist philosophy of non-violence, and became a fervent advocate of the dictator. The subject of episcopacy is a priori encumbered with political connotations as the king is "defender of the faith" (*defensor fidei*) by right and episcopacy is respectively a support of the monarch. This type of attack against the episcopate was reflected in a popular image of Cromwell in those times, depicting him with a sword in one hand and the Bible in the other, a case in which Milton definitely was no dualist but rather an aggressive politician. A new element when the explosion of political passion took him beyond Bogomil thought and lifestyle.

Milton's affiliation to Bogomil theology consequently found itself preserved in another way, transformed as it was by him into poetics. In terms of a period in life this corresponded with his complete exclusion from politics after the Restoration. In other words, a return from politics to poetry and dualistic philosophy. Some would object to this, quoting the numerous battles and clashed of force in *Paradise Lost*. These, however, are no blood battles but raging emotions, which gradually raise man above the kingdom and the temptations of Satan, which call upon a spiritual feat, an appeal resounded with repeated insistence in *Paradise Regained*. Therefore I think one could make such a summary in advance as

---

[1] Paradise Lost. Book VI, verses 45-46:
    Gabriel, lead forth to Battel these my Sons
    Invincible, lead forth my armed Saints

it would allow a more precise understanding of the exceptionally varied Miltonian life and world. By the political sign of Puritanism Milton left the New Testament world of Bogomils, Cathars and Lollards and **returned to the Old Testament practice that was history then and is history today. Later, after his political downfall, he raised Bogomil theology to the firmament of poetry, which is a world of spiritual evolution and of beauty. Maybe close to the heavens of the good Father where the dualists dreamed of returning.**

Now we have to answer the second question: why did such an engagement of Milton's with basic tenets of dualistic theology in the frequently lexical coincidence of images and expressions with dualistic texts remain unrevealed for nearly 250 years? As time will probably provide the comprehensive answer here we shall just outline two visible peculiarities.

The first is that, both in the 20th century and today, English medieval and heresy studies adopt the axiom that the island remained untouched by the major medieval heresies on the continent.

One of the reasons for that is that the English heretics, the Lollards with whom Wycliffe was associated, concealed their continental origin very carefully to avoid large-scale persecution of the type of the destructive internal crusades Pope Innocent III organized in Provence, France, in the beginning of the 13th century. Such skillful concealment of identity and history did not allow the Catholic Church in England to gauge what its opponents actually were and whose spirit they were bringing to the island. Even today we find the following thesis in the *Catholic Encyclopedia*: "Till the latter part of the fourteenth century England had been remarkably free from heresy. The Manichean movements of the twelfth and thirteenth centuries, which threatened the Church and society in Southern Europe and had appeared sporadically in Northern France and Flanders had made no impression on England. The few heretics who were heard of were all foreigners and they seem to have found no following in the country."[1] This is an erroneous assertion for at least two reasons. First of all it is impossible that the Lollards, who constituted widespread and influential communities in the 14th century, who sent a petition to Parliament in 1395 and had their own schools and literature, did not previously undergo a period of inception and growth in order to achieve the various dimensions of all that varied activity. In other words, judging by

---

[1] Catholic Encyclopedia. Robert Appleton Company. 1910. Vol. IX, p. 333.

174

the familiar rates by which a culture developed in the Middle Ages, as the Lollards were a most active factor in social life at the end of the 14th century such a culmination should have been preceded by at least two centuries of development.

Besides, the term Lollard is of proven continental origin, as the *Encyclopaedia Britannica* states[1]. In the 19th century authors like Nikolai Osokin or Jacques Jusserand wrote about English relations with continental heresies but their studies – particularly Osokin's – remain beyond the field of vision of our British colleagues. It seems that the problem, which hinders their communication with major authors like Nikolai Osokin or Lev Karsavin, is a linguistic one. Or maybe sometimes one should speak of a certain dose of conservatism, for the excellent bibliography of Krastina Gecheva on Bogomilism[2] where she has quoted works containing proof of Lollard continental origin and the dualistic character of their teaching, a book published in 1997, has not been mentioned in any of the recent English publications to the best of my knowledge.

That Milton's dualistic philosophy was not gauged may also be due to the fact that most of his scholars see the politician but overlook the theologian in his essays. These writings of Milton's pay due to the political passions of the period, in terms of style they constitute publicist pieces sometimes, as Milton aficionados have noted to their chagrin, reaching the point of crude attacks on opponents. These essays are not only pamphlets, however, for half or at least one-third of them contain theological disputation.

To underestimate the theological aspect is an inadequate and unproductive approach. Thus the *Cambridge History of English and American Literature* finds that Milton's prose is not an easy subject to study, that it has been repeatedly overlooked – at least in the general reviews of his work[3]. What this history offers, however, is no alternative as his essays are practically analysed only in terms of style to reach the conclusion that, with the exception of some passages, this prose was below the poet's own level[4]. Neither their ideological dimensions have been mentioned

---

[1] Encyclopaedia Britannica. Vol. 14, 1970, p. 256.
[2] Гечева, Кр. Богомилството. София. 1997.
[3] The Cambridge History of English and American Literature in 18 Volumes (1907–21). Volume VII. Cavalier and Puritan. V. Milton, p. 56.
[4] Ibidem, p. 67.

nor their significance as expressing one of the most energetic positions of the Reformation[1]. In this respect older English publications register more interest in Milton's treatises. In his preface to Milton's 1659 essay *Considerations Touching the Likeliest Means to Remove the Hirelings out of the Church* J. John wrote in 1883: "Few readers perhaps expect the rare display of learning and logic which they will find in this treatise."[2]

This study has no claim to being comprehensive for it is a beginning which explains principles of Milton's philosophy and imagery, a formidable task which necessitates further intensive work. Fascinating problems continue to sprout in the field of research as a forgotten reality begins to speak, wanting to be reborn. Since the poet used apocrypha and other dualistic literature so abundantly what are those sources. Although he expressed affiliation to the work of the Waldensian and Cathar churches or to the heretical John Wycliffe Milton did not name his direct sources. Historically amassed dust or the cautious witholding of truths that could be used against the ongoing reform – these are questions that could be considered, especially after additional facts are found.

One should also take a closer look at Milton's correspondence or his associates. He shared some of his meetings and contacts of anticlerical pathos. Thus in 1638 he visited the aged Galileo in Italy[3] and paid attention to his meetings with Jean Diodati (1576-1649), a noted Protestant theologian who made a new translation of the Bible in Italian and published the treatise *De fictitio Pontificiorum Purgatorio* (1619), which rejected the idea

---

[1] It is in a similar way that the *Cambridge History* presents William Tyndale – primarily as a theological pamphleteer. The Cambridge History of English and American Literature. Vol. 3. II Reformation Literature in England, p. 32. Further on the analysis leaves out the definition theological and lays the stress on the pamphlet, the word itself being mentioned on another two occasions in the same chapter. At one point the author even heaves a sigh of relief: "It is a relief to turn from the pamphlets to Tindale's Biblical translation."(Ibidem, p. 33). This relief, however, means that further analysis has been given up, for the works described as pamphlets are in fact important theological treatises with which Tyndale motivated his translation and explained some of its peculiarities. This theology has neither been recognised nor analysed.

[2] John, J. Preface to 'Considerations Touching the Likeliest Means to Remove the Hirelings out of the Church where is also Discoursed of Tithes, Church Fees, and Churche Revenues; whether any Maintenance of Ministers Can Be Settled by Law...' in: The Prose Works of John Milton. V.III. London.1883, p.1.

[3] "...I found and visited the famous Galileo, grown old a prisoner to the Inquisition, for thinking in astronomy otherwise than the Franciscan and Dominican licensers thought." – In: Areopagitica and Other Prose Works of John Milton. London, Toronto, New York. 1927, p. 25.

of purgatory. Milton should have left a trace somewhere, be it in letters or in memoirs of his peers and friends. A letter of Milton's to Emeric Bigot mentions the Cotton MSS, the first part of which contains the dualistic *Dialogue between Salomon and Saturn*, as well as a fragment of the *Gospel of Nicodemus* used by the dualists[1]. In other words, those were older dualistic sources possibly on English territory since the 12th century. At that the letter is dated March 24, 1658, i.e. the period in which the already blind poet was probably in the atmosphere of his great work, *Paradise Lost*.

Naturally, the scarcity of details about Milton's direct contacts with heretical literature does not invalidate the arguments in favour of his dualism presented here. Dualism acquires the significance of a flight in the heavens. It turns out that the grandest trips in different worlds, man's most encompassing view of the Universe and human elevation to a general view of God's deeds were achieved through poetics borrowed from dualism. Because Dante's *Divina Commedia* relied on it in its construction of the worlds and Milton's epic, dedicated to the universal struggle between good and evil, is full of its imagery and theogony. This super-scope was also noticed by J. Goodridge who wrote that Dante's *Divina Commedia*, Milton's *Paradise Lost* and William Langland's *Piers Plowman* worked with the widest of all themes "the meaning of man's life on earth in relation to his ultimate destiny. Like Milton, Langland seeks to 'justify the ways of God to men'."[2] By the way, *Piers Plowman* acquired this scope once again from dualistic poetics, for this poem also has the aspect of a Bogomil-Cathar treatise.

What are the similarities and the differences between the poetics of Dante and that of Milton? Above all, Dante was not a dualist. He was carried away by a struggle with the church on principle. With his treatise *De Monarchia* he wanted the church to be subordinate to the state, he was familiar with dualistic apocrypha like *Visio Paoli*, from which he borrowed the idea of the descent into the underworld and the trip there. Milton embraced *The Secret Book of Bogomils* and other fundamental apocrypha of theirs. An embrace of dual meaning in the sense that on the one hand he borrowed the universal scope and on the other – he shared the finalist views of the Bulgarian dualists that were harbingers of defeat for the devil and his

---

[1] Milton, J. To the accomplished Emeric Bigot. – In: The Prose Works of John Milton. V. III. London. 1883, p. 513.

[2] Goodridge, J. Introduction to Langland, W. Piers the Ploughman. London, 1959/1977, p.11.

demons. Naturally, in *Paradise Lost* the poet updated their views with the culture and the humanistic leanings of the 17th century. Spatially speaking, Dante took the drama of the underworld, i.e. the antechamber of catharsis and redemption, for it is in the Inferno that he is most powerful. Milton took the entire universe in order to give Christ the final victory in *Paradise Regained*. A victory of the Son that man is destined to repeat. In other words, the English poet nevertheless succeeded in compiling a positive epic of Christian humanism. The works of Dante and Milton seem to persuade us that the picture of the universe in literature can be achieved most successfully through a dualistic prism.

And now a modern aspect. In the great work of *Paradise Lost* Bogomil philosophy and imagery have found a happier reproduction than in Bulgarian literature itself. This is the most convincing possible example of cultural interaction or *interculturalité*, to use the French term. Besides such a statement, however, there are things that remain unsaid. What does this mean – that ideas have some law of their own of materialising regardless of the place of their genesis? Or vice versa – that their more comprehensive materialisation elsewhere predicts a new, more impressive one on their own cultural and historical soil? In any case, with the material development of mankind that should leave us free for more spiritual occupations we are embarking upon times of interaction, when the spiritual wealth of the world is revealed not only as accessible to all, but also as a result of processes of shared creation and as a prospect to renew the most sublime meanings, the still resourceful aspects of the same processes.

Bibliography

Primary sources

Cyrillics

Ангелов, Б. М.Генов. Стара българска литература (IX-XVIII век). София, 1922

Анонимен катарски трактат - в: Ръкописите на катарите. София, 1999

Байрон, Дж. Каин - мистерия. В. Търново, 1992

Българската литература и книжнина през XIII век (Съст. и ред. Божилов, Ив., Ст. Кожухаров). София, 1987

Видение на светия апостол Павел, който бе възнесен от ангел на третото небе - в: Стара българска литература 1.Апокрифи. София,1982

Геновъ, М. Антология на старобългарската литература. София, 1947

Гечев, Ст. Голготата на Варава. Пиеси. София.1999

Данте, А. Божествена комедия. Прев. от ит. Ив. Иванов и Л. Любенов. София, 1975

Зигавин, Е. Догматическо всеоръжие - в: Богомилството в България, Византия и Западна Европа в извори. Съставит. Д. Ангелов, Б. Примов и Г. Батаклиев. София, 1967

Ивановъ, Й. Богомилски книги и легенди. София, 1925

Катарски требник (XIII век) в превод на Йордан Иванов - в: Богомилски книги и легенди. София, 1925

Легенда о братстве - в: Памятники старинной русской литературы (Сказания, легенды, повести, сказки и притчи) под ред. Н. Костомарова. Вып.I. Санктъ Петербургъ, 1860

Никодимово евангелие - в: Апокріфі і легенди з украіньских рукописів. т.II. Львів, 1899

Охридски, Кл. Събрани съчинения. т.II. София, 1977

Охридски, Кл. Слово за Пасха - в: Стара българска литература 2. Ораторска проза. София, 1982

Памятники отреченной русской литературы, собраны и изданы Н. Тихонравовымъ. т.I. Санкт Петербургъ, 1863

Патриарх Теофилакт до Петър, цар на българите - в: Богомилството в България, Византия и Западна Европа. София, 1967

Писмо на Евтимий от Акмония (XI век) - в: Богомилството в България, Византия и Западна Европа. София, 1967

Писмо на иерусалимския монахъ Атанасий до Панка - в: Стара българска литература (IX-XVIII). Съставит. Б. Ангелов и М. Генов, 1922

Повест за кръстното дърво - в: Стара българска литература 1. Апокрифи. Съст. и ред. Донка Петканова. София, 1982

Повест за кръстното дърво - своден вариант в Презвитер Еремия (дисертация на Пейо Д. Пеев). Шумен-София, 1990

Полемично съчинение срещу босненските богомили - в: Богомилството в България, Византия и Западна Европа в извори.София, 1967

Попруженко, Б. Синодикъ царя Борила. София, 1928

Похвално слово за Мойсей, за сплитането на дърво от от ела, кедър и кипарис - вариант на Повест за кръстното дърво. Jagič, V. Novi prilozi za literaturu biblijskih apokrifa. Starine V. Zagreb, 1873

Презвитер Козма. Беседа против богомилите - в: Стара българска литература 2. Ораторска проза. София, 1982

Прение на антихрист с господа наш Исус Христос - в: Стара българска литература 1. Апокрифи. София, 1982

Пространно житие на Теодосий Търновски от патриарх Калист - в: Стара българска литература (4). Животописни творби. София, 1986

Райнов, Н. Сатанаилово царство.Богомилски апокриф. -в: Съчинения в 5 тома. т.2. София, 1990

Сказание за кръстното дърво (Ркп в Сборник N925 на Солов. манастир в Казанската Духовна Академия) - в: Стара българска литература (IX-XVIII в.). София, 1922

Слово за Адам и Ева от началото до свършека - в: Стара българска литература 1.Апокрифи. София, 1982

Снегът зеленина сънува (Антология на провансалската лирика). Подбрал и превел от провансалски Симеон Хаджикосев. София, 1990

Сперанскій, М. Славянскія апокрифическія евангелія (общий обзоръ). Москва, 1895

Цезарий от Хайстербах. Диалог на чудесата. София, 1999

Latin

XXIV conclusiones Wycclyf damnatae Londoniis in synodo - in: Fasciculi Zizaniorum magistri Johannis Wyclif cum tritico. Ed. by Walter W. Shirley. London, 1858

Anglo-Saxon poetry. An anthology of Old Englisn poems in prose translation with an introduction and headnotes by S.A. Bradlley. London, Melbourne, Toronto, 1982

Ariosto, L. Orlando furioso. Samsoni- Firenze. 1957

Blake, W. The Complete Writings (With All the Variant Readings. Edited by Geoffrey Keynes). London, New York, 1957, p.150. An abridged version of this topic we see in plate 24: "Note: This Angel, who is now become a Devil..." (A Memorable Fancy), p.158

Borenius, T. and E.W. Tristram. English medieval paintings. Ed. Pantheon. Casa editrice Firenze; The Pegassus Press. Paris, 1927

Boulton, M. Anglo-Norman texts. Les enfaunces de Jesu Christ. London, 1985

Byron, G. Cain (Mystery) -in: Complete poetical works. Oxford, 1970

La Chanson de la Croisade Albigeoise (Canzos de la Crozada) Editée et traduite par Eugène Martin-Chabot

t.I, La Chanson de Guillaume de Tudèle. Paris, 1976

Confessio Johannis Tyssyngton de ordine Minorum - in: Fasciculi Zizanorum

Concilium Lateranse III. Cap. XXVII De hereticis. Mansi. t.22

Christian dualist Heresies in the Byzantine World c.650-c.1405. Selected sources translated and annotated by Janet Hamilton and Bernard Hamilton. Manchester & New York.1998

Chronicon Henrici Knighton vel Cnitthon Monachi Leycestrensis. Ed. By J. R. Lumby, D.D. London. vol. I, 1889

Cursor mundi. Ed. by Morris. Four versions: British museum Ms. Cotton Vespasian A.III; Bodlean Ms. Fairfax 14; Gottingen university library Ms. Theol. 107; Trinity College Cambridge Ms.R. 3.8. Seven parts. London, 1874/1961

Dante, A. Il convivo. Trat.II. Cap.VI -in: Dantis Alagherii Opera Omnia II. Leipzig, 1921

Dante, A. La Divina Commedia. Le rime, i versi della vita nuova e le canzoni del convivio. G. Einaudi editore.1954

Dante, A. Vita nuova. Canzone II -in: Dantis Alagherii Opera Omnia II. Leipzig, 1921

De Corbian, P. Prière à la Vierge - in: Anthologie des troubadours XIIme - XIIIme siècles (Edition refondue). Paris, 1974

181

Döllinger, Ign. v. Dokumente vornehmlich zur Geschichte der Valdesier und Katharer herausgegeben. t.II.München, 1890

Dondaine, A. La hiérarchie cathare en Italie - in: Archivum Fratrum Praedicatorum XIX (1949). Roma

Douais, C. La somme des autorités à l'usage des prédicateurs méridionaux au XIIIe siècle. Paris, 1896

Du Cange. Glossarium Mediae et infimae latinitats. t.I, t.V

Duvernoy, J. Le régistre d'inquisition de Jacques Fournier 1318-1325. Toulouse. t.I, 1965

L'Evangile de l'enfance - in: Migne. J.-P. Dictionnaire des apocryphes ou collection des tous les livres apocryphes. Paris. t.I, 1856

Foxe's Christian Martyrs of the World. Westwood. New Jersey, 1985

Great Voices of the Reformation (Anthology). New York, 1952

Gouillard, J. Quatre procès de mystiques à Byzance (vers 960-1143). Inspirations et autorité. Paris, 1978

The Holy Bible, containing the Old and New Testament with the apocryphal books, in the earliest English versions made from the Latin Vulgate by John Wycliffe and his followers. Edited by J. Forshall and Fr. Madden. Vol. IV. Oxford, MDCCCL.

Heresy Trials in the Diocese of Norwich, 1428-31, ed. Norman Tanner. Camden Fourth Series, Vol. 20. London, 1977

L'Homélie d'Epiphane sur l'ensevelissement du Christ (édition par A. Vaillant). Radovi Staroslavenskog instituta. Zagreb, 1958

Ingressus fratris Jonahhis Kynyngham Carmelitae contra Wicclyff - in Fasciculi zizanorum. Ed. by Walter W. Shirley. London, 1858

Kent Heresy Proceedings 1511-12. Edited by N. Tanner. Kent. 1997

Langland, W. The vision of Piers Plowman (A complete edition of the B-text). London, Melbourne, Toronto, New York, 1978. A critical edition of the B-text based on Trinity Colledge Cambridge MS B.15.17 with selected variant readings, an introduction, glosses, and textual and literary commentary by A.V.C. Schmidt.

Langland, W. Piers the Plougman translated into modern English with an introduction by J.F. Goodridge. New York etc.,1959/1977

Langland's Vision of Piers the Plowman (Text B). Ed. by W.W. Skeat. Original series 1869, reprinted 1881,1898, 1930, 1950, 1964, 1971. London, New York, Toronto

Lazar, M. La Légende de «l'Arbre de Paradis» ou «bois de la croix» - poème anglo-normand du XIIIe siècle et sa source latine, d'après le Ms.66. Corpus Christi College. Cambridge.(Inédit). - in: Zeitschrift fur Romanishe Philologie, 1960 (76)

Medieval English Prose for Women. Ed. by B.Millet&J. Wogan-Browne. Oxford, 1990

Meung J. et G. Lorris Le roman de la Rose (mis en français moderne par André Maury). Paris, 1949

Rački Fr., Prilozi za povest bosankih patarena - in Starine 1869

Lollards of Coventry 1486-1522. Edited and translated by Shannon Mc Sheffrey and Norman Tanner. Cambridge university press. 2003

Michel, D. Ayenbite of Inwit or Remorse of Conscience. v.1. Text - R. Morris transcription now newly collated with unique manuscript British Museum Ms Arundel 57 by Pamela Gradon. London, New York, Toronto, 1886/1965

Migne, J.-P. Dictionnaire des apocryphes. t.I,II. Paris, 1856

Milton, J. Areopagitica and other Prose Works by John Milton. London, New York. 1927

Milton, J. On the late massacre on Piedmont - in: Selected Shorter Poems and Prose. London, New York, 1988/9

Milton, J. Paradise lost – in : The Poetical Works of John Milton. London, Oxford University Press, NY, Toronto. 1958.

Milton, J. Paradise regained - in: Complete English Poems. Ed. by Gordon Campbell, 1909/1990

Milton, J. Of Prelatical Episcopacy, and whether it may be deduced from the Apostolic Times by virtue of those Testimonies which are alledg'd to that purpose in some late Treatises; one whereof goes under the Name of James, Archbishop of Armagh. London 1641

Milton, J. The Reason of Church Government urged against Prelaty – in: Milton Prose. Oxford, London, New York, Toronto. 1931/1949

Milton, J. A Treatise of Civil Power in Ecclesiastical Causes. – In: Milton's Prose. Oxford, London, New York, Toronto. 1925/1949

Moreri, Le grand dictionnaire historique ou mélange curieux de l'histoire sacrée et prophane... M.DCC.XL. t.VIII

Muratori. t.II. part.V. Rerum italicarum scriptores (Historia fratris Dulcini heresiarche). ed. Citta di Castello. M.DCCCCVII.

Nouveau Testament. Traduit au XIIIe siècle en langue provençale suivi d'un rituel cathare. Reproduction photolithographique du manuscrit du Lyon publiée avec une noùvelle édition du rituel cathar par L. Clédat. Paris, 1887

Patrologia Graeca, 130

Petrarca, Fr. Le Rime del Petrarca. Tomo secondo. Firenze. M.DCCCXXXII

Plotin. Ennéades. Paris. t.I, 1924

De Rougemont, D. L'amour et l'Occident. Paris, 1939/1970

Sacconi, R. O.P. Summa de catharis par Fr. Sanjek O.P. - in: Archivum fratrum praedicatorum. vol. XLIV. Roma, 1974

Salve Burce. Supra stella - in: Dokumente vornehmlich zur Geschichte der Valdesier und Katharer herausgegeben von Ign. v. Döllinger. Munchen, 1890

Sciptorum veterum (quorum pars magna nunc primum e MSS. Codibus in lucem prodit) qui Ecclesiae Rom. Errores & Abusus detegunt & damnant necessitatem que Reformationis urgent. Londini MDCXC

Tanner, T. Heresy Trials in the Diocese of Norwich, 1428-31. London,1977

Tanner, N.(Ed.) Kent Heresy Proceedings 1511-12. Kent Archeological Society. 1997

Tischendorf, K. Evangelia apocrypha. Leipzig, 1852

Thomae Aquinatis Summa Theologica. Romae. Ex Typographia Forzani et S. M DCCCXCIV. Pars Tertia, Quaestio LII, Articulus VIII

Lou tresor dou felibrige. Dictionnaire Provençal-Français. t.I, Paris, 1932

Les troubadours (anthologie bilingue). Paris, 1971

Tyndale, W. An Exposition upon the V,VI, VII Chapters of Matthew, Antwerp, 1533

Tyndale, W. Doctrinal Treatises and Introduction to Different Portions of the Holy Scriptures by William Tyndale, martyr, 1536. Cambridge. M.DCCC.XLVIII

Tyndale, W. The Independent Works of William Tyndale. An answer vnto sir Thomas More. Dialogue. Washington, 2000

Tyndale, W. The Obedience of a Christian Man. London. 2001

Tyndale, W. The Parable of the Wicked Mammon. Antwerp.1528

La vie de M. Jean VVicleff avec la copie de la lettre que le Pape envoya au Roy d'Angleterre pour persécuter ledit VVicleff, M.D.LXV

(de) Voragine, J. La légende dorée. Traduite de latin par T. de Wyzeva. Paris, 1920

Wycliff, J. The Anticrist labour to destroy the holy Writ -in: Great voices of the Reformation (anthology). New York, 1952

Wyclif, J. De compositione hominis. London, 1884

Wyclif, J. Miscellanea Philosophica. vol.II. London. 1905

Wyclif, J. Johannis Wyclif Operis evangelici (lib.III and IV). London, 1896

Wyclif, J. Opus evangelicum. t.I, II. London, 1895

Wycliffe, J. Summae in theologia (Tractatus tertius). De civile domino (Liber primus). London, MDCCCXXXV

Wyclif, J. Tractatus de Benedicta Incarnatione. London, 1886

Wycliffite Manuscript. The New Testament. England, 1400-1450. Ed. by Bridwell library and Octavo edition. CD.1999

Zend Avesta. Ed. et traduct. Darmsteter, J. t.I. Paris, 1892

Secondary works

Cyrillics

Алексиев, М.П., Из истории английской литературы (Видение о Петре Пахаре). Москва-Ленинград, 1960

Ангелов, Д. Богомилството. София, 1993

Ангелов, Д. Богомилы и катары - в: Славянские культуры и Балканы. т.I. София, 1978, с.85

Ангелов, Д. Българинът в средновековието (светоглед, идеология, душевност). Варна, 1985

Ангелов, Д. История на Византия. I част. София, 1976

Арнаудов, М. Фолклор от Еленско. Сбну XXVII

Богданов, Б. Орфей и древната митология на Балканите. София, 1991

Бърлиева, Сл. Агиографските творби за св.св. Кирил и Методий в Legenda Aurea на Яков Ворагински - в: Кирило-Методиевски студии. Книга 11/1998

Бояджиев, Ц. Философия на европейското средновековие. София,1994

Василев, Г. Български богомилски и апокрифни представи в английската средновековна култура. София, 2001

Василиев, А. Ермении. Технология и иконография. София, 1976

Василиев, А. Социални и патриотични мотиви в старото българско изкуство. София, 1973

Веселовский, Ал. Калики перехожие и богомильские странники - във: Вестникъ Европы. II, 1872

Веселовский, Ал. Соломонъ и Китоврасъ. Санкт-Петербургъ, 1872

Вълчанов, Сл. Отражения на старозаветната апокрифна традиция в средновековната българска култура - в: Годишник на Духовната академия «Св. Климент Охридски». т.XXVIII (LIV),3. София, 1978/1979

Въргов, Хр. Революционери. София, 1924

Галаховъ, А.Исторiя русской словестности - дрѣвной и новой. т.1. Санктъ Петербургъ, 1880

Гечев, Ст. Предговор за Палатинската антология и за други древни неща - в: Палатинска антология. София, 1994/1996

Гечевъ, Ст. Къмъ въпроса за славянския физиологъ. София,1938

Гечева, Кр. Богомилството (Библиография). София, 1997

Георгиева, Ив. Българска народна митология. София, 1983

Гинчев, Ц. По няколко думи. София, 1988

Голенищев-Кутузов, И. Средновековая латинская литература Италии. Москва, 1972

185

Елдъров, Г. Св.Франциск и исляма -in: в.Абагар. бр.1, януари 1997

Жюсеранъ, Ж. Исторія англійскаго народа въ его литературѣ. С. Петербургъ, 1898

Зайцев, В. Богомильское движение и общественная жизнь Северной Италии эпохи Дуеченто. Минск, 1967

Зайферт, Л. Световните революционери (от поп Богомил през Хус до Ленин). София, 1994

Иванов, Й. Българските народни песни. София, 1959

Иванов, Й. ф.52. опис 1.арх. ед.61. Централна библиотека на БАН

Илчев, Ст. Речник на личните и фамилните имена у българите. София, 1969

Иречек, К. История на българите (под редакцията на Петър Петров). София, 1999

Йоан-Павел II. Да си признаем греховете. в. Абагар. год.VIII, бр.10 (93), октомври 1999

Йоан-Павел II, Енциклика «Славянските апостоли» - в: Кирил и Методий (Благовестие и екуменизъм). София, 1996

Карсавинъ Л. Очерки религиозной жизни в Италіи XII-XIII вѣковъ. Ст.- Петербургъ, 1912

Кенанов, Д. Йордан Иванов и «Тайната книга» на богомилите - в: Известия на Исторически музей.Кюстендил. т.IV, 1992

Кирило-методиевска енциклопедия. I, 1985

Клибанов, А. Богомилството като световно явление (разговор с В.Велчев и К. Мечев)- в: сп.Проблеми на културата, 1/1981

Кодов, Хр. Бележки към Охридски - в: Климент. Събрани съчинения. т.II. София, 1977

Кръстанов, Тр., А.-М. Тотоманова, И. Добрев. Ватикански палимпсест. София, 1997

Кръстев, К. Българският принос в Боянските стенописи - в: сп. Изкуство, 4-5/1965

Лавров, П. Материалы по истории возникновения древнейшей славянской письменности. Ленинград, 1930

Лазаров, Ст. Проучвания върху културата на богомили и катари: театър и музика (Автореферат на дисертация). София, 1989

Лурье, А. Коментарии к Послание Геннадия к Йоасафу - в: Памятники литературы древней Руси (вторая половина XV века). Москва, 1982

Милтенова, А. Бележки в: Българската литература и книжнина през XIII век. София, 1987

Милтенова, А. Текстологически наблюдения върху два апокрифа (Апокрифен цикъл за кръстното дърво, приписван на Григорий

Богослов и апокрифа за Адам и Ева) – в: Старобългарска литература, кн.11/1982

Мишев, Д. България в миналото. София, 1918

Николов, Й. Ересите в Западна Европа XII-XIII век (Социалнополитически проблеми). София, 1989,

Осокинъ, Н. Исторія Альбигойцев до кончины папы Иннокентія III. Казань. т.I, 1869

Панайотов, В. Сведения за богомилството в «Писмото до Панко на Атанасий Йерусалимски» - в: Старобългаристика, бр.3/1987

Пеев, П. Презвитер Еремия (автореферат за присъждане на научна степен кандидат на филологическите науки). Шумен, 1991

Петканова, Д. Апокрифната литература и личното творчество на старобългарските писатели - в: Старобългаристика, 3/1981.

Петканова, Д. Апокрифни мотиви в творчеството на Климент Охридски - в: Кирило-Методиевски студии. кн.8. София, 1991

Петканова, Д. Към въпроса за връзката на фолклора с богомилството. Известия на Иститута за българска литература.6. София.1958

Старобългарска литература. Енциклопедичен речник. Съст. Донка Петканова. София, 1992

Петканова, Д. Бележки в: Стара българска литература.1 Апокрифи. София, 1982

Православная богословская энциклопедия. т.VI. Санктъ Петербургъ,1905

Примов, Б. Бугрите (книга за поп Богомил и неговите последователи). София, 1970

Примов, Б. Българското народностно име в Западна Европа във връзка с богомилите - в: Известия на Института за българска история. София, 1956

Полный православный богословскій энциклопедическій словарь. Изд. П.П. Сойкина.т.II (s.l.;s.a.).

Попов Г. и Кр. Станчев. Климент Охридски. София, 1988

Радченко К. Этюды по богомильству. ИОРЯС. т.XV. СПб, 1910

Рѣчникъ на светото писаніе. Цариградъ, 1884

Рънсиман, Ст. История на първото българско царство. София, 1993

Сапрыкин,Юл. Взгляды Джона Уиклифа на общность имущества и равенства - в: Средные века 34. Москва, 1971

Соколовъ, М. Материалы и замѣтки по старинной славянской литературе. выпуск 1. Москва, 1888

Сперанскій, М.Славянскія апокрифическія евангелія (общий обзоръ). Москва, 1895

Софийски, Ст. Българската църква. София, 1932

Стоилов, А. Легендата за грешна майка - в: Българска сбирка. год.VIII, 1901

Тодоров, Е. Древнотракийското наследство в българския фолклор. София, 1972

Фол, Ал. Тракийският орфизъм. София, 1986

Франко, I. Передмова - в: Апокріфі і легенди з украінских рукописів.II. Львів. 1899

Хаджикосев, С. Към изворите на новоевропейската поезия - в: Снегът зеленина сънува. София, 1990

Шишманов, И. Литературна история на Възраждането в Италия. София, 1934

Шурбанов, А. Светотворчеството на Милтън. – In: Изгубеният рай. София, 1981

Latin

Aers, D. Chaucer, Langland and the creative imagination, Boston and Nenley, 1980

Abels, R. and E. Harrison The participation of Women in the Languedocien Catharism - in: Medieval Studies. t.41, Toronto

Ancelet-Hustache, J. Maître Eckhart et la mystique rhénane. Paris, 1971

Aston, M. A. Lollardy and Sedition 1381-1431. – Past and Present, apr. 1960

Aston, M. A. Lollards and Reformers (Images and Literacy in Late Medieval Religion). Hambledon Press, 1894

Autran, Ch. Mithra, Zoroastre et la préhistoire aryenne du christianisme, Paris, 1935

Baggiolini, C. Dolcino e i patareni. Novara, 1837

Baugh, A. and K. Malone - in: A literary history of England. Vol. I. The Middle Ages (the Old English period to1100). London and Henley, 1985

Bayet, M.C. L'Empire Byzantin - in: Histoire générale du IVe siècle à nos jours (sous la direction de M.M. E. Lavisse et A. Rambaud). Paris. t.I (Les origines 395-1095). Paris, 1893

Biller, P. Women and texts in Languedocian Catharism - in: Women, the Book and the Godly. Selected proceedings of St Hilda's conference. vol.I, 1993.First published 1995. Cambridge.

Bompiani, Dictionnaire des oeuvres. Paris, 1952

Borst, A. Les Cathares. Paris, 1978

De Beausobre, M. Histoire critique du Manichée e du Manichéisme. Amsterdam. MDCCXXXIV

Brenon, A. Les archipels cathares. Dissidence chrétienne dans l'Europe médievale. Cahors. 2000

Brenon, A. Le catharisme des montagnes (à la recherche d'un catharisme populaire) -in: Heresis 11/1988

Brenon, A. Localisation des manuscripts vaudois. Centro studi piemontesi. Torino. 1978

Brockett, L.P. The Bogomils of Bulgaria and Bosnia (The Early Protestants of the East. An Attempt to Restore Some Lost Leaves of Protestants History). Philadelphia, 1879

Bruffaut, R. Les troubadours et les sentiments romanesques. Paris, 1945

The Cambridge History of English literature. vol.I (from the beginnings to the cycles of romances). Cambridge, 1932

The Cambridge History of English and American literature in 18 volumes (1907-1921). Vol.II. The End of the Middle Ages

Cantu, C. Les hérétiques d'Italie - discours historique de César Cantu (Les précurseurs de la Réforme). Paris, 1869

The Catholic Encyclopedia, Robert Appleton Company Volume II. 1907

Daniell, David. William Tyndale. A Biography. New Haven&London, 2001

Deanesly, M.A. The Lollard Bible (and other medieval biblical versions). Cambridge, 1920/1966

Delaruelle, E.L'état actuel des études sur le catharisme - in: Cahiers de Fanjeaux 3. Toulouse, 1986

Delmaire, B. Un sermon arrageois sur le «bougres» du Nord de la France (vers 1200) - in: Heresis N17/1991

Doane, A. The Saxon Genesis (An edition of the West Saxon

Genesis B and the Old Saxon Vatican Genesis). The University Wisconsin Press, 1991

Dondaine, A. La hiérarchie cathare en Italie - in: Archivum Fratrum Praedic. XX (1950)

Dondaine, A.Un traité néomanicheen du XIII siècle, Le liber de duobus principiis. Rome, 1939

Drout, M. Piers's Good Vill: Langland's politics of Reform and Inheritance in the C-text - in: Social Practice in the Middle Ages. Chicago, 1996

Džonov, B. Le modèle de confession chez les Bogomiles et les Cathares - in: Paleobulgarica 4/1980

Duvernoy, Jean L'acception «haereticus» (iretge) – in : The Concept of Heresy in the Middle Ages. Paris-La Haye. I. 1967-1077

Duvernoy, Jean Les origines du movement Vaudois. – In: Heresis N13 et 14. 1990

Eames, E. English Medieval Tiles. London, 1985

Enciclopedia Italiana. Roma MCMXXXXV-XLII. vol.XXVII. s.v. Franceschi. tav. LVIII

Encyclopaedia Britannica vol.3. 1970

Enev, M. The Apocalypse. Sofia, 1996

Fines, J. Heresy Trials in the Diocese of Coventry and Lichifield, 1511-12. - in: Journal of Ecclesiastical History. vol.14, 1963

Forsyth, N. The Satanic Epic. Princeton University Press. 2003

Funk&Wagnalls. New Standart Dictionary of the English Language. New York-London, 1933

Füssly, J. K. Neue und unparteische Kirchen und Ketzerhistorien der mittler Zeit. T. 1-3. Frankfurt am Main etc. 1770-1774. Quoted according to the bibilography: Гечева, Кр. Богомилството. Библиография. Sofia, 1997.

Gairdner, J. Lollardy and Reformation. v.I., London.1908

Gaster, M. Ilchester Lectures on Greeko-Slavonic Literature and its Relation to the Folklore of Europe During the Middle Ages. London, 1887

Gillet, L. Dante. Paris, 1941

Le Goff, Jacques. La naissance du Purgatoire. Paris, 1981

Goodridge, F. in: Piers the Plougman translated into modern English with an introduction and notes by J.F. Goodridge. New York. etc.,1959/1977

Grand Larousee encyclopédique. Paris. t.VIII, 1963

Gray, M. A Chronology of English literature (from Anglo-Saxon times to present day). Ed. Longman and York Press, 1989

Guéorguiev, St. Les Bogomiles et Presbiter Kosma. Lausanne, 1920

Gui, B. Manuel de l'inquisiteur, édité et traduit par G. Molat. Paris. t.I, 1926

Giuraud, J. Cartulaire de Notre Dame de Prouilles, précédé d'une étude sur Albigéisme languédocien au XIIe et XIIIe siècles. t. 1-2. Paris, 1907

Gouillard J., in Quatre procès de mystiques à Byzance. IV. Les évêques «bogomiles» de Cappadoce. Paris: Institut des études Byzantines,74)

Gurteen, S. H. The Epic of the Fall of Man (A comparative study of Caedmon, Dante, and Milton). New York, 1896

Guzelev, V. The Bulgarian version of the Apocalypse - the 'Secret book' of the Bogomils or John's Gospel - in: The Apocalypse. Sofia, 1996

Hamilton, B. and Janet Hamilton. Christian dualist Heresies in the Byzantine World, C.650-c.1450 (Manchester Medieval Studies). Manchester University Press, 1998

Hamilton, B. Wisdom from the East: the Reception by the Cathars of Eastern dualist Texts. – In: Heresy and literacy. Cambridge, 1994/1996

Hargreaves, H. The Marginal Glosses to the Wycliffite New Testament. Studia Neophilologica (Upsalla), 33, 1961

Haskins, Ch. The Renaissance of the Twelfth Century. Cambridge (Mass.), 1927

Hearnshow, F. Some great political idealists of the Christian era. London, Bombay, Sidney (s. a.)

Hotchkiss, V. Outlawed English - in: Formatting the Word of God. Ed. by V. Hotchkiss and Ch. Ryrie. Dallas, 1998

Hristova, R. The Influence of Ancient Unofficial Religious Doctrines on William Blake's Art and Writings. Paper presented on 34th annual conference of British Society for Eighteenth-Century Studies (BSECS), 6-8 January 2005, St. Hugh's College, Oxford.

Hudson, A. 'Laicus literatus': the paradoxe of Lollardy - in: Heresy and literacy, 1000-1530. Ed. by P. Biller and A. Hudson. Cambridge, 1994/1996

Hudson, A. Lollards and their books. London, 1985

Hudson, A. Selections from English Wycliffite Writings. CUP. London, New York, Melbourne.1978

Hupe, H. The filiation and the text of the Mss. - in: Cursor Mundi. part VII

Jackson, A. Zoroaster, the Prophet of Ancient Iran. New York, 1898/1926

Jeanroy, A. Avant-propos - in: Anthologie des troubadours XIIme - XIIIme siècles. Edition refondue. Paris, 1974

James, M.R. Rare medieval tiles and their story - in: The Burlington Magazine for Connoiseurs. London. vol. XLII, Jan.-Jun.1923

Jolliot, A. Les communautés vaudoises des Hautes Vallées alpines aux XVe et XVIe siècles. Fédération historique du Languédoc méditerranéen et du Roussillon. XLIVe Congrès (Privas, 22-23 mai 1971). Université Paul Valéry – Montpellier. 1972

Jorgenson, J. The Debate Over the Patristic Texts on Purgatory at the Council of Ferrara-Florence, 1438 - in: St. Wladimir's theological Quarterly. New York 4/1986

Jusserand, J.J. L'épopée mystique de William Langland. Paris, 1893

Knowles, M.D. et D.Obolenski Nouvelle histoire de l'Eglise.v.2 Le moyen âge. Paris, 1968

Kurth, B. Milton and Christian Heroism. Berkeley and Los Angeles. 1959

Lagarde, G. La naissance de l'esprit laïque au déclin du Moyen âge. Wien, 1934

Lambert, Malcolm. The Cathars. Oxford&Malden(USA),1998

Lambert,M. Medieval Heresy (Popular movements from the Gregorian Reform to the Reformation).Oxford, 1977/1992

Lea, Ch. A history of the inquisition of the Middle Ages. vol. I, II. London, 1888

Legouis, E. A History of English Literature. 1.The Middle Ages and the Renaissance. Modern Times by L. Cazamian. Revised edition. London. 1957

Le Roy Ladurie, E. Montaillou, village occitan de 1294 a 1324, Paris, 1975/1982

Life and times of John Wycliffe (the morning star of the Reformation). London, 1884

Lombard, A. Pauliciens, Bulgares et Bons-hommes en Orient et Occident (Etude sur quelques sectes du Moyen âge). Genève et Bâle, Paris, 1879

Loos, M. Dualist heresy in the Middle Ages. Praha, 1974

Mâle, E. L'art religieux du XIIIe siècle en France (étude de l'iconographie du Moyen âge et sur ses sources d'inspiration). Paris, 1919

Maury, A. Essai sur le legendes pieuses du Moyen-âge. Paris, 1843

McSheffrey, Sh. Literacy and the gender gap in the late Middle ages: women and reading in Lollard communities - in: Women, the Book and the Godly. volume I. Cambridge, 1995

McSheffrey, Sh. Women and Lollardy: a reassessment - in: Canadian journal of History 26(1991)

Manly, J. Piers the Plowman and its sequence - in: The Cambridge history of English literature. vol.II. The end of the Middle Ages. Cambridge,1932

Manselli, R. Dolore e morte nella esperienza religiosa catara - in: Todi. Presso di l'Academia Tudertina, 1967

Merrifield, J. The Perfect Heretics (Cathars and Catharism). With Contributions from Yves Rouquette, Michel Roquebert and Anne Brenon. Lyme Regis, 1995

Mincoff, M. A History of English Literature. Part I: From the Beginnings to 1700. Sofia, 1970

Monnier, J. La descente aux enfers. Paris, 1904

Morghen, R. Problèmes sur l'origine de l'hérésie au Moyen âge - in: Revue historique. 90e année. tome CCXXXVI, 1966

Moore, R. The Origins of the European Dissent. New York, 1977/85

Morris, R. Preface, notes and glossary - in Cursor mundi. Part VI

Nauèrt, G. Jr. Editor's preface in: Lollard themes in the Reformation theology of William Tyndale (Sixteenth Century Essays&Studies, vol.6), 1986

Naumov, Al. Apocryfy w systemie literatury cerkiewnos³owianskiej. Wroc³aw. Warszawa. Kraków. Gdansk.1976

Nelli, R. Contribution à l'Iconographie du Catharisme: La Croix Cathare - in: Revue d'ethnographie méridionale, t.XVI, 26-e année. N3, automne 1963

Nelli, R. Dictionnaire des hérésies méridionales et mouvements hétérodoxes, apparus dans li Nidi de la France depuis l'établissement du Christianisme. Toulouse, 1968

Nelli, R. Préface vers J. Ivanov - Livres et légendes bogomiles (aux sources du Catharisme). Paris, 1976

Nelli, R. Le phénomène cathare (perspectives philosophiques et morales). Toulouse, 1988

Nelli, R. La vie quotidienne des Cathares du Languedoc au XIIIe siècle. Paris. 1969.

Niel, F. Albigeois et cathares. Paris, 1959

Nelson, D. Society, theodicy and the origins of medieval heresy - in: Schism, heresy and religious protest. Cambridge, 1972

Nuttall, A. The Alternative Trinity: Gnostic Heresy in Marlowe, Milton and Blake. Oxford, 1998

Obolensky, D. The Bogomils (A Study in Balkan-Neo-manichaeism). Cambridge, 1948

Obolensky,D. Papas Nicetas: A Byzantine dualist in the Land of the Cathars - in Harvard Ukrainian Studies Okeans. v.VII, 1983

Olivieri, D. Dizionario etimologico italiano (concordato coi dialetti, le lingue straniere e la topo-onomastica).Milano, 1953

Partridge, E. A short etymological dictionary of modern English. London, 1958/1966

Onions, T. The Oxford dictionary of English etymology. At Clarendon press, 1966

The Oxford English Dictionary. I. Oxford, At the Clarendon Press, 1933

Paterson, L. Chaucer and the subject of history. London, 1991

du Perron, A. Zend-Avesta, ouvrage de Zoroastre. Paris, MDCC.LXXI. t.II

Pelikan, Y. with Valerie R. Hotchkiss and David Price. Yale University Press, New Haven and London, Bridwell Library, SMU, Dallas

Planiscig, L. Luca della Robia. Zweite Auflage.Wien, 1940

Prati, A. Vocabulario etimologico italiano. Torino,1951

Poole, R. Wycliffe and movements for reform. New York, 1978 (reprint of the 1889 ed.)

Puech, H. -Ch. Le Manichéisme (Son fondateur. Sa doctrine). Paris, 1949

Puech, H. A. Vaillant. Le traité contre les Bogomiles de Cosmas le Prêtre. Paris, 1945

Renwick, W.L., H. Orton, The beginnings of English literature to Skelton 1509. London. v.1, 1939/1952

Resnicov, S. - The cultural history of a democratic proverb - in: Journal of English and German philology, 3/1937

Robinson, F. Commentary. – In: Wycliffite Manuscript. The New Testament. England, 1400-1450. Ed. by Bridwell library (Dallas) and Octavo corporation.CD.1999

Rosén, T. The Slavonic Translation of the Apocryphal Infancy Gospel of Thomas. Uppsala, 1997

(Le) Robert, Dictionaire de la langue française. Paris. t.VII, 1985

Rousseau, J.-J. Discours sur l'origine et les fondements de l'inégalité parmi les hommes. Paris, 1903

Roubaud, J. Introduction à Les troubadours (anthologie bilingue) Paris, 1971

Runciman, St. Bogomil and Jeremiah - в: Сборник в памет на проф. Петър Ников. София, 1940

Schmidt, C. Histoire et doctrine de la secte des cathares ou albigeois. t.I,II. Paris-Genève, 1849

Seifert, L. Die Welte revolutionäre. Von Bogomil über Huss zu Lenin. Wien. 1931

Skeat, W. An etymological dictionary of the English language. Oxford, 1956 (reproducing the edition of 1879-1882)

Smeeton, D.D. Lollard themes in the Reformation theology of William Tyndale (Sixteenth Century Essays&Studies, vol.6), 1986

Solovjev, A. Svedocanstva pravoslavnih izvora o bogomilstvu na Balkanu - in: Godisnjak istorikog drustva Bosne i Hercegovine. godina V. Sarajevo,1953

Stoyanov, Yu. The Hidden tradition in Europe (The secret history of the Medieval Christian Heresy). Penguin books/Arkana, 1994

Summers, W. The Lollards of Chiltern Hills. London, 1906

Summers, W. Our Lollard Ancestors. London. 1904

Tischendorf, K Nota -in: Evangelia apocrypha. Leipzig, 1852

Thomov, T. Les appellations de «bogomiles» et de «Bulgares» et leur variantes et équivalents en Orient et Occident - in: Etudes Balkaniques N1/1973

Thomson, Cl. ch.XVI Later transition English I.Legendaries and Chroniclers - in: Cambridge history of English literature. v.II. Cambridge, 1933

Thomson, J. The Later Lollards 1414-1520. Oxford University Press, 1965

Thode, M. Saint François d'Assise et les origines de l'Art de la Renaissance. Paris, 1885

Thouzellier, Chr. Hérésie et hérétiques (Vaudois, Cathares, Patarins, Albigeois). Roma, 1969

Vaillant, A. Préface - in: L'Homélie d'Epiphane sur l'ensevelissement du Christ, Radovi Staroslavenskog instituta. Zagreb, 1958

Vattier, V. John Wyiclff (sa vie-ses oeuvres-sa doctrine). Paris, 1886

Venckeleer, T. Un recueil cathare: le manuscript A.6.10 de Dublin. Une apologie. – In: Revue Belge de Philologie et d'Histoire. t.38. 1960, pp. 815-834; Une Glose sur le Pater. – In: Revue Belge de Philologie et d'Histoire. t. 39. 1961, pp. 759-762

Webster's Third International Dictionary. Massachusets, 1961

Weis, R. The Yellow Cross. The Story of the Last Cathars'Rebellion against the Inquisition 1290-1329. New York. 2002

White, H. Langland, Milton and felix culpa. – In: The Review of English Studies. 1994. V. 45, No. 1

Wilks, M. Reformatio regni: Wyclif and Hus as leaders of religious protest movements - in: Schism, heresy and religious protest. Cambridge, 1972

de Wyzeva, T. Préface -in: La légende dorée. Paris, 1920

Workman, H. John Wycliff (a study of the English medieval church). Oxford, 1926

Index

178, 181, 182, 194
- apostles of Christ, 6, 42, 63, 138
- Christ Ploughman,120, 121, 125, 126, 127
- Christ teaches Peter to plough, 122, 150
- harrowing the hell, 12, 13, 47, 51n, 13, 112, 113, 113n, 116, 117, 120, 129, 130, 158, 159, 162

Comnena, Ana, 7, 7n

(De) **Corbian, P. Prière à la Vierge**, 50, 177

Cross
- negation of the cross, 21, 22, 39, 76, 78, 100, 138, 139, 140
- readopting the cross, 92, 106, 119

Cyril and Methodius, 27n, 33, 64, 78, 84
- Cyrillo-Methodian, 64, 66, 77, 84, 85, 86, 88, 109n, 169

Dante, 30, 60, 61n, 131, 131n, 146, 150, 150n, 151, 166
- Il Convivio, 156, 181
- De Monarchia, 146
- La Divina Commedia, 147, 147n, 151n, 177, 181
- Vita nuova, 177

David, Daniell, 8, 10, 89, 87
- William Tyndale. A Biography, 8n, 87, 87n, 91n, 108, 185

Deanesly, Margaret, 31, 64
- The Lollard Bible, 24n, 30, 32n, 64n, 76, 77, 77n, 185

Döllinger, Ignatz von, 5, 6, 180
- Dokumente vornehmlich zur Geschichte der Valdesier und Katharer herausgegeben, 5n, 6n, 13, 20n, 45, 52, 67, 69, 72, 73, 74, 75, 94, 97, 97n, 98, 105, 118n, 130n, 141n, 151n, 156n, 168n, 171n, 172n,

Dominic d'Osma, 55
- Dominican inquisition, 42, 46, 176

Donatio Costantini, 134, 139, 145, 145n, 146, 149, 150, 151n

Dualist myths
- the fall of Lucifer and his angels, 13, 14, 15, 16, 16n, 43, 57, 59, 70, 112, 116, 117, 120, 124, 132, 153, 160,
- the secondary creation of Satan, 49, 152, 154
- incarnation of the souls in the human body, 49, 71
- the Devil as impious steward of this world, 17, 70, 109

Dualist practice
- baptism in Saint Spirit, 70, 80, 80n, 94, 94n, 98, 110, 110n, 141, 168
- condemnation of bloodshed, 15, 15n, 27
- official Church is seen as a community of Herod, or of the Anti-Christ, 15, 20, 102
- Church buildings are thought of as synagogues, crossroad and wastelands, 15, 20, 102, 140
- direct confession to God, 6, 14, 19, 73, 95, 97
- negation of hell and purgatory, 15, 19, 22, 102, 104, 105, 106, 111, 170, 177
- negation of icons, 15, 16, 16n, 22, 76, 95, 96, 104, 137, 138, 139, 140, 141 (stokks and stonys)137
- negation of liturgies, 21, 75
- negation of legal authority and oath-taking, 15, 19, 74, 75, 86n
- negation of liturgy, 75, 96, 102, 139, 140
- negation of transubstantiation, 15, 21, 25n, 71, 72, 100, 101, 101n, 111

To be continued... instead of a summary

The summary of the book may begin with the following words: We documented, that since the 12th century the presence of dualist apocrypha in England is clearly denoted, right until the 17th (i.e. in the works of John Milton), and that there was an infusion of a potent cultural and philosophical trends in English culture, trends, which were founded on the basis of dualist Bogomil-Cathar heresy. The Lollards with their iconography, the reformers John Wycliffe and William Tyndale, the poet William Langland, the apocryphal volume *Cursor mundi*, as well as the Anglo-Norman variants of *The Legend of the Tree of the Cross* and *Les enfaunces de Jesus Christ*, are all profoundly keen to the word in John Milton's great poems *Paradise Lost* and *Paradise Regained*. All they converge within this time span, in a rich blend of ideas and strongly perceptible imagery or cognitive concepts.

Yes, we are faced with a chain of dualist events, works and outstanding individuals who frequently reach the pinnacles in English culture. At this moment is important to glance forward, facing new essential surprises in the field of our scholarly exploits. Dear readers, we entered in a very engaging domain, where explaining one event immediately leads to discovering another. These links of the events are marked by their own temper, they are true revelations with an impressive connectivity. As usual, history outdoes fiction. Now we are meeting a new episode of the process of the dualist philosophy's transfer in the English isle. This time the action takes place in the 18th century and we are introducing the most interesting personality of Johan Heinrich Fussli, born to an artist's family in Zurich, Switzerland, 1741.

In England he was known as Fuseli or Fussly. Under his father guidance he tried to become a preacher, but confronted by a powerful magistrate moved to London, where he earned living as translator and after seven years of study in Italy, as a painter. As an artist he won European fame and attracted the interest of Göthe, also became a close friend of Blake. Currently Fuseli is considered as a precursory of the symbolists and even of the surrealists. Died in 1825 after serving as a professor of painting at the Royal Academy in London. Created 200 paintings, presently in the best European museums and the Tate Gallery in London has an entire collection of his oeuvre.

Why are we focusing on this man? Because his deeds lead to answers of a recently pressed question by A.Nuttall: What is so particular about the philosophy of William Blake? While labeling generally his universe as a "Gnostic heresy", Nuttall asks: "By what means could have Blake known of Gnosticism?"[1] However we see in the poet's philosophy a discernible trace of the dualist heresy and now we introduce an initial answer to the evolving of his thinking. Of course the poet underwent a number of other influences. Blake mentioned six times the name of the Swedish mystic Swedenborg in *The marriage of Heaven and Hell*, yet the imported dualist features which we intend to unveil are also present in this work.

While claiming that John Milton depicted the Satan with a greater craft, William Blake emphasized the dualist fabric by a specific mention of the fundamental Bogomil-Cathar myth about expelling Lucifer from heaven (plate 5): "And the original Archangel or possessor of the command of the heavenly host, is call'd the Devil or Satan and his children are call'd Sin & Death"[2]. Our forthcoming answer will gain additional supportive facts and will be enriched consequently.

For example William Blake creates a particular image of Jesus – as *The Good Farmer* (1780-5), "where Jesus advises people how to sow, plough and reap the wheat from which they will produce bread"[3]. The prevailing till now interpretation was that this group of seven sketches images "all appear to illustrate the Parable of the Wheat and the Tares from St. Matthew's Gospel". But their imagery and sens seem to be much closer to the beloved to Bogomils and Cathars apocrypha *Infancy Gospel* (see more in Chapter VI), and the author Rumyana Hristova quite correctly associates them with "ancient unofficial religious doctrines".

And now we discover the conveyance, the medium... It also happened that Blake's personal and highly valued friend[4] Henry Fuseli defended in Bern, Switzerland during 1761 a most unusual doctoral thesis *Dissertatio de fanaticis seculo XII in Anglia repertis* (Bernae, MDCCLXI). The dissertation was written in Latin, discussed the migration and the expansion of the middle ages heresies as Waldensians, Albigenses, Patarenes, Publicans

---

[1] Nuttall, A. The Alternative Trinity. Gnostic Heresy in Marlowe, Milton, and Blake. Oxford, 1998, p.200. This scholar associates the eccentricity of Blake's behavior with the Begards, but does not elaborate on a specific conceptual connection (p. 194).

[2] The Complete Writings of William Blake (With All the Variant Readings. Edited by Geoffrey Keynes). London, New York, 1957, p.150. An abridged version of this topic we see in plate 24: „Note: This Angel, who is now become a Devil..." (A Memorable Fancy), p.158

[3] Hristova, R. The Influence of Ancient Unofficial Religious Doctrines on William Blake's Art and Writings. Paper presented on 34th annual conference of British Society for Eighteenth-Century Studies (BSECS), 6-8 January 2005, St. Hugh's College, Oxford.

[4] Blake praised his friendship with Fuseli with the following words: "The only man that e'er I knew / who did not make me almost spew". Also it is well known that Fuseli stimulated Blake's creative environment.

in England during the twelfth century. In addition Fuseli published three volumes in German about the middle ages heresies as well.[1]

He described personally his work as impartial (unparteishe) history of the middle age church and heresies. Now we claim with a greater credibility that this academically bona fide established authority on Bogomil-Cathar infusion in England has directly impacted Blake and led him to sharing to considerable degree the heretics'philosophy. Consequently we identified Fuseli as a highly motivated contributor to the Bogomil-Cathar philosophy in England during 18th-19th century and as a cordial friend of William Blake's. The spiritual friendship of the both creators supported the dualist doctrine and it is heightened by the fact that Fuseli nursed intense spiritual interest for the greatest dualist epic of John Milton - the *Paradise Lost*. Indeed he created forty illustrations for the poem, named his gallery in London after Milton and painted "Milton When a Youth".[2]

After that far manifesting the spiritual incentive of Fuseli, we may expect that such true, academically and scholarly documented emissary of the Bogomil-Cathar morphism, positively would have extended a further close soul communion with the prominent intellectuals in Switzerland, England and Germany. This would be a new testimony to the latest generation wave of Bogomil-Cathar hermeticism revived in England by the central European artist. So all these findings and events are calling for further research – to be continued....Before us, a book published by the American Baptist historian Dr. L.P. Brocket declared in 1879 a vital connection between the Bogomil-Cathar teachings and the Reformation spawn protestants. The book title speaks stronger then any *comments: The Bogomils of Bulgaria and Bosnia (The Early Protestants of the East) – an attempt to restore some lost leaves of protestant history*[3]. This unprecedented documentary of a vital bond between the Middle Ages Balkan Bogomils and the late 1800 American Protestants noted by a prominent Baptist historian deserves the greatest attention possible. He is the first American to our knowledge to link the medieval heretics to the solid ground the New World uncompromising Protestants, relieved from the Mary's and saints' cults and worshiping solely Christ.

---

[1] Füssly, J. K. Neue und unparteische Kirchen und Ketzerhistorien der mittler Zeit. T. 1-3. Frankfurt am Main etc. 1770-1774. Quoted according to the bibilography: Гечева, Кр. Богомилството. Библиография. Sofia, 1997.

[2] The French title is longer and sounds more romantic: "Milton adolescent, contemplé par une dame italienne."

[3] Brockett, L. P. The Bogomils of Bulgaria and Bosnia (The Early Protestants of the East). Philadelphia: American Baptist Publication Society, 1879.

Contents

Georgi Vasilev

**Dualist ideas in the English
Pre-Reformation and Reformation**

(Bogomil-Cathar influence on Wycliffe,
Langland, Tyndale and Milton)

www.cl.bas.bg/Balkan-Studies/bogomilism/index.html;
www.geocities.com/bogomil1bg
E-mail: aba1@bulgaria.com

• • •

Edited by: Bistra Roushkova
Translation into English: Bistra Roushkova
Cover layout: Ognian Iliev
Desktop publishing: Mitko Ganev

• • •

Publication of the BULKORENI
1784 Sofia, Bulgaria
Tel./fax: +359-2/760 600, 779 363
E-mail: koreni@mobikom.com
ISBN 954-798-019-X